# ROAD TO HEURTGEN
# FOREST IN HELL

PAUL BOESCH

To Eleonore
and to the wives of all Infantrymen
who gave them hope when they
needed it the most.

**Road to Huertgen—Forest In Hell**

Paul Boesch

Printed in the United States of America.

ISBN-13: 978-1497434479
ISBN-10: 1497434475

*Road to Huertgen,* by Paul Boesch, was first published in 1962 by Gulf Publishing Company, Houston, Texas. The original book is now in the public domain.

TYPEFACE: Paperback 9/12.5

# Foreword

*In considering this Foreword, it seemed as if there were two persons so closely linked with the Huertgen battle that the book would be almost incomplete without a word from each. Fortunately, both of them, Maj. Gen. William G. Weaver and Maj. Gen. P. D. Ginder consented to pen their thoughts here.*

The Huertgen Forest defenses of the Nazis were meticulously and diabolically planned. They, with the Ruhr River positions, constituted the Eastern-most section of the Siegfried system. Capture of Huertgen, followed by crossing the Ruhr would mean that the much vaunted German West Wall had been completely crushed.

The Germans intended to use Huertgen not only as a defensive structure but also as an area from which to launch part of their Argonne offensive later.

To show the importance of the Huertgen Forest, the Nazi Commander issued an order that if any of the fortifications fell into American hands, those responsible for their re-capture would be awarded Iron Crosses and given furloughs.

Victory at Huertgen required not only superb efficiency and unwavering determination but inspired valor and leadership. The situation demanded and produced a superlative degree of dedicated Americanism, spirit and faith. In the forest proper, our gains came inch by inch and foot by foot, delivered by men with rifles—bayonets on one end and grim, resolute courage on the other. There was no battle on the continent of Europe more devastating, frustrating or gory.

Lt. Paul Boesch, leading "G" Company of the 121st Infantry through screaming shells and deadly small arms fire captured a vantage point on the edge of the town of Huertgen. There, completely surrounded, he demonstrated outstanding leadership. He and his depleted company hung onto this valuable conquest and their unconquerable determination gave a springboard from which the final attack was successfully launched.

In decorating Lt. Boesch with the Silver Star for his work in this attack (his third award in less than 2 months) I wrote his wife that her husband was a brave and efficient soldier, whose actions upheld the highest military traditions.

Today, I find in his book a poignant memory of the work done by the men with the rifle that must evoke pride in every American, and a true but little told account of what it means to be an Infantryman.

WILLIAM G. WEAVER
MAJOR GENERAL, U.S. ARMY (RE'TD.)
COMMANDING GENERAL, 8TH INFANTRY DIVISION
HUERTGEN ATTACK.

\* \* \*

From 1944 to 1962 seems like only a week or two when I clearly recall those great soldiers whose heroism made possible the capture of the town of Huertgen, Germany, one of the key spots of the entire Second World War.

In December, 1944, I received sudden orders detaching me from the 2nd Infantry Division and sending me to report for temporary "task force" duty with the 8th Infantry Division in Huertgen Forest. My orders were very simple: "See what you can do about capturing the town of Huertgen."

A number of Divisions had tried to crash through to this key town, but the combination of weather, natural obstacles, mines and the German resistance had taken a terrific toll of all our attacking units. However, one unit, Company "G" of the 121st Infantry, had been able to take a small piece of the town and hang on to it. This badly depleted Company, led by Lt. Paul Boesch, gave me the springboard to complete the capture of Huertgen, although I was able to assemble little more than a company of soldiers and tanks to do the job.

I have seen much war, before Huertgen and after, but the memory of the way that small band of brave men responded that day will always remain as proof to me that the American soldier is among the world's finest fighting men.

Road to Huertgen not only describes the ferocity of the fighting with an accuracy and feeling possible only to someone who was there, but it pinpoints the feelings of all men under fire and their reaction to combat . . . and the battles they have within themselves as well as those they fight with the enemy.

Later I led troops in Korea as Commanding General of the 45th Infantry (Thunderbird) Division, and more recently directed the Army's Reserve Program as Assistant Chief of Staff, Reserve Components. I have always felt the necessity of explaining battle to men who had never experienced it.

To accomplish that task is quite a problem, but as I read Paul Boesch's account of his heroic struggles in combat, I realized that it is not impossible.

He has done it.

To an old soldier this book will arouse memories; to the man in uniform who has never heard a shot fired in anger this book will stimulate reflexes which are life savers when the chips are down; to the youngster who eventually will be given the opportunity and privilege of wearing the uniform of his country, this book demonstrates the heights of heroism Americans can reach under the most deadly and difficult circumstances.

P. D. GINDER
MAJOR GENERAL, U.S. ARMY (RE'TD.)

UNCOMMON VALOR SERIES

*Road to Huertgen* is part of a series entitled *Uncommon Valor*, taken from the quote by Admiral Chester W. Nimitz, U.S. Navy:

"Uncommon valor was a common virtue,"

referring to the hard-won victory by U.S. Marines on Iwo Jima. The intent of the series is to keep alive a number of largely forgotten books, written by or about men and women who survived extreme hardship and deprivation during immensely trying historical times.

Steve W. Chadde
SERIES EDITOR

[TOP LEFT] *Farmhouse where Lt. Boesch and his men found five wounded Americans.*

[MIDDLE LEFT] *Another view of the farm. The open shedded area is where the men were huddled waiting for help.*

[BOTTOM LEFT] *This cross beside the road marks the point where Lt. Boesch deposited a badly wounded man after carrying him several hundred yards through heavy enemy fire.*

[BELOW] *Men of the 121st Infantry Regiment guard an assortment of German prisoners captured in the heavy fighting around Dinard, France.*

*The anti-tank barrier that prevented armor supporting the 121st
from breaking through at Dinard, France. Mortars and machine
guns sighted along the barrier also held up the infantry.*

*Madame Blanche Vallois, an American in France during the occupation whom the author met in one of the war's most unique "battles."*

*Madame Vallois' home as it was before Lt. Boesch and his men inadvertently blew in the front door and living room.*

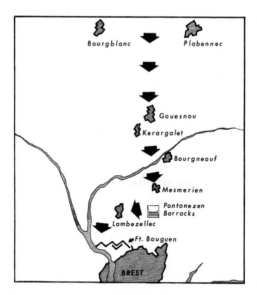

Map shows route of advance to Brest, eventually held up at the ancient Ft. Bouguen [BELOW]. Germans mounted 88's and machine guns in the fortification which combined to halt American tanks and Infantry.

*Fighting in the streets of Brest and the surrounding towns was as tough and bitter as any on the European continent.*

*Map shows why long Crozon peninsula was strategically important in capturing and retaining Brest.*

Air Force Major Harry Stroh, son of Major General Donald Stroh, Commanding General of the 8th Infantry Division, was killed as he flew in support of his Father's division which was attacking Brest. General Stroh witnessed the crash that sent his son to his death, not knowing at the time who piloted the plane.

One of the huge naval guns protecting Brest and the Crozon peninsula. The Germans turned them around and used them on advancing American infantrymen.

*The author [RIGHT] and his close friend, Lt. Jack Bochner between the capture of Dinard and the attack on Brest.*

*French boxcars. Capacity: 40 men or 8 horses.*

[TOP] *German pillboxes and installations like this one were the heart of the German defense in the Huertgen Forest.*

[LEFT] *First Sgt. Fred Foy, whom Lt. Boesch calls one of the best noncoms he ever served with.*

*Rocket launchers support the 121st Infantry in its attack through the Huertgen forest.*

*Three officers who played a prominent part in the capture of Huertgen. [LEFT] Capt. John Cliett, Atlanta, Ga., CO Company F; [CENTER] Capt. Jack Christiansen, who took over the author's company in the battered town of Huertgen; [RIGHT] Lt. John Terzella, Fords, N. J.*

*Infantrymen of the One-Two-One advance cautiously through the dank, mine-laden Huertgen Forest where the next step might mean loss of a leg or life.*

*Tanks made quagmires of the narrow, winding roads of the Huertgen Forest.*

*A scant 500 yards from the fighting, a Graves Registration unit evacuates American dead while a reconnaissance unit brings up armor to hold the hill taken just an hour earlier.*

*Companies F and G advanced from the woods astride the road in their attack. Bulls-eye shows where Lt. Boesch and his men were pinned down for almost 48 hours.*

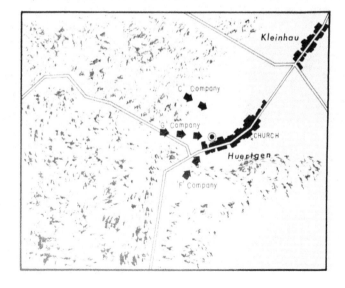

*Once inside the town of Huertgen, the fighting continued from house-to-house, and from room-to-room.*

[BELOW] *A proud moment as Lt. Boesch and three other members of the 121st receive Silver Stars.* [LEFT TO RIGHT] *Capt. McKenna, Lt. Boesch, Sgt. Barber, Sgt. Hobbs. Several months later, Lt. Boesch was the only one of the four left alive.*

[ABOVE] *Huertgen, after the attack by the 121st Infantry reduced it to a rubble heap. The battered church stands as evidence of the fury of the attack. Inside the church* [LEFT] *the altar and painting of Christ suffered comparatively small damage.*

*To some* [UPPER LEFT] *the fall of Huertgen marked the end of their individual efforts; to others* [UPPER RIGHT] *it meant the first hot meal in more than two weeks; to still others* [LOWER LEFT] *it was little more than a stopping point on the road to Berlin; and finally, to some* [LOWER RIGHT] *it was the end of everything.*

# ROAD TO HEURTGEN FOREST IN HELL

*Two lieutenants from H Company are Oid Wineland, Alton, Kansas and Macon Roberts.*

*Shortly after the war, Medic Cpl. Theodore Haerich, Hackensack, N. J. visited the grave of Sgt. William F. Hobbs.*

*Remnants of an American steel helmet as it still stands today somewhere in the Huertgen Forest.*

# Introduction

LT. COL. CHARLES B. MacDONALD
OFFICIAL DEPARTMENT OF THE ARMY HISTORIAN

Speak of the Huertgen Forest and you speak of hell.

During a seemingly interminable three months, from mid-September to mid-December 1944, six American infantry divisions—the 1st, 4th, 8th, 9th, 28th, and 83d—and part of the 5th Armored Division fought at one time or another in the Huertgen Forest. These divisions incurred 28,000 casualties, including 8,000 due to combat exhaustion and rain, mud, sleet, and cold. One division lost more than 6,000, a figure exceeded for a single World War II engagement—if indeed it was exceeded—only by the bloody Marine battle on Tarawa.

The name Huertgen Forest is one the American soldier applied to some 1,300 square miles of densely wooded, roller-coaster real estate along the German-Belgian border south and southeast of Aachen. It actually embraced several forests—Roetgen, Wenau, Konigl—but the name Huertgen caught on with the American soldier to the exclusion of the others. Few could distinguish one dank stretch of evergreens from another; one abrupt hill from another; one expanse of boggy, mine-infested forest floor from another. The forest lay athwart the path which the First U.S. Army had to take to reach the Rhine River, and thus American commanders considered it essential to conquer it. By the time both American and German artillery had done with it, the setting would look like a battlefield designed by the Archfiend himself.

The Huertgen was the Argonne of World War II.

In my position as official Department of the Army historian for the campaign of which the Huertgen Forest fighting was a part, I have studied millions of words about the Huertgen action. Much of it is couched in the dry language of official reports, but much of it also is more personal—the experiences of individuals. Yet few of these personal accounts seemed to me to transcend the rather limited experience which one man alone can glean from war.

One day not long ago another personal manuscript, much of it about the Huertgen fighting, crossed my desk. This one, I soon discovered, was different.

This was a lengthy narrative written by a former lieutenant, Paul Boesch. It was obviously too long for publication, yet the combat sections of it revealed a genuine, first-hand grasp of what war is like at the shooting level and what it does to the men involved. It was too human a document to be ignored. It too faithfully mirrored the experiences, not of one man alone, but of millions, to go unnoticed. It too sharply underscored the innate faith, humor, devotion, and even the weaknesses of the American soldier to be forgotten.

With Paul Boesch's permission I went to work with him to prepare this combat portion of his manuscript for publication. The result is The Road to Huertgen.

I have yet to meet Paul Boesch in person. I want to do this and someday intend to, but it is not really necessary. As anyone will feel who reads this book, I already have met him—a warm, human, forthright, intrinsically honest man. I have met too his friend Jack, his wife Eleonore, the men who served with him. For me, it has been a moving experience.

Many of us who fought in World War II—whether in Europe, the Pacific, the Mediterranean—will quickly recognize that someone has at last emerged to tell our story as it actually happened. It is more than one man's story. It is a microcosm of one of the great mass human experiences of all time.

It is, in fact, history in human terms.

# 1

Faster and faster the shells came as if Satan himself urged the gunners on. Shell fragments, rocks, and clumps of dirt rained down. The air became nothing but acrid, choking dust filled with confusing, terrorizing sound.

I lay there, hugging the ground and holding my steel helmet in an iron grip. At last I spotted a few feet away, a small crease in the earth, a tiny mark of erosion barely three inches lower than the soil I was burying my face in. But three inches looked like the Grand Canyon, and I wormed my way toward the crevice and wriggled into it.

From somewhere came an occasional scream as jagged shell fragments struck a human mark, but I found that strangely I was not frightened. I kept comparing it to the training problems we had run with the 63rd Division back at Camp Van Dorn, Mississippi, and I expected it would end at any moment. A poor comparison, but it occupied my thoughts and spared me the full impact of what was actually happening. The dust choked, and the pungent fumes from exploding powder burned my throat. From a dirty pocket I pulled a package of Charms, the fruit-flavored candy drops that came with some of our rations. Very slowly and deliberately I unwrapped one and popped it into my mouth—it tasted good.

Jerry eventually either tired of plastering us or decided to conserve his ammunition. With the lull, men started to stream back from the head of the column around the farm buildings we were trying to take. I knew they were from Company F, Jack's company, but for a long time I looked in vain for Jack among those who were fleeing.

It was only after another ear-splitting barrage of nauseating fury had come and gone that I spotted Jack. He saw me at almost the same time, rushed over, and flopped on the ground beside me.

It was more than good to see Jack. I wanted to jump up, say to hell with the Germans, and clap him on the back. We had been apart no more than a week now and not really apart at that, for with a luck uncommon to two friends in a big, cold, impersonal army, we had somehow landed in the same battalion, Jack a rifle platoon leader in Company F, me a machine gun platoon leader in Company H. On the other hand, for the past week we might have been engaged in two different wars for all we had seen of each other. I had watched from a distance that morning as Company F moved out toward the farm buildings and had known that somewhere in that mass of men was Jack, but I couldn't know which of the incredibly slow-moving brown spots in the big, open field was he. Then my platoon, attached in support of Company G, had begun to advance, and life suddenly became too complex for me to spend time trying to determine which brown spot was my friend.

In a few words Jack told me how not only his platoon but all of Company F had taken a licking from the shelling and machine gun fire. His company commander had ordered withdrawal.

Reluctantly—for we would have liked to stay together—Jack left to round up his platoon. I watched uneasily as he dashed across the field in bounds until at last he disappeared behind a rise in the ground. I wanted to follow, to get the hell off this exposed slope, to go some place—any place. But up ahead of me were the men of Company G, and I had to keep close—ready on a moment's notice to signal my machine gunners to positions from which they could fire in support of the riflemen ahead.

Again the enemy shelling increased in intensity. Shell fragments whined close and I got a strange, uneasy feeling in the pit of my stomach which no amount of Charms would dissipate. For the first time in my life I was scared, really scared. I felt naked and alone.

I began to crawl around, looking for better protection than that afforded by the little crevice. The dust choked me. One shell exploded particularly close, filling my mouth, my nose, and my eyes with dirt. I could do nothing but chew harder on the candy and search harder for a protected position. I finally found a partially completed foxhole partly under a fallen tree. With unabashed relief, I threw myself into the bottom of it.

I scarcely had time to examine my new surroundings before I saw a man crawling toward me. He was bleeding from wounds in the thigh and hip. Blood covered his torn uniform. Dragging his legs, he made his way slowly, painfully toward me. I watched him, transfixed.

"Help me, Lieutenant," he moaned, drawing slowly closer. His voice was frighteningly plaintive. "Help me! Please help me!"

I stared at the man in amazement. The blood seemed to rush from my head to my stomach, and my insides churned in confusion. This man wanted me to leave the hole I had just found and go again into the open to help him! The thought put my brain in a whirl. All I could think was that he wanted me to become as bloody and helpless as he was.

For perhaps half a minute, or maybe it was an eternity, I stared at the man, unblinking, unmoving. My mind was a turmoil of contradictions. I knew I had to help him, but I wanted to hide. I hated him for finding me. Why did he have to find me? It wasn't a problem at Camp Van Dorn any longer. We never had this kind of realism at Van Dorn, bloody, helpless men struggling on their bellies while the shells rained down—this was for keeps. Sweat broke out on my forehead, and I began to tremble.

The man opened his mouth to speak, and it was a cry from some other world.

"Help me, Lieu tenant!"

His words slowly penetrated my senses. I knew what I had to do. I forced myself to begin to climb from the hole. The lead left my feet and I found my heart again.

I dragged the man close to my hole and looked at his wounds. They were bad. I knew I had to get a medic, but a quick glance told me that while I had been occupied with my search for protection, everybody else had left. There was nothing to do but head for the rear and take the man with me.

Slowly, laboriously, I helped him move. I could hear the shell ing start again, but I couldn't take time to look where they were landing. A burst of machine gun fire tore into the ground up ahead of us. I wanted to hit the dirt, but dared not stop. Another burst sounded, but the bullets hit well off to our right.

It was a long, slow, arduous journey until at last we came to a religious shrine, a cross which stood by the side of the road that had served as our line of departure that morning. I eased my burden into a ditch and called out for medics. Other men passed my call along to the rear.

When the medics came, I watched them place the man on a stretcher. I never did find out his name or his company or where he came from, but that wasn't important. What was important was that he didn't know the tremendous turmoil his sudden appearance had caused in my life.

I hoped he might never know.

In some respects it seemed like weeks had passed since I had left my platoon at seven that morning, yet in other ways I had been so occupied that it hardly seemed any time at all. I found most of my men just where I left them, but my platoon sergeant was missing. One section leader, a soft-spoken Georgian, T/Sgt. Arthur M. Clarke, explained his absence.

"Lieutenant," Clarke said slowly, "Jim left. The first time that machine gun fired he handed me his tommy gun and said he couldn't take it any more. He took off."

I listened—stunned.

"He said for me to take charge of the platoon," Clarke continued. "That crazy Indian left with him."

I could hardly believe it. The platoon sergeant was the same man who, less than a week before when I had first joined the platoon, had stepped forward, his eyes shifting a bit, and regaled the replacements who had arrived with me.

"Listen, you guys," he had barked harshly, "I don't want any of you guys to turn yella, see? A yella belly sonofabitch is worse than a damn Jerry! If you see a man turn yella and run, shoot him in the back like a dirty damn dog!"

I had been shocked and could see by the faces of the new men that they too could hardly believe what they had heard. Yet I too was new, a replacement officer; the sergeant had been with the outfit a long time. Perhaps he knew his business.

"Well, Sergeant," I had said, not really to him but to those men he had threatened without cause, "anyone can see we don't have any of that kind in our group. I'm sure we're going to have the best platoon in the regiment."

Those few words had appeared to ease the situation, but I hadn't forgotten. Now, as Sergeant Clarke told me what happened, Jim's words to the new men came rushing back, mocking. I swore at myself, angry that I had not told him off with the harsh words that had welled up within me that first day.

"This," I thought, "was the man who was going to shoot the first 'yella belly' in the back."

I knew that Jim had incurred a touch of battle fatigue in the engagement the company had been through just before I arrived, but he also had been to the medics for rest and treatment and had been returned as fit for duty. There was no denying that to leave the platoon this way was plain desertion, and the penalty for desertion in the face of the enemy could be death!

Looking along the column of men lying in the ditch, I wondered how Jim's leaving had affected their spirits.

"Hey, Lootenant," one of the men shouted, "is that the guy who was going to shoot us in the back?"

A chorus of similar remarks reassured me. These men would hang on with their teeth, if for no other reason than to prove they had more guts than their spineless Platoon Sergeant.

"Perhaps," I reflected to Sergeant Clarke, "it'll be for the best. I hate to do it, but I'm going to have to court-martial him. You can't let a man get away with something like that."

I hardly had time to designate Clarke as the new platoon sergeant when Jerry started throwing more artillery at us. As the fire grew heavier, men from the rifle companies began to stream past us toward the rear. Word had been passed along, they said, to pull back, but no one had stopped to verify the source. What began as a sudden withdrawal suddenly turned into a full-scale rout. In unbridled panic they fled down the road toward a woods about two hundred yards behind us.

Their fear threatened to spread like a disease to my platoon. Eyeing the running troops, the men turned to me with restless anxiety. One of the squad leaders came to me.

"Lieutenant, my men think we ought to get out of here too."

"Our orders," I replied, making sure my voice reflected no uncertainty, "were to follow G Company, sergeant. G Company is still up there, and we stay with them. If they pull back, then we'll follow, but not before."

Another sergeant joined us and said his men were worried too.

"Just where do they want to go?" I asked.

Both sergeants pointed toward the woods behind us where the riflemen were fleeing.

"No," I said. "We're doing O.K. here. Not a man hit. We'll mount the machine guns to cover their pull-back and stay where we are. I promise you, if G Company comes back, we'll go too."

With reluctance, they passed along my orders, but as the shelling continued and even increased, the urge to join the dash for better protection grew visibly stronger. With every shell the men were becoming more and more dissatisfied and I was beginning to weaken a bit in my own resolve when at last the fire lifted. But it did not stop. It shifted to the woods behind us just as the bulk of the fleeing riflemen got there.

Then all hell broke loose. It was the heaviest, most concentrated firing of the day. Though the woods was too far away for us to see the terrible damage of the shelling, we could hear the screams of those caught in the deadly combination of flying splinters and shrapnel.

The men in my platoon looked back at the woods and then at each other.

"Is that where you fellows wanted to go?" I shouted.

No one answered.

# 2

When word came that afternoon to dig in for the night, we dropped our packs and went to work. The gun pits slowly took shape, but it was hard work. A hot sun beat down, and sweat soaked our clothes.

As we dug, somewhere to our front a man began to call for help, a plaintive, pleading, wailing voice. When I first heard it, I looked around for the medics. They had heard, but they were waiting for darkness. A litter party, they said, plainly marked with white patches and red crosses on helmets and arm bands, had gone out earlier, only to come under heavy German fire. The Germans had killed one of the medics.

I explained the situation to the men of my platoon and we went back to work, trying not to notice the voice. But we could not help but hear, and once you heard that miserable cry, you couldn't ignore it. As the voice weakened, everyone grew increasingly nervous. I knew I had to do something.

Keeping low, guided by the voice, and all but oblivious to the crack of bullets overhead, I worked my way forward until at last I found the man. A shell fragment had caught him in the hip. He obviously could not walk. Though it was a painful wound, he had remained calm through most of the day, taking his sulfa tablets and bandaging his wound as best he could, confident that the litter bearers eventually would come. Yet as the day had worn on, shells passing overhead and crashing nearby had made him jumpy. And as the day began to wane, he had begun to fear we might pull back, that we might not find him in the dark, that he might lose consciousness and be unable to guide the medics to his position. That was when he had begun to cry out.

When I first went forward, all I meant to do was comfort him and mark his position so he could be found when night came. But the thought of staying there alone was too much for the man, and the thought of leaving him after I had seen his condition was too much for me.

It was a devil of a job getting the guy on my shoulders while at the same time trying to keep from hurting him and from exposing us too much to the Germans. The man was heavier and more helpless than the one I had helped that morning. I could tell that moving was painful to him, but he gritted his teeth and refused to cry out.

"It's all right, lieutenant," he said. "I can take it."

I breathed a silent prayer for my long years of wrestling experience as a civilian, for without it I'm sure I couldn't have managed the burden. Somehow I got him to my shoulders, and despite the awkward stance I had to assume, I struggled and puffed my way slowly back toward our positions. I couldn't tell if the Germans fired at us. Somewhere I heard a machine gun, and a barrage of mortar shells fell not far away, but I couldn't know if the fire was directed at us.

At the cross by the side of the road, the medics again took over. This should have been enough rescue work for one battle green lieutenant for one day, I knew, but something the wounded man said would not permit me to rest. During the day he had heard cries of other wounded from a group of farm buildings which the rifle companies had tried to capture. Having heard nothing more for the last hour or so, however, he figured that either they had died or else the Germans had gotten them. Nevertheless I couldn't put the thought out of my mind that some of our wounded still might be there. Over and over I pondered how miserable it would be for any man to lie helpless through the chilly night, belonging half to the enemy, half to us.

In the end I telephoned battalion headquarters and asked permission to leave after dark with a patrol of riflemen from Company G to search the farm buildings. I didn't propose to take any of my own men, since normally machine gunners don't go on patrols. Not that it was the job of the machine gun officer either, but this patrol was my idea and I could hardly suggest that someone else be given the assignment. The colonel said O.K.

Darkness seemed a long time coming, even though there was much to do before the patrol. Within my own platoon we had to issue rations, portion out the water, and dig our firing positions. We stacked ammunition around the pits and made sure the guns were clean and ready. Though I started work several times on my own foxhole, the interruptions were so frequent that I did little more than scrape away the topsoil.

I also had to find the Company G commander to borrow a squad of his riflemen. It turned out he had taken a bullet in the arm and a tall, blond fellow, First Lieutenant Walter Black, had taken over the company. Black was glad to cooperate. We agreed that I would start as soon as it was completely dark.

When I met the riflemen, I recognized several men who had come through the replacement mill with me in England. Exchanging whispered greetings in the darkness, I told them what we were to do. When we were about to start, the sergeant in charge of the riflemen stepped forward and hissed through clenched teeth.

"I'll drill the fust sonofabitch that opens his yap!"

He sounded just like Jim. I started to say something, then decided against it. Still conscious of my inexperience and aware that these men were not from my own platoon, I was reluctant to start a controversy over ethics even before the patrol set out. Though I could not approve, he could handle his squad his own way so long as it didn't interfere with our mission.

We made our way forward slowly while shells passed overhead and nervous Jerry machine gunners fired occasional bursts. Because flares constantly burst with blinding brilliance, we had to hit the ground time after time to avoid detection. When at last we drew close to the farm buildings, the men ahead of me came to an abrupt halt. I worked my way forward from the middle of the column to learn the trouble. I found the squad leader cursing vehemently.

"The bastards got the place mined, Lootenant," he said. "We can't go in."

By the light of the next flare, I made out the words scrawled on a piece of board:

ACHTUNG! MINEN!

The Germans, I had already learned, always marked their minefields this way to keep their own men from wandering into them by mistake. But sometimes they marked unmined areas as well in order to delay us while we determined whether or not the warning was genuine.

We circled the buildings at a distance, looking in vain for a marked route through the minefield. At last I decided we would have to take our chances by going right through. Some of our troops had been in the buildings earlier in the day; surely they must have passed through this same marked area to get there. We passed the word along to stick close together and to step in the footsteps of the man ahead. I led the way, half holding my breath and treading as lightly as I could, as if my 220 pounds were capable of a really light tread.

It was slow. It was nerve-wracking. Any step might have blown one or all of us to kingdom come. But there was no explosion.

As we neared the buildings they appeared deserted, but we still could not be sure. We were feeling our way closer when suddenly there was a great cracking noise all around us. To ears overly attuned for the sound of exploding mines, it was deafening. We froze in position, only to realize at last that we were making the noise ourselves when we stepped on slate roofing shingles which artillery fire had strewn all over the farmyard. We stood there, wondering whether to go ahead or give up. The noise obviously was loud enough to be heard for some distance, but we had already made such a hell of a racket, I decided finally, that if the Jerries were there, they would have already opened fire—so we moved deeper into the farmyard. Like most French farms, the buildings were constructed in a square with the bam an integral part of the unit. It was in the barn, in a stable where the farmer had kept his horses, that we found what we were looking for. I breathed a prayer of thankfulness to God, for I believed He had given me the suggestion for the patrol. We found five wounded men.

One of the wounded was an officer, a Lieutenant Harris. When the rest of his company had withdrawn that morning, he had gathered the little band of wounded together. Painfully, for he too was seriously wounded, he tended them, treating their wounds as best he could and comforting their fears through a day that seemed never to end. Yet neither Harris nor the men had doubted that eventually they would be rescued. I didn't tell them that our being there was due entirely to a chance remark of another wounded man.

We had brought along no litters or litter bearers, uncertain about what we might find. Yet none of the five wounded could walk. So, there was only one thing to do—go back for the medics.

Directing the sergeant to post his men defensively around the farmyard lest Jerry get the same idea we had and search the farm, I left with one man through the same path we had used in entering. A seemingly interminable trip across the noisy, flashing field began. In my impatient desire to get help for the men in the stable as soon as possible, the shelling and bursts of small arms fire seemed even more pronounced than before—and our halt for flares even more frequent.

We went back through the same outpost we had used in leaving and I immediately contacted battalion on the field telephone. The colonel was quick to promise help, but since it would take 20 men to carry the five stretchers properly, we had to wait while battalion called regiment for additional men. It seemed an eternity before the litter bearers arrived, and even then they were short four men. But short or not, we couldn't wait for others to arrive; we'd use riflemen to help carry the stretchers and take our chances that we wouldn't have to fight our way home.

On the trip back to the farm I led the group, and the man who had accompanied me brought up the rear to make sure none of the litter bearers got lost. Knowing that we were fairly certain to meet our own men at the end of the journey and not the Jerries gave us a good feeling we didn't have the first time out.

We no sooner reached the stable than the squad leader gave me the alarming news that he thought there were Germans in some of the buildings. With the wounded still uncared for, the sergeant had been careful to avoid a fight. Finally we decided the Jerries were probably confused about our intentions and would stay quiet if we did. We got on about our business.

By the light of tiny candles, the medics began to examine the wounded. One man, they discovered, had died while we were away for the litters. The news made me sick. What a horrible, lonely way to die—in a dirty, evil-smelling horse stable in a strange and far-away land. It took much more heroism to face death calmly in the dank darkness of that bam rather than in some dashing act in the face of the enemy. I hoped that his parents or his wife and family might never know how the end had come, that they might always believe that death took him as he ran gallantly up the side of a hill in the sunlight, a picture-book hero.

But our job was for the living, and the medics set out in workmanlike manner to prepare them for the rough trip back. They were about half through when we began to hear a sound which there was no mistaking. A sound which brings fear into the heart of every infantryman.

Tanks!

Somewhere not far away, the churning motors of tanks—German tanks!

As the minutes dragged on, the riflemen began to get edgy. I went from man to man, convincing them that no matter what happened, we were going to wait until all the wounded were ready, then leave together. I don't know how long I could have kept them convinced. Fortunately, the medics, spurred by the same rumble in the background, were soon ready. Loading the stretchers we warned each man to be careful of too much speed or jolting lest we lose another of our wounded. Then we stepped out of the barn into the farmyard.

I was the last to leave. It could have been my imagination, but I would have sworn the tanks were entering the farmyard just as we left.

The shells took no holiday as our column moved back toward relative safety. They seemed to scorch the air overhead on a never-ending schedule of death and ruin. When they burst not far from us, I could see in the quick flashes of light the strained faces of the litter bearers and the wounded.

At last we made it to Company G's outpost, where I discovered that only two of the stretchers were with us. The others had lost contact.

For a brief moment I thought of them wandering into some other part of our lines where the men on guard would not be expecting a patrol to come through. Perhaps, I thought, some of my own machine gunners would open fire on them. Quickly I retraced my steps. In the end, the very flares I had been cursing all night revealed them and I was able to shepherd them back to safety.

When we reached the cross by the side of the road, litter jeeps were waiting. We placed the wounded on board. Lieutenant Harris reached out and pressed my hand.

"Thanks," he said.

That was all he said, but it was enough to give me a lump in my throat. I turned and thanked the sergeant and the men in the rifle squad. They headed back to their holes.

With a tremendous feeling of relief, I searched for my own shallow foxhole and sank down, exhausted. A fog began to settle over our positions, and it started to drizzle, lightly but persistently. The shells kept up their terrifyingly monotonous whispering and crashing. I pulled my raincoat around me and huddled near a fallen tree. I didn't want to think, but a million thoughts kept rushing through my mind.

I thought of the wounded man that morning, the other one that afternoon, of the man who had died in the stable. I thought of home, long, lingering thoughts of home and my own, dear Eleonore. I thought too of Jack.

"So this," I said to myself, half aloud, "is combat. I've had only one day of it. How does a man stand it, day in and day out?"

# 3

With the first signs of light, I visited my gun positions to make sure the men were alert. Hardly had I returned to my hole to give a little attention to my personal needs when Lieutenant Black, Company G's commander, went past me like a man pursued.

Without pausing, he shouted: "Get ready. We move out at seven!"

A dozen questions welled to my lips. I wanted to know where we were going, what preparations to make, what was our objective, where did he want my guns placed. But he was gone. As leader of a machine gun platoon, usually detached from the parent heavy weapons company to support a rifle company, I would become accustomed to learning less than all I wanted to know about a situation, but this was the shortest order I ever received, before or after. On that fragmentary information we had to risk our lives.

I knew we were heading toward the resort town of Dinard on the north coast of the Brittany peninsula, just across a bay from the port of St. Malo—at least, we had been heading in that direction the day before, and I assumed we would continue. Through the soldier's newspaper, *Stars & Stripes* I knew that the 83d Division was attacking St. Malo and finding it difficult. Our regiment, the 8th Division's 121st Infantry, was attached to the 83d Division to move to the other side of the bay and take Dinard, thereby relieving pressure on the 83d.

Orienting my men as best I could under the circumstances, I told them to get the guns ready to displace forward. Then I tried to get a little breakfast. All I could find was the dinner portion of a K-ration, a can of cheese and an envelope of powder which some imaginative soul had chosen to call lemonade. In the chilling drizzle of that late August morning, I would have given many a dollar for a cup of coffee instead.

Finally, word came to move out. I watched the men take their guns out of action with the skill and confidence of veterans. We stepped out of our holes and started forward.

We had not gone ten yards when German machine guns opened fire. Less than ten feet to my right one of the bullets caught Second Lieutenant William Carroll, a rifle platoon leader from St. Louis, in the leg. As he fell into a vacant foxhole, an alert medic jumped in to help him. I looked at him, wet my thick, dry lips, and muttered the only words of condolence I could find in my heart.

"You lucky bastard," I said.

I had no way of knowing at the time, of course, but my path would cross again with Bill Carroll's, next time under even more unfavorable circumstances than these.

The machine guns did not stop, nor did we—at first. Advancing across a slight rise in the ground, we took off toward open fields in the direction of Dinard. Off to my left, a rifleman fell into a foxhole and started sobbing like a baby.

We had gone about 150 yards when the men ahead of us abruptly hit the ground. I tried my best to see what was holding us up, but without success. Word came back to dig in. Jerry machine guns continued to fire and artillery shells began to strike dangerously close. We dug while lying flat on our faces, like clumsy, over-sized gophers. No further explanation came from up front.

Later in the day word passed from man to man that we were to attack again, this time behind a heavy artillery preparation. Our artillery was at its best as round after round passed overhead. We had a feeling we could have reached up and touched the shells as they passed, and the earth actually trembled when they hit. A slight wind blew dust, dirt, and the yellow smell of powder back on us.

As the fire ceased, I scrambled to my feet and ordered my platoon forward, but most of Company G's riflemen still hugged the ground, uncertain that the final shell had fallen. I swore out loud. The basic idea behind an artillery preparation is not only to kill the enemy but to drive him to shelter so he can't man his guns and stop your advance. You presumably will know when the barrage will lift, he will not; thus you can advance close on the last shell and get on top of his position before he knows what's taking place. Though the men of Company G responded to my urging, we lost precious minutes that meant the difference between success or failure. The German machine guns again opened fire, and their artillery again began to fall around us.

When word came down the column to go back from where we had started, I determined to work my way forward to find out what was happening and why my machine guns were not being used. I had gone only a little way when German shelling came so close that I dived into an empty foxhole. I was about to get moving again when two GI's dived right on top of me.

This hole, it developed, was theirs. With some scrambling, we worked out a compromise. Since it was their hole they got in first, then I got on top of them. Despite my weight, they were delighted with the arrangement. Not only was a covered foxhole a luxury, but a lieutenant for a roof was more than a rarity.

As the shelling slacked, I continued to work my way forward until at last I reached Lieutenant Black. He showed me in an instant why we were stopped. Across the entire front of the company stood a steel antitank fence. The Germans had zeroed their machine guns along the face of it and already had taken a heavy toll of the men who had tried to climb it. The scattered bodies offered mute testimony to the effect that we wouldn't get through here, not in daylight at any rate.

When I got back to my platoon, I found my men had assumed something had happened to me, and two of them already had started on a search. Though it gave me a good feeling to know they were concerned, I easily convinced them any report of damage to me was considerably exaggerated. However, I could not as readily dismiss the injury to two gunners. A shower of shell fragments had ripped into one man's face, while a machine gun bullet had struck another in the stomach. Both had been evacuated by the time I got back and never did return to the platoon.

Having seen at firsthand the antitank barrier, I assumed we would stay in this position for some time. We prepared the gun positions, then I started my own foxhole.

Throughout the day I dug, wondering with each exchange of shells where Jack was and how he was faring. When the shells passed overhead and crashed near where I knew Company F to be located, I prayed hard for him and knew that he was doing the same for me. It would be a crushing blow to be separated from Jack at this point by some errant German shell after we had conquered all the vicissitudes of the Army's personnel system to stay together since our friendship had first begun at Non-Commissioned Officers' School. How many experiences we had shared, through Officers' Candidate School at Fort Benning, through assignment to a division at Camp Van Dorn, then successively through shipment as replacement officers to Camp Shanks, New York, then to England, to a replacement depot in France, and at last to the same battalion of the 121st Infantry.

Yet the day passed, as would many others, with no word from Jack. I would have to be content with the maxim that no news is good news.

I slept soundly that night, exhausted from the previous night and the tension of the day. Only occasionally did the chattering of my teeth bring me back to consciousness. It was incredible how cold it could be in Brittany in August.

I had not fully realized how soundly I had slept until, as a foggy daylight came, I stirred from my hole and saw, only inches away from the lip of my hole, a dead man. I learned later that medics evacuating wounded during the night had discovered one man was dead and had rolled him off the stretcher in the inky night.

As I stood gazing at the poor fellow one of my section leaders, Staff Sergeant Louis Mazza, grinned at me.

"I can just imagine the wrestling match you would have had, Lieutenant," Mazza said, "if they had rolled him in on top of you in the dark."

I laughed.

"But this is one match I would have won," I said, "that is, if it hadn't scared me to death."

Were we irreverent to the dead? Perhaps. But who had a better right to be irreverent, even callous, than the men who might join the dead before another sun set? And who could live with death and horror as constant companions unless he found something to balance the score?

The Battalion S-2 (intelligence officer), First Lieutenant Bob Fay, meanwhile had set up an observation post (OP) only a short distance from my platoon's positions.

"Plenty's been going on," Bob said when I wandered over to see what was happening. "The 3d Battalion broke through the barricade but has been cut off ever since. Nobody's been able to reach them."

The 1st Battalion, Bob told me, had been committed on our left to take the farm buildings. This left my platoon at this point on the extreme right flank of the regiment—a "wide open" right flank. In a way I was pleased with this news, half wishing that something would develop on that flank so we would have something tangible to shoot at. I was beginning my third day in combat and my machine guns still hadn't fired a single round.

It is hard to recall now how many days we stayed on the hill or just which event happened on which day. Company G was not called upon to attack the antitank barrier again; we stayed in place to protect that flank while other units tried to open a road so our supporting tanks could get through. Meanwhile, we tried to make the best of a cramped, underground life.

During one of the enemy shellings, Sergeant Clarke called to me above the din of exploding shells:

"Hey, Lieutenant, ain't this a helluva way to spend my birthday?"

Somebody in another hole started singing, and others took up the chorus. I found myself joining in with my tin-eared baritone.

"Happy birthday to you. Happy birthday to you.

"Happy birthday, dear Sergeant C-l-a-r-k-e . . .

"Happy birthday to you."

Once established on the hill, I had little to do. I frequently checked the guns, the positions, my men, but I never had to wander far from my foxhole. It was not long before I began to feel strangely naked and exposed outside my hole. I kept telling myself, with an appealing and convincing philosophy, that having no real duties outside the hole, it would be stupid to wander and get wounded or killed for no gainful reason. The fact is, I was developing a serious foxhole complex, and so were some of my men. Each time artillery fire fell near us, its terrifying crash was followed by the metallic clank of men digging just a little deeper into the earth—me included.

Often I lay on the bottom of my hole reading the letters from Eleonore I had received in England and looking at pictures. But I didn't write to Eleonore. For the first time in my life I was involved in something which I did not want to share with my wife, at least not until I could better measure my own reactions and find some way to transmit the strange feelings that were surging through me.

One sunny day as I lay there, wishing I were almost any place else in the world, I began to watch two strange little insects vainly trying to climb the steep sides of my foxhole. Each time they would reach a point about half way up, then slip and fall back to the floor. I watched them through several valiant attempts until finally I reached out, tenderly picked them up, one by one, and set them outside.

"You might as well go," I said out loud; "no use in all of us staying here."

One pleasant thing about our little sojourn on the hill was that it gave me an opportunity to get to know my men better. On the surface they were a fine bunch of fellows, and I was pleased to find that they withstood close-range inspection with even better results. Many were devout with deep religious roots—others could trace their religious conviction to the time they heard their first German artillery. But no matter what their religion, almost all were closer to their God than they had been for years. One man gave me a small Catholic prayer book, whereby I became closely acquainted with the soldier's saint, Saint Sebastian. The religion of the foxholes was a serious matter to all of us, and no man hid his piety.

As a former Georgia National Guard regiment, the 121st Infantry— we called it the One-Two-One—entered combat with a preponderance of men from Georgia, but by the time I got to my platoon, the Southern accents were tempered with tongues from all parts of the U.S. My new platoon sergeant, Sergeant Clarke, was one of the originals from Georgia. One of the section leaders, Gerald D. Smith, was equally soft-spoken but came from Illinois. The other section leader, Sergeant Mazza, was a Northerner whom we knew as Lefty. I admired Lefty's spirit, and we often collaborated in little gags in an effort to keep the men in good humor.

While looking through my wallet one day for something to read, I came across an unused pass from Camp Shanks. It was an extra one Jack and I had prepared as insurance in case something should happen and we needed it on the spur of the moment to get away to Norma and Eleonore. None of the statistics on it had been filled out. I made it out now to Sergeant Mazza and authorized him to visit the town of Dinard, our objective.

"Hey, how about it, guys?" Lefty yelled as he left my foxhole, waving the pass. "I got a coupla broads lined up in Dinard and a three-day pass!"

It was funny at the time.

One of my squad leaders, Sergeant Vincent Gulaza, a swell youngster from Ohio, was certain the war was going to end on a specific day because he was doing a Novena and saying a certain amount of prayers each night. One day he came to see me a little crestfallen.

"Lieutenant," he said, "we'll have to postpone the end of the war. I fell asleep while saying my prayers last night. That breaks my

Novena. Now I'll have to start all over again."

I sympathized with him and asked that he let me know the new date so I could be ready.

Another squad leader, Woodrow W. Edwards, was almost completely deaf. How he had gotten in the infantry and stayed there, I could never understand. He couldn't even hear the shells come in. He had to watch the other men and take his cue from them when they hit the ground. I subsequently instigated proceedings to have Edwards transferred to a position in the rear where his handicap would not endanger him and his squad.

The men in the squads represented a varied assortment. Young Bob Osterberg of Chicago had been in college when summoned to the Army and hoped after the war to study for the ministry. Bob Nachtingall (whom we called Nightingale) was a physical culturist who somehow managed to further his interest in body building even in the foxholes. Blackie Napoli tan was another sincere youngster from Philly. Jerry Schwartz was a Brooklynite whose high school French, when practiced on the natives, contained more than a smattering of Brooklynese. Johnny Tardibuono, also from New York, delighted in being called "Broadway Johnny" and looked and acted like the movie version of a racketeer. He might even have been one for all I know.

Of two men who alternated as messenger, Hugh Perkins had run a couple of cigar stands in civilian life back in Indiana and studied magic as a hobby. The other, Jimmy Hearld, came from the hills; we all swore they had to tie Jimmy down to get shoes on him the day he joined the Army.

So we stayed on the hill and got acquainted.

Meanwhile, I continued to worry about Jack. From my foxhole I could see the group of houses around which Company F had dug in, and I could see when the positions came under enemy fire. One day I happened to be in contact with Battalion by telephone when Jack was there and had a chance to speak with him.

"Don't forget," I told him, "Norma, Eleonore, and I wouldn't like it if you weren't there for the reunion."

Jack Bochner was the one really close friend I had made in the Army; in fact, one of the few genuinely close friends I had ever made. There had been little time for friends before, struggling from high school into the hard knocks of the wrestling profession. Strange, too, that it should have been Jack, for we had little in common in background or temperament except that we both came originally from New York. Jack was an advertising artist who played the piano beautifully. I had made my living by more rugged pursuits. We had first come to know each other when we occupied adjoining bunks at Camp Wheeler, Georgia, and found ourselves sitting up late at night doing the same thing, writing long letters home. It was many months later when we had been able to introduce Norma and Eleonore. We had been delighted when the girls established a friendship apparently as deep as ours.

Maybe it would have been easier on both of us had we not succeeded in landing in the same battalion, if we had experienced our combat miles or even continents apart. I do know it would have been impossible to convince either of us at the time that this would have been best.

# 4

Lying there in my hole on the hill, I mused from time to time about how the war had suddenly diminished in size. Heretofore I had always tried to keep abreast of the broad strategy, to read about developments in all theaters of operations. There on the hill, when we were lucky enough to receive a few copies of *Stars & Stripes* along with our rations, we could read about how our armor was making gigantic strides across France; how we were slaughtering the Germans in the Argentan-Falaise pocket; how the Russians were also making sweeping advances; how we were taking great leaps in the Pacific. But now I found I didn't give a damn about these things. It wasn't a question of how far Patton's tanks had gone that day or how the Russians were faring; I wanted to know how our 3d Battalion was getting along, how many casualties Company F was taking from the shelling, what was being done to blast the stalemate which had developed in our own particular, private little war.

But these answers were almost impossible to come by.

Though we might not know immediately all the efforts being made in our behalf, the fact was that things were taking place designed to get us through the antitank barrier. Our first inkling came when we saw a group of prisoners being herded back and noticed a strange silence on the part of our own artillery. Next we thought we saw some of our own men moving in an area that had definitely been enemy territory. We buzzed about all these things excitedly, confident that they foreshadowed something important, though we didn't know what. We just sat there, protecting the flank of the regiment, waiting and hoping.

Finally one day we saw our own light tanks roll down the road toward Jerry-land, disappear from view in a hollow, then reappear on what we knew was the other side of the antitank fence. We cheered lustily. It meant the end of our clay pigeon existence and a chance to get where we could do some real damage to the enemy for a change. Without awaiting orders, I told my men to begin packing up, to get ready to move forward.

It was not long before orders came for us to stick with Company G in the advance. Happily, we hoisted the paraphernalia of battle on our backs and headed for the break in the antitank fence. It was good to be able to stretch our legs and get a good look at the barrier that had proven so formidable. It was a high steel fence, resembling a huge picket fence, made in sections so Jerry could move it wherever he needed a sturdy roadblock. Machine gun fire from well-camouflaged dugouts by the road had added to the effectiveness.

Night came not long after we passed the antitank fence. Though we halted and started to dig in our machine guns, the pause was only temporary. New orders came to forge ahead. We left our half-dug emplacements with little regret, confident that our best protection lay in moving as far and as fast as we could while the Germans were off balance.

Throughout our march, flares and artillery slowed our movement considerably, but it was a new weapon that proved the most effective, not because it produced so many casualties but because it scared us half to death. We were hustling along the side of a paved road when we first heard it, a weird, agonizing sound—a sound which grew louder and more terrifying as the projectiles approached. It sounded for all the world like a ghost tearing a board from the wall of a haunted house on Halloween. We needed no urging to hit the dirt.

It was our first experience with the "Screaming Meemy," or, as Jerry called it, the *Nebelwerfer.* It was a multiple-barrel rocket launcher, fired electrically so fast that the rockets came over in great numbers almost simultaneously. The rockets plowed into an empty field behind us with spectacular concussion.

Upon reaching our destination we had to get our guns in place by intuition for the night was pitch black. Thoroughly weary, we lay down and slept. But it was good to be tired from exhaustion of movement instead of the nervous strain of sitting and taking mental punishment.

In the morning Lieutenant Black took me along to a company commanders' meeting at battalion to plan the next jump forward. The meeting was held in a deep gully which served as a battalion command post. Hardly had it broken up when Jerry pounced on the area with his artillery, pounding it unmercifully. The direct fire wham-wham of 88's followed quickly. These were high-velocity 88mm dual-purpose pieces—antitank and antiaircraft, and, as many infantrymen will testify, antipersonnel as well.

About a hundred yards to the left of my foxhole a tank destroyer took a direct hit and blew up with a tremendous explosion. It was an awesome sight. Two bodies hurtled from the destroyer, while a third rose in the air and fell back on the burning hulk. A column of black smoke rose high in the air. Then the tank destroyer itself became a dangerous weapon as the ammunition inside began to ignite. High explosive shells and machine gun bullets erupted with enough force and numbers to give the impression of a full-scale battle. Pieces of shells and great hunks of the vehicle itself flew in all directions.

Then, danger came from another quarter when the other tank destroyers decided to get as far from the burning hulk as they could, as quickly as they could. The roar of their engines filled the air. With little regard for the men in the foxholes, they raced away barely missing several of the foot soldiers. I cursed loudly but breathed a sigh of relief when they got out of the area without injuring anybody.

That same day I discovered an antidote for the foxhole complex I had developed in front of the antitank barrier. Taking charge of a patrol to search a wooded area on our flank, I found that the greatest cure for concern over my own safety was to have something to do. Company G was down to one officer by this time, Lieutenant Black himself. Thus, I volunteered to take over some of the duties of a rifle company officer. I led the patrol through a number of small farms, looking for likely places where the enemy might be hiding. We gathered a few docile prisoners without firing a shot, though we came under heavy artillery fire several times. But the good thing was that I found myself losing the feeling that I needed a portable foxhole wherever I went.

During the afternoon while turning in our captives at an improvised prisoner of war enclosure, I came upon Lieutenant Mike Germusa. Mike had been in the group of replacements which I was in charge of on the voyage across the Atlantic, but I had not seen him since being assigned to the One-Two-One. Mike told me that on his first day in action he had been called upon to take over Company C when the rest of the company's officers were killed or wounded. He was elated that he had proven equal to the assignment.

"That'll be something to tell my son," Mike bubbled excitedly.

"Your son?" I asked. "I didn't know you had any children."

"I haven't—yet," Mike replied with a grin, "but when we were in England, I got a letter from my wife saying we're going to have one. She promises it'll be a boy I"

I slapped Mike on the back, wished him good luck, and went back to the business of getting into Dinard.

The next morning brought no change in orders at first. Company E was to take the lead, and again we were to stay with George Company and maintain protection for the right flank. This time we were to go all the way into the city itself. But as we formed to move out, Jerry artillery came down with a terrible ferocity, catching the men of Company E in the open and filling the air with flying pieces of steel and flesh. Several were killed, some wounded, and the company disorganized.

Plans were changed quickly. Company G moved into the lead, and my platoon stayed with them. But from the very start as we picked our way along hedgerows, we caught hell time after time.

Once between shells I looked up and there was Jack on the other side of the hedgerow I was hugging. I leaped over the embankment to greet him. The first thing he did was give me a Luger pistol he had been saving for me. I returned the gift in the form of a cheap watch I had taken the day before. Though the German artillery failed to appreciate our reunion, we fell to the ground and carried on an animated conversation despite the barrage. As Company G pulled ahead, Jack and I agreed to meet again in Dinard.

A few hundred yards down the road we joined forces with some medium tanks and for a while fitted our pace to theirs. The noise of the tanks apparently alerted every one of Jerry's gunners, for he began to favor us with a devastating artillery barrage. Sergeant Walter Price and I crawled close to a big hedgerow, but we turned out to be on the wrong side of it, the side where the shells were falling.

It was terrifying. Dust, dirt, and shell fragments flew everywhere. Great jagged fragments hitting the hedgerow above knocked clods of earth down on top of us. We huddled and hoped and prayed, even as we coughed and spluttered to get the dirt out of our eyes, nose, and throat.

Then suddenly it was over and we waited for the head of the column to go forward again. Though we waited and waited, nothing stirred. I checked my men and found that the leading man in the platoon was in contact with the last man of a group of engineers who were between us and George Company. We settled down to an impatient wait.

Finally, when the tanks started moving around again, the Germans again renewed their artillery barrage. I cursed the luck that had put us in such an unenviable position without apparent remedy, but our orders were to stick with George Company, and that's what we had to do.

No sooner had the artillery stopped than the engineers began to run pell-mell for the rear. I reached out and stopped several of them and demanded to know what was the matter. Their answers left me flabbergasted.

"Our squad leader got killed!" one of the men panted, eyeing the rear anxiously.

"Who's keeping contact with George Company?" I shot back.

"Nobody. We ain't had contact for a long time. We were waiting for somebody to come and get us."

Choking back a string of epithets, I turned away before I did something for which I might be sorry. I knew that somehow I had to regain contact with Company G, but what made me angrier than anything was knowing that we had endured the artillery fire without reason. Checking my men quickly, I found that only one had been injured. Sergeant Mazza had been hit in the left heel—of his shoe! He would limp his way into Dinard.

Taking part of the first squad as a patrol, I made a rapid search. Fortunately, we found George Company with little of the difficulty I had anticipated. The riflemen had been advancing cautiously and had been virtually oblivious of the heavy shelling to their rear. I sweated and swore at the absent engineers responsible for stretching our nerves to the breaking point with such careless neglect of a duty that was fundamental in the infantry.

As the advance progressed, we passed through beautiful hilly country studded with magnificent estates and stately homes. Searching our way through each of the dwellings systematically, we came to a big estate on the very edge of the city. We made our way through the grounds, helping ourselves to bunches of delicious grapes and other fruit right off the vines and trees. At last we reached a group of houses, empty and surrounded by a high concrete wall.

I went forward with Company G's commander, Lieutenant Black, to survey the situation. Just beyond the concrete wall was the first paved street of Dinard itself, and across the street was another building which looked to us like some kind of fort with a high wall around it similar to the one around our buildings. From a vantage point in a house, we could see firing apertures in the farther wall with connecting trenches behind the wall. In one or two places the muzzles of rifles protruded. As several of our men ventured into the street, the Jerries opened fire. Since we were too close to this new obstacle for artillery fire, it looked to us like a job for mortars. We called forward one of the officers from the 81mm mortar platoon, Lieutenant Lee Norman, to do the job.

Our plan was to put both mortar and machine gun fire against and beyond the wall. As this fire fell, the riflemen were to breach the wall with bazooka rockets, whereupon the attacking platoon was to rush across the narrow street onto the objective.

Lieutenant Norman's mortars began to do their job. My machine guns opened fire. A bazooka-man fired three rounds into the wall. The riflemen tensed, ready to assault.

Rubble and dust were still settling and the riflemen had not begun to move when the street suddenly filled with German soldiers. They marched in parade formation, their officers at the head waving white flags of surrender.

Though it took a moment or two to get over this pleasant shock, we hardly could be expected to turn down the German offer. There were about 175 of them. We herded them into an open courtyard and I set up my machine guns just in case they should change their minds.

While searching the Germans for concealed weapons, I looked for a good wristwatch as mine had been broken in the morning's shelling. I never permitted my men to rob the enemy, but we did not consider taking a man's watch an act of thievery. A watch is a legitimate item of military equipment, and I wanted every man in my platoon to have a good one. The only other items we took from Jerry were knives, scissors, and other sharp instruments. Pistols, of course, were prized items.

I finally found a watch fitting my requirements and motioned my prisoner to remove it.

"Kaput," the German said, pointing to the watch.

We had long since learned from the French what kaput meant, for the French constantly used the word in relation to the Boche; finished, broken, done for, all washed up.

"Nix kaput," I said firmly, staring as hard and firmly at the German as he was at me.

The German made one more try.

"Kaput," he said again, this time with a shrug of the shoulders.

I made a definite motion of my outstretched hand. He reluctantly removed the watch from his wrist and handed it to me.

Far from being kaput, the watch kept time magnificently, and I figure it helped me to do my small part in the war.

Our bag of prisoners was a strange crew of all ages and sizes, but it was their bland attitude toward surrender which amazed me more than anything else. They seemed to think that because they had surrendered without a fight to the finish, we should look on them as allies. They bowed and grinned at us obsequiously, all the while muttering that they had not fired at us. I wondered just who the hell had been doing all the shooting the past week. Surely the scores of dead piled up in front of the antitank barrier, the wounded man who had died a lonely death in the farmhouse —these would not have appreciated the grins and repulsively friendly overtures of our captives.

As in every group of prisoners, some claimed they once had worked in the United States or for one reason or another were practically American citizens. Many insisted they had kinfolk in Milwaukee, Chicago, Brooklyn. Making our way through the group we had a hard time avoiding being buttonholed by Jerries who wanted to tell us about the store they had owned in New York, the brewery they had managed in St. Louis in wonderful, wonderful America. How naive did they think we were? How could they possibly have expected to gain special treatment by revealing this kind of information? If they actually had lived and worked in America, then this made it all the worse. After accepting our country's hospitality, they had turned and killed our country's soldiers.

It was interesting to see the amount of equipment the Jerries carried to their surrender rendezvous. We, the victors, were stripped to bare essentials, carrying neither messkits, blankets, shaving kits, nor other comforts. Not so our captives. They were loaded with items we would not have thought of carrying. We gathered, for example, the fanciest array of cutlery you have ever seen outside of a hardware store display. There were knives, razors, and scissors of all sizes, shapes, and purposes. Each man in my platoon managed to select an interesting and useful knife or two in the haul and not for a long time did we need new hair-cutting supplies for the platoon barber.

One of the first things a German did upon surrendering was to throw away his gas mask and gas protective equipment. They obviously were as happy as we that gas had not been used, and just as we had our suspicions that they might use this monstrous means of waging war, they had similar suspicions about us. The second thing

Jerry disposed of was his steel helmet. Indeed, some of them seemed to think that tossing away the helmet was in itself a sign of surrender.

One thing that amazed us particularly was the amount of pornographic literature and photographs Jerry carried with him. The men of my platoon were delighted with the items they took but became concerned lest the Germans had appropriated the entire supply in France.

"We better hurry to Paris," Blackie Napolitan insisted, "before these guys get all the postcards."

The officers in particular were elaborately prepared for surrender. Some carried bulging suitcases with changes of uniform and other bulky items. Since it obviously would have taken hours to pack the bags, they must have anticipated the capitulation long before it came.

I suppose our general impression of the prisoners was best expressed by one of my men while he sat glaring at them.

"Supermen?" Dick Wheelden asked sarcastically, spitting on the ground. "Supermen, hell! There ain't a real he-man in the whole damned bunch."

Just about the time we finished frisking our quarry, orders came to turn the job of guarding the prisoners over to headquarters men and join Company G inside Dinard. Hoisting our weapons on our backs, we trailed the riflemen down the main street. Everywhere we could see evidence of defense preparations; foxholes in the streets, smaller holes for housing mines, barricades by the sides of buildings, and holes punched in the walls as apertures for rifles. But the men who were to have manned these defenses had thrown up their hands.

When we reached our objective and halted, we became aware that other units were not having the same good fortune we had met, for we could hear sounds of heavy fighting in other parts of the city. The sharp blast of tank cannon mingled with the crack of rifle and machine gun fire. Wisely sticking to orders, Lieutenant Black held his company on its objective to avoid being hit by our own fire as other units advanced. But as we waited it was hard to ignore excited French civilians who constantly came to us with reports of German concentrations in various parts of the city. We finally decided to send out small patrols to investigate these reports. Though the patrols brought in a few Jerry stragglers, on the whole we found that the volatile French informants had exaggerated German strength.

I took over one of these patrols and in the process of investigation came across the command post of Charlie Company, Mike Germusa's unit.

"Sergeant," I said to a man who was splicing wires together, "have you seen Lieutenant Germusa?"

"Lieutenant," the sergeant replied, scarcely looking up from his work, "he just got killed. Ten minutes ago, I guess it was. Too bad too. He was one hell of a swell officer."

I was shocked—stunned by the news. All I could think of was my last meeting with Mike, only yesterday, when he had told me his wife was going to have a baby.

I asked the sergeant how Mike died. A man who had been near him at the time volunteered that Mike and his messenger had set out to investigate reports of German resistance at a nearby hotel. Just as they rounded a bend in the street, the Germans cut Mike down with machine gun fire.

Sadly, I turned and started back. And as we walked along the rubble strewn street, I seemed to hear a familiar voice saying proudly:

"She promises it'll be a boy."

# 5

Dinard must have been a beautiful place in peacetime. It was a seashore resort. From where we set up our defense, we could see from a high bluff down into the waters of the bay, and we marvelled at the beautiful, sparkling, inviting sea. Most of the houses were handsome, many extremely modern and well placed to make the most of the magnificent view. Dinard was not completely destroyed like other towns we had seen in France, though some of the buildings were still burning and the local fire department rushed around in an old truck trying to put out all the blazes at once. In spite of ourselves, we had to laugh at the Frenchmen going about the task. It was like an old Keystone Kops comedy. The amount of chattery, screams, and gestures that apparently went with putting out a fire would have quenched all the flames easily had words been water.

Since we had no definite idea where the remaining enemy were in Dinard, we set up our guns at a street intersection so we could fire in any direction. What had once been a rifle platoon of 40 men and an officer—now reduced to but 12 men—joined our positions. Just as we got preparations under way, word came that we would have a hot meal, our first in many days. I sent a patrol to the company command post (CP) to pick up the food.

I was looking around for a place to locate myself when the crack of a rifle shattered the comparative silence we had been enjoying. The shot came from a patrol leader crouched behind a brick wall which ran around a stucco house.

"What's up, Sergeant?" I asked, dropping down at his side.

"Snipers in that house, Lieutenant."

"I didn't hear anybody fire at you," I said.

"They didn't have a chance. I saw the shutter move and I fired first. Look! There's another one of the bastards!"

Glancing toward the house, I saw one of the big iron shutters move slowly. When someone fired, the movement ceased, but the same suspicious movement started again on the bottom floor. A shot from the sergeant put a stop to that one.

"Looks like the place is crawling with them," I observed, "and our chow's getting cold."

Spreading out around the house until we had surrounded it, I bellowed in English for the occupants to come out with hands up. When this produced nobody, I tried again in my special version of German. Someone else tried in French. It was not long before all of us were yelling encouraging or threatening remarks in some language. But none produced a response.

Because of the long, unprotected run from the wall to the house, I hesitated to assault.

"But our chow's getting cold, Lieutenant," one of the men complained.

"Okay," I replied. "And it's getting dark. We can't leave them there tonight or we'll never get any rest. Who's got a rifle grenade?"

The sergeant produced a grenade, the infantry's tiny, portable artillery, and fitted it to the end of his rifle. I told him to fire at the front door. As soon as the grenade exploded, we would rush the door.

The explosion was deafening. As a cloud of smoke and dust rose from the house, we charged through a gate in the wall. We drew no fire as we dashed across the open space to gain the protection of the side of the house. Inching forward, we made it to the front door. Inside I could hear sounds of movement, and in the dim, dusty light I made out two figures. I pounced into the room and collared them.

"Come on, you sonsofbitches," I yelled. "Get the hell out of here!"

To my astonishment, they weren't Germans at all. The big, strong Paul Boesch, professional wrestler and fearless soldier had collared two old French women!

For a few minutes, confusion was king. The old women wept and screamed, all the while keeping up a verbal barrage that would have done credit to a machine gun. We couldn't understand a word they were saying—the fact is, I doubt they were making much sense in their own language. When one of the women began waving papers under my nose, I took them and looked them over. They were identification papers required by the Germans. These women thought we were Jerries I By gently taking one of the women by the shoulders,

I managed to shut her up for a moment.

"Nix Bodies," I said slowly and deliberately. "Nix Boches. Americains! Americains!"

For a split second, silence—but before I could sigh with relief, the torrent of weeping and screaming began again; only this time in a different vein. They fell on my neck and hugged and kissed me, all the while shouting hysterically, "Americains! Americains!"

I felt embarrassed and confused and wanted to get away, but one of the women kept shouting something about "Madame" and pulling me farther into the room. I finally gave up and followed her through shattered plaster and broken crockery across the room and into a hall. There we came across another woman, this one older than the other two, bent at the waist and supported by a cane. All three chattered briefly, then dragged me toward the stairs and half-pulled, half-prodded me up the steps. I felt distinctly foolish.

"Better keep your weapons ready," I said to the men behind me, however unconvincingly, "you never can tell where the hell this will lead to."

At the head of the stairs, my antiquated guides turned to the right and burst through a door into a bedroom. There in a large, daintily draped bed lay another old woman. Hers was the pale face of someone who has been confined indoors for a long time.

One of those who had led me upstairs rushed to the bedside and in an uncontrolled flow of words told what had happened. The patient, who obviously was the "Madame" referred to downstairs, shot question after question back. None of us could understand the questions or the answers, and I doubt if either of the women got much from the exchange, for neither appeared to listen to the other.

Disgusted and perplexed, I plumped my weary body into a frilly chair near the bed and dug out my French phrase book in search of some means of telling these people to stay away from windows, act in the open and not surreptitiously, and let us leave after suitable apologies for the damage we had wrought. But all the phrase book told me was, "What is the price of tomatoes?" or "Can you direct me to the railway station, please?"

In utter desperation, I said to myself in a harassed voice, half plea, half prayer:

"For the love of Pete, can't anybody around here speak American?"

My words miraculously produced a delightfully soothing silence. All the old ladies looked at me as if I had shot off another rifle grenade.

"Why, I do!" exclaimed the lady on the bed. "I'm a Yankee. I was born in Brooklyn."

For a while none of us could speak. We hardly could have anticipated finding an American in that house, least of all one from Brooklyn. Of eight men in the room, at last six were from Brooklyn. They crowded around the little old lady's bed.

In a few minutes we determined that the woman's name was Blanche Vallois, but before her marriage to a Frenchman after the first world war, her name had been Stebbins. She had been living in France since her marriage and, as far as she knew, was the only American to stay in Dinard during our attack. The Germans had given the population a chance to leave the city, which most people had done, but plucky Madame Vallois would not go. During the entire period of German occupation she had not once stepped into the street lest she meet a German. Proudly and confidently she had waited in her home for the day when her native countrymen would come, but I am sure she never anticipated that her countrymen would burst in so noisily and unceremoniously.

In spite of our attack on Madame Vallois' home, she remained unruffled, gracious and charming to us all. She had come from an old American family, as evidenced by photographs covering her bedroom walls. Some showed her and her father with President McKinley.

When I explained that she and her companions had better behave in a less mysterious manner in the future, she waved a finger at me severely.

"Just what did you do, young man," she demanded, "to my dining room?"

When she saw the look on my face, a twinkle came to her eyes, and I knew that Madame Vallois was indeed a gracious lady.


Taking reluctant leave of Madame Vallois, we found that our chow had arrived in our absence, but now it was cold and unappetizing. The night was as dark as the inside of a boot and we were tired, much too tired to care about anything. I lay down under a big tree and promptly fell asleep.

The next morning I examined a nearby house and found it to be a stately structure which must have been a show place when properly maintained. It was uninhabited; rumor had it that the owners were pro-Nazi and had left town some weeks before. Though some windows were broken, a few big ones with an unrivalled view of the bay remained intact. There was no water and no electricity, but we hardly noticed these deficiencies in our delight with soft chairs and sofas. We bounced around from one to another.

Wandering upstairs to the bathroom, I looked into a mirror and gasped.

Staring back at me was a horrible apparition that bore no more than a faint resemblance to the real me. Though conscious that I had neither shaved nor washed for more than ten days, I was quite unprepared for the result of such cumulative neglect. My beard was twice as thick and twice as black as I had thought it must be. For the first time I realized why some of the Jerry prisoners had stared at me with such obvious concern. Looking in the mirror, I wondered why I bothered to carry a carbine—I could have scared the Germans to death.

Jack arrived to see me just as I was about to start. As I scraped the beard from my face with a borrowed razor, he watched in open-mouthed amazement. I also got a few helmets full of water and managed a bath that made me feel clean even though I had to put the same dirty clothes on again.

Having improved my appearance, I took Jack over to see Madame Vallois. She hardly recognized me with my bare face hanging out, but a few words brought back the experience of the previous day. We brought her some butter, sugar, and soap from the company kitchens, for we figured she deserved some of the things she had been missing for so many years in return for her loyalty to her homeland.

Jack and I discussed many things with the grand old lady as we sat there in her home that afternoon. Despite intermittent shelling that was still going on within the city, it was like taking a vacation from the war. We learned that part of Madame Vallois' family still lived in the States and that her sister had been visiting her when the war broke out and had been forced to remain in France after the Germans came. When the attack started, her sister had elected to go stay with friends in the country.

Knowing that Madame Vallois' resources probably were limited, Jack and I offered her some of the money we were carrying around somewhat superfluously in our wallets, but she was as independent as she was gracious, and refused to accept. But we could do her one favor. She had been unable to write to the States since the war began and unable to receive dividends from her investments in America. As a civilian, it still might be some time before she could establish contact with her family and her bank, so I wrote to them through military channels. Months later I was to receive an appreciative letter from her nephew, but by that time I had left Dinard and Madame Vallois far behind in all but my thoughts.

After our visit, I went with Jack to his CP located in a badly damaged building in which everything seemed half demolished except a piano. Jack already had treated his men to a few tunes.

Now, as shells fell outside, he agreed to another concert in my honor.

From Jack's CP I went to my own company headquarters, there to be shocked at the complete cessation of discipline that had set in. Wine was flowing freely. Empty bottles littered the floor.

I searched out my company commander to perform an unpleasant duty. I had to prefer court martial charges against Jim, my platoon sergeant, and the private who had deserted with him. Both men were hanging around the CP, enjoying the liquid fruits of victory. Their brazen attitudes infuriated me. The private had even become involved in a shooting scrape, details of which still were obscured in drunken and argumentative testimony. He wasn't very brave when it came to facing the enemy, but he wanted to shoot his friends the minute he got a few drinks under his belt.

The Captain was full of wine too and was feeling maudlin about those of his men who had been killed. He pleaded with me not to start anything.

"They had a tough time before we got here, Boesch," the Captain droned, none too convincingly. "I'll bust both of them and get them transferred to another outfit. What's the use killing any more men?"

I was hardly anxious to have either of the men shot—no man likes to make a decision like that—but I had to do something that would show the rest of my men there was no reward in letting their buddies down. Even though I knew that the court martial penalty for desertion in the face of the enemy was "to be put to death by musketry," I also knew I had to act.

"When will you do it?" I asked. "It's been almost two weeks now. That Jim is still wearing his stripes and walking around here like he's a hero. A little more of that and we'll have the whole company hanging around the CP the minute a little shooting starts."

"Don't worry, Boesch," the Captain coaxed, "I've been busy too, you know. I'll make sure it's done before the day is out. And if any more guys get the idea they can goof off, I'll show them who's boss of this outfit. Is it a deal? We bust 'em and send 'em someplace else."

He put an arm around my shoulder and breathed wine-laden

breath in my face.

Disgustedly, I accepted. It was not without a sense of some relief that I gave in, but I have always questioned whether or not I did the right thing by taking the easy way out. Certainly the many men who died in action on the way to Dinard would have preferred reduction in grade and transfer to another company to a cold soldier's grave. Perhaps if I had been more experienced at the time, I might have insisted on court martial. Then again, after all I saw later, would I have been more mellowed perhaps, more understanding?

Returning to my mansion, I checked on the men of my platoon and then set about my favorite work; for the first time in almost two weeks, I sat down to write a letter home. Now that the fighting was over, I knew what to say. Though I recognized that it was useless to try to conceal from Eleonore the fact that I had seen combat, I felt now that this particular phase was over I would not have to tell her anything that would worry her unnecessarily. My experience with Madame Vallois pointed the way, for it was easy to tell that story. As I wrote, I poured out my heart with the realization that a long period of anxiety would be ended when Eleonore got my letter. At the same time I yearned for mail of my own. Now that the tension of the fighting had eased, I began to feel terrible pangs of homesickness and loneliness which for the next few days would almost get me down. I longed for the sight of Eleonore, to feel her arms warm about me, to tell her I was well and safe.

# 6

In a few days the 121st Infantry assembled in a heavily wooded area astride the main highway to Brest. A carnival spirit reigned. Some of the men came well supplied with liberated bottles of wine from Dinard, and this together with lots of good hot food, warm tents and no enemy made us feel as though we were on maneuvers back home.

We looked on small luxuries as minor miracles, so much so that we could scarcely believe the major miracle when it took place—some thoughtful magician produced hot showers I In keeping with a timetable set up for each company, we armed ourselves with cakes of soap and towels and fell in with gusto at the head of a column of men. It was a three-mile hike down a long, dusty road, but this didn't even begin to dampen our enthusiasm.

The shower unit was typically Army. Men streamed in from various outfits all over the area, and a clock-like system had to be put into effect if every man was to get a chance. They gave each of us a number. When this came up, they ushered us into a large tent where we removed our clothes and waited, naked and impatient, until they called our number again. Thereupon we whooped with joy and rushed into the shower tent to gaze upon a long line of needlepoint showers from which the water ran at a delicious temperature.

A sergeant blew a whistle and shouted for quiet.

"All right, you guys," he yelled, "you've got five minutes to take your shower and get out. The next time you hear the whistle, we expect all of you to move out on the double and make room for the next bunch."

A chorus of groans greeted his announcement, but we knew we hardly could hope to change the rules at this stage. Instead of wasting time with idle argument, we began to soap furiously. When the whistle blew again, all too soon, we walked lingeringly under the whole length of the shower line to get the last delightful dashes of water and then wandered reluctantly into the drying tent. Though we had hoped to soak in the water until it literally came out our ears, we consoled ourselves with the fact that at least we were clean, even if we weren't soggy.

The march back to camp was just as hot, just as long, and just as dusty as the march out, so that when we reached the company area, we neither looked nor felt like we had had a shower. But the man who was producing the miracles gave us no time to gripe about it, for no sooner had we reached our tents when an announcement came that a GI band and an all-soldier entertainment unit were on hand. It turned out to be a good show, packed with laughs which we sorely needed.

I relished the times when we were busy like this, for otherwise with time on my hands I found the loneliness overpowering and the desire for mail so strong that when the joyous shout of "Mail Call!" sounded, I wanted to hide. I had shifted from one address to another for so long that it might be weeks before any letters caught up with me. On the other hand, I knew that Eleonore had been writing every day to whatever address she thought was current and that some day all her letters would reach me in huge bundles. But I wanted them now!

Jack and I managed to get permission to revisit the area we had fought over near Dinard and take photographs of the places we had been. It turned out to be a strange and sobering experience to walk around the same fields in safety, peace, and quiet. Jack showed me the area where he had spent the days in front of the antitank obstacle, and I showed him my first foxhole.

We made our way down the path to the group of farm buildings that had been our first objective and met the owner and his family. They had just returned and were repairing the house and preparing to resume work in the fields. The farmer showed us through the buildings to point out the strong-points Jerry had established to repulse our attack. With a prayer in my heart I quietly entered the stable and showed Jack the bloodstains the floor where the soldier had died while I went for help.

It was hard to believe that a battle had been fought and that men had died so violently in the peaceful, sunny fields around the farm; but as we returned to our jeep, the sight of five bodies piled by the side of the road brought back the grim reality that war really had passed this way. Since Graves Registration obviously had missed these bodies, we made pencilled notes of the exact location in order that we might report it. One of the dead had been an officer in Jack's company.

"There but for the grace of God, we might be lying," I said to Jack. He did not answer.

Our combat experience had given most of us the idea that we were veterans, finished products as far as the art of war is concerned. Thus our inflated egos were rudely punctured when orders came down to begin training schedules just as though we were back in basic training. At first we treated the training to bitches and groans that could have been heard on a quiet night as far as Berlin, but as I examined the idea and explained it to the men, I found myself in full agreement with it. Particularly if we stuck to the essentials required in combat. Many of the replacements who had joined the unit recently had received only a minimum of training in the States—a mere two weeks of combat obviously could not have made experts of them.

The big brass had one selling point in favor of continued training: our next battle was already in the planning stages. The other two regiments of our division, the 13th and 28th Infantry Regiments, had moved westward toward the big port city of Brest at the tip of the Brittany peninsula. Since they had experienced a fairly easy time while we were driving into Dinard, they would get the jump-off role when D-Day arrived at Brest. For the first time since arriving in France, the 121st Infantry drew the reserve assignment.

A common sight during our stay in the rest area was the heavy traffic which passed en route toward Brest. The artillery was particularly impressive. We saw guns we never thought existed except on battleships. It was interesting to note the reactions of the men to these weapons. I listened to two of them one day as they watched the traffic rumble by.

"Damn, look at the size of that pistol!" exclaimed one man as a 240mm artillery piece passed. "This next fight oughta be a lead pipe cinch if we got all that stuff behind us."

"Son, you talk crazy," his companion said soberly. "You ain't been in the army long enough to know how to lace your leggins. Don't you know they wouldn't be sending us those things if they didn't think

Brest was going to be the toughest nut to crack on the whole damned continent of Europe?"

I wondered with some degree of trepidation which of them had the right slant.

Strange as it may sound, one part of the training I thoroughly enjoyed was the hiking. The countryside was beautiful and the marches never so strenuous that we could not enjoy the scenery as we plodded along. Standing in front of much of the scenery were the ubiquitous youngsters of France with their eternal plaintive chants:

"Cigarette pour Papa?"

"Bon-bon pour baybee?"

"Chocolat pour Mama?"

Yet our hearts were as big as our pockets. We seldom refused a request that was accompanied by the proper gesture or plaintive look, even though we suspected that the kids were a lot smarter than we gave them credit for and might be using our good will as a stepping stone to a lucrative if minor venture into the black market.

I got to know one French youngster quite well. His name was Emile, he was 12 years old, and he had a vibrant personality. Emile hated *les Boches* and could hardly believe that my name was pronounced exactly like this French name for the enemy. It was some time before he accepted the fact that I wasn't joking and decided I could be his friend if he could get around the name problem by calling me Paul.

One day as we were making a hike, rain began to pelt down unmercifully. To our surprise, they treated us like fragile recruits, cut the hike short, and turned us loose to go to our tents. Drenched, I piled into my tent to dry off and had just removed my outer garments when I heard the cry, "Mail Call!" I could hear the rush of eager feet past my tent, and then I heard the happy shouts of those on whom fortune had smiled. I tried hard to disregard the sounds and was not making a bad job of it when my tent flap opened wide.

Sergeant Mazza, a grin on his face, thrust a handful of letters at me.

"What the hell's the matter with you, lieutenant?" he asked. "Don't you want your mail?"

He was off to his own tent before I could express the thanks that dribbled out of my mouth in a choked-up whisper.

Letters from home! Letters from Eleonore! It was a miraculous, wonderful day. The rain pelted down but the sun was shining. Everything was crazily, beautifully mixed up.

I opened the treasured letters eagerly, my hands almost trembling, and drank in every word. Though I wanted to read each of them again and again, I went to see Jack since many portions of my letters referred to things Norma and Eleonore were doing together.

As it turned out, this was a special day for Jack too, for later at another mail call, he too hit the jackpot. We squatted in my tent and read his letters, first silently, then aloud. Occasionally he had to stop and choke back the lump in his throat. It was such a happy experience, this hearing from home, that if we had not had that false pride that prevents men from enjoying life as women do, I am sure each of us would have broken down and cried on the other's shoulder.

But we had mail from home. Now nothing could be too tough to take!

It was just as well too, for word came the next day that we were leaving, heading for Brest.

The ride toward Brest was an experience that made us forget the war and the fact that we were headed for another uncertain existence. France, so beautiful in the summer, and the Brittany peninsula, one of the more picturesque sections. The war fortunately had passed quickly through this area of Brittany and had left few tell-tale marks to indicate its heavy-footed path. In every ancient village the people gathered by the roadside to give us a liberator's welcome. Even though countless troops had passed before us, the thrill for these people who had waited so long for freedom would not soon wear off.

As the crowds gathered, we noticed that these people were different from the other French we had seen, for the Bretons are an independent folk who pride themselves on preserving their native speech and costumes. The men wore great, broad-brimmed black hats with bows hanging down the back. The women, particularly the elderly, wore magnificent lace caps that perched on their heads with dignity, stiffly starched and spotlessly clean.

Something else changed on this trip. In most of the towns through which we had passed, the people had strewn flowers in our path, but here on the Brittany peninsula they threw handfuls of onions into our trucks. I searched at first for some caustic meaning behind this unusual offering until I saw the enthusiasm with which the men devoured the onions. Onions here were plentiful, and the natives had discovered early that the GI liked them.

One aspect of the countryside which did not change but still served to amaze me was the incredible number of religious symbols at various spots along the road. One came upon them in all parts of France, at road junctions, along forgotten country lanes, on main highways, on private farms. Some were rather impressive statues of angels or of one of the saints, sometimes of Jesus himself, while others were more simple, like the cross which had served as a landmark on my first day of combat. Because men of our Signal Corps sometimes used these shrines to support some of the thousands of miles of telephone wire they had to string, it was not uncommon to round a bend in the road and see the Lord holding a half dozen strands of wire in His outstretched hand. I liked to think He was happy doing this little bit extra to help our side win.

At the end of our journey, we were assigned tactical sectors, though we still were not to be engaged in the fighting—at least, not immediately. We were to protect the division flank against any surprise attack or penetration by German patrols.

My platoon dug in well on one flank of the regiment, where we found excellent machine gun positions among the hedgerows. But the situation was still fluid as the army massed for the attack on Brest, and artillery units arriving each day to add to our strength often went into position directly in our line of fire. We had no alternative but to shift positions.

It would take time before the drive on Brest would begin. With the main Allied armies pursuing the Germans across northern France, Brittany had become a backwash in the overall picture of the war. Most of the transportation and supplies went to support the main advance, while Brest would get only what was left. We particularly needed a stockpile of ammunition before striking the concrete fortifications which ringed the big port.

The job was not to be the 8th Division's alone, for which we were thankful. We were to attack as part of the VIII Corps, which included also the 2nd and 29th Infantry Divisions and several Ranger Battalions. Added to this was tank support and plenty of big artillery. I heard it estimated we were to have more than 600 big guns ready to fire.

But no matter how much help, it would not be an easy job. At least that was what our intelligence officer, Bob Fay, told us.

"Jerry has a weird assortment of troops in Brest," Bob said, "but they're all under a tough paratrooper general named Ramcke who has a lot of backbone. What's more, he's got orders from Hitler himself to defend Brest to the last man."

Pointing to a map, Bob gave us some idea of the formidable collection of obstacles, both natural and man-made, which ringed the city in what seemed an endless length and depth. Yet with the everlasting optimism of the GI, we took refuge in the fact that our regiment was still in reserve, the battle had not yet begun, and anything might happen before we got into it.

"Maybe," a few men ventured hopefully, "the war will end before we get back in the line."

But we weren't awaiting miracles without preparing for reality. Each day we cleaned and oiled our guns to make sure they were in perfect condition. We constantly improved our positions.

Since we were assigned a definite flank protection mission, being in reserve outside Brest did not mean USO shows and showers. On the other hand, during this period my platoon was attached to Fox Company, so that Jack and I were able to spend a lot of time together under relatively peaceful conditions.

The good fortune of that period extended even farther when I received my first mail direct from home. Eleonore had at last received my permanent address. From that time I knew I could depend on a steady flow of mail.

One day we had visitors, Big Brass. Our regimental commander, Colonel J. R. Jeter, made an informal inspection of our positions. I was looking forward to his visit, hoping he might say a few words of praise to the men about their work at Dinard.

When the Colonel arrived, we were busy cleaning our guns according to our daily routine. As I showed him around our positions, I waited anxiously for him to unbend a trifle, in which case I intended to ask that he mention the Dinard fight. But when at last he did break down a bit, I wished he hadn't.

I noticed that the Colonel was staring fixedly at Jerry Schwartz. Horrified, I saw that Jerry was wearing a German belt. Turning to me, the Colonel administered a first-class chewing that made me shrivel to the size of a pea. Then he spun       on   one   heel   and   left without a kind word, either for me or the men.

I sat down dejectedly.

"Don't worry, Lieutenant," Mike Juki said consolingly, "when you get to be a colonel you'll find something more important in combat than whether or not a guy's wearing the right belt."

"But the Old Man's right," I said, a little reluctantly, "he wants us

on our toes. If we slip in the little things, we'll slip in the big things."
But I don't think I was very convincing.


Our positions were the closest we had ever held to units of other types besides Infantry, and we made the most of the opportunity to get acquainted with other races of people. But the visits only aroused our envy and made it all too apparent what a gap existed between the Infantry and the other branches. True, every unit in the army experiences a certain amount of real or potential danger, but when most of them were not actually engaged at their job, they had many of the comforts of home right along with them. Outside of the Infantry, men almost always were able to find blankets at night when it got cold, food when they were hungry, water when they wanted to drink. Their vehicles carried extra rations, small stoves, and other comforts we could only dream about.

Often one of the comforts was a radio.

When I first heard music wafting across our positions, it drew me like a magnet. It came from a radio belonging to a nearby artillery unit. It had been so long since I had heard music that I sat before the set entranced. Yet as I listened I discovered that the music filled me with a nostalgia that was hard to control. Thoughts of home danced before my eyes. I hated the Germans, the war, everything that kept me away from home. They played one tune I had never heard before, and as I listened I thought I could hear Eleonore singing it to me.

*"Goodnight, wherever you are.*
*May your dreams be pleasant dreams, wherever you are.*
*If only one little wish that I wish comes true,*
*I pray that the angels will watch over you.*
*Goodnight, wherever you are.*
*I'll be with you dear no matter how near or far.*
*With all my heart I pray everything is all right.*
*Wherever you are . . . goodnight."*

With the song finished, I had to leave. I mumbled something to the men about thanks, I'd enjoyed listening, maybe I'd get back sometime. Then I turned and almost ran all the way back to my foxhole where I poured out my thoughts in a long letter home.


It was not long after that when the planes began to bombard the defenses of Brest and the big guns opened fire. Nor was it long before the One-Two-One got ready to join the fight. Jerry was being stubborn. We would have to help.

I slung an extra box of ammunition under my arm as the column moved out through a dark night. But my thoughts were far away from the business of going into battle, and in my ears and in my heart the sound of the big guns served only to provide a deep accompaniment as Eleonore sang a song she probably didn't even know existed. Stumbling down the highway, I stared moodily into black space and listened to a wonderful, comforting, phantom voice that consoled and pleased me . . .

> *With all my heart I pray everything is all right.*
> *Wherever you are . . . goodnight.*

## 7

For several hours we made our way through the dark along the road toward Brest, then stumbled into fields near a group of battered farm houses to pass the rest of the night. The ground was littered with German equipment, ammunition, and weapons, obviously left behind in a hurried withdrawal. When it got light, we again took up the march, this time advancing cautiously in two columns on either side of the road in deference to enemy artillery. Some rounds came fairly close whereupon we invariably crouched low in the ditches or fell to the ground.

I felt a trifle foolish when I looked up from one of these quick dives to see a number of French farmers walking nonchalantly down the middle of the road. Their indifference to the danger was in sharp contrast to our actions and although we admired their courage (or was it ignorance?) we wished they would find some other place to stroll. They made us nervous.

"Those silly bastards don't know there's a war on," growled Johnny Tardibuono.

Our objective turned out to be a position only recently vacated by two companies of the 28th Infantry, which had been captured *en masse*. It happened following particularly heavy fighting when the Germans had asked for a medical truce to evacuate their dead and wounded. But when it was granted, they took advantage of the lull to infiltrate behind the two companies. The ruse had enabled the enemy to capture or kill all the men in one quick blow.

We were thoroughly shocked at the shambles we found. Though we had become accustomed to seeing Jerry's belongings scattered all over an area, it came as a jolt to see U.S. Equipment spread about in the same manner. Not only was there issue equipment like belts, packs, raincoats, and helmets but also clothing and personal effects of every conceivable nature—well-worn letters from home, half-written letters of reply, shaving kits, combs, tooth brushes, writing paper, and pictures of sweethearts, wives, and kids.

I felt my blood chill as I examined the tragic scene.

"We got to give those bastards a taste of their own medicine," was the way Mike Juki, usually an easy going fellow, summed it up.

After considerable work, we managed to make the area presentable and began to dig in while waiting for our assignment. But reminders of the tragedy continued to crop up. One man was completing a foxhole he had found half dug when he uncovered the arm of a GI who had been completely buried by the explosion of a shell. He came upon the mutilated corpse so suddenly he almost fainted.

During our first day there the weather cleared, and with this first absence of clouds, air activity increased considerably. We watched in awe at the antics of our P-39's and P-47's as they delivered huge demolition bombs, smaller fragmentation bombs, machine gun fire, and Napalm bombs which exploded in a great, spectacular gush of flaming oil. The planes zoomed low over our heads as they streaked for Jerry's lines to support our attacking units, and we were loud in our praise of the airmen we had so often vilified during training because we thought they had an easy life. Taking back most of the mean things we had said about them we were ready to admit they were our allies. We were even ready to admit out loud that they were soldiers, which was quite a concession for infantrymen.

Just as we were shouting the airmen's praises without restriction, a pair of Thunderbolts roared out of the sky. To our horror we could see their bombs release and come screaming straight at us. In open-mouthed amazement I stared, then let out a bellow:

"Hit the dirt!"

The bombs landed about a hundred yards away with terrific blasts. I had no sooner scrambled shakily to my feet and checked my platoon to make sure everybody was all right when the P-47's returned to strafe. This time the men needed no urging to embrace the hedgerows. The planes zipped past, spitting blatant messages of death, then zoomed off. We stood up, brushed off and hardly had time to cuss before two others roared out of the sky on a bombing run. Again we hugged the earth, but these bombs fell well to our rear.

"Lieutenant," one of my squad leaders sputtered, "we better put out our panels. Those crazy bastards are after us!"

"Take it easy," I cautioned, even though I shared his misgivings. "We've got no orders to put out panels. They've probably got those planes stopped by radio by now."

The panels to which the sergeant referred were identification panels about four feet wide and ten feet long, made of a light-reflecting material, a bright cerise on one side, white on the other. They were to be displayed to mark the front lines of our units as a guide to our pilots but strictly were not to be used except on specific authorization. We soon found out why.

My field telephone rang and an angry voice demanded. "Have you got your identification panels out?"

I could truthfully say no.

"Don't ever put them out," the voice roared, "unless you get specific orders from this headquarters."

It turned out that a unit of the 28th Infantry, well in rear of our position, had grown nervous during the air attack and had put out its panels without instructions. The result had been tragic. Our planes had flown over, spotted the panels, and naturally assumed that everything forward of the panels was enemy. One of the bombs hit close to regimental headquarters and killed two men.

In the bombardment of Brest, we not only had constant support of the small fighter planes but also the big fellows—the B-17's. Squadrons of the big ships flew over in tight, massed formations to drop huge blockbusters on the enemy defenses and on the enormous submarine pens in Brest. One day we had two separate attacks by the B-17's. My boys were so elated at the sight that they got out of their foxholes and cheered lustily as the bombs fell in clusters toward the German positions.

The cheers suddenly caught in our throats however as we saw one of the planes swerve into another, knocking off the tail. Both the big ships seemed to fall apart in the air, and pieces hurried earthward as harbingers of the remains. It seemed to take forever for the main body of the planes to crash to earth, and yet not a parachute appeared. From where we watched, untutored as we were in the problems of the men in the sky, it seemed that some of the crews should have been able to escape, and we prayed to the last for the billowing silk that would indicate they had succeeded.

The tragedy made us feel closer to the men of the Air Corps and impressed on us that we had no monopoly on death.

As the air attack continued the next day we again watched with the awful realization that we might witness another tragedy. This time Jerry antiaircraft guns opened up with fire that looked like harmless little puffs of black smoke in the sky. We watched in astonishment as one of the puffs appeared directly under one of the planes. The big craft disintegrated in a great burst of smoke and flame. We surmised that the German fire had exploded one of the big bombs, for the end came with dramatic but merciful suddenness. And again, no parachutes.

Not all the tragedy in the air was so impersonal. Our division commander, Major General Donald A. Stroh, was in a forward position watching an attack by fighter-bombers when one of the P-47's, hit by enemy fire, plunged out of control. With a blazing roar it crashed into the side of a hill. The General turned away from the sickening sight. He did not know it at the time, but the pilot of the plane was Major Harry R. Stroh, the General's son. Major Stroh had volunteered to fly the support mission to give his dad's Division the help it needed.

From our vantage point we could trace the progress of the battle by watching the way our artillery fire gradually crept forward.

About 800 yards ahead of us was a thick woods which our artillery was giving a heavy pounding when we first reached the position. We watched the shells hit the trees and burst spectacularly in the air. We saw brilliant white phosphorous shells create a gaudy pyrotechnic display and wondered what Jerry thought of the might of our artillery. His reaction probably was reflected in the answering shells he sent toward us, constant reminders that punishment in war works both ways. At Dinard we had already acquired a healthy respect for Jerry's accuracy with artillery; here at Brest we gained a new esteem for the size of the shells he threw. They screamed in with frightening noise like a speeding freight train, and the, accompanying blast convinced us that at least a train load of explosives came with each one. The answer to these enormous shells lay in the fact that the French had fortified Brest from attack by sea, and we were paying the price for French thoroughness—the big guns which had been mounted to duel with warships were now turned around to fire at us.

The Germans made every effort to stop the Infantry because they knew that until we advanced and actually occupied the ground, they were not licked. Though we noted that they soon stopped firing at our attacking aircraft, we did not know why until one day someone captured a prisoner carrying an order saying the Germans were to reserve all their fire for our Infantry, including the fire of antiaircraft guns. General Ramcke was conserving his ammunition for a long siege. This meant we would get not only exclusive attention from the 88's but also from the 40mm and lesser-caliber pieces whose shells arrived with silent suddenness and exploded above us in deadly little puffs of smoke.

When the shelling gradually moved ahead of the woods where it had been concentrated for so long, we knew our men had taken that objective. Shortly afterwards we received word to move forward. Our 3d Battalion now was ahead of the woods attacking the Pontenezan Barracks, an old French installation where many American troops had been quartered during World War I, including some of our own 8th Division. As the 3d Battalion became involved in this fight, our battalion moved into a gap in the line between the 3d and a battalion of the 13th Infantry on our right. With this protection, the men of our 3d Battalion were able to focus all their attention on the barracks and take their objective, clearing the way for an attack the next morning on the town of Lambezellec.

With my section leaders I moved ahead to reconnoiter positions from which we could support the attack on Lambezellec. Our path took us through the still burning woods which had been so heavily shelled, and we could see why Jerry had been able to withstand so much punishment. The place was honeycombed with thick concrete pillboxes. We had to make sudden use of them when Jerry turned his own big guns on the woods.

Following a trail of wounded men streaming back from the barracks area, we reached the spot from which the attack was to jump off the next morning. I made a detailed investigation to make sure our guns would be in the best possible positions, for the scheduled attack was somewhat complicated. The 13th Infantry had been stopped cold on a ridge, whereas our 121st Infantry had advanced several hundred yards farther. Our battalion was to be committed against the flank of those Germans who were holding up the 13th Infantry so that we actually were to attack directly across the 13th Infantry's front. They were to support us with fire if possible. It was a tricky maneuver that could fail easily if not properly co-ordinated.

Unsatisfied with several positions which I looked over, I decided to go forward on the ridge to see if I could do better. The Germans must have had the ridge under observation for even though I was careful to conceal my movements, they picked me out and began to plaster the area with 50mm mortar fire. This small mortar was one of the most accurate weapons of the German army. In this case their aim was off by only ten feet! My messenger and I crouched on one side of a tall hedgerow while about forty shells landed just on the other side. We could feel the shell fragments lash the dirt above us. Concerned lest the enemy mortarmen make a quick adjustment of their fire, I motioned for my messenger to follow and headed for the rear.

In the end I chose a position near a tank destroyer which looked down into a gully through which our attacking battalion was to move. The men in the tank destroyer warned us to be careful moving about on the ridge. Earlier in the day, as Jerry was throwing artillery at them, one shell had hit within two feet of their lightly-armored vehicle. The men were still somewhat groggy from the concussion. They were lying there quietly in the hope that Jerry would think his marksmanship had been totally accurate and forget about them.

While waiting for my messenger to go back for the rest of the platoon, I moved to the right to contact the adjacent company of the 13th Infantry, where I looked at some of the Jerry positions through field glasses at one of the 13th's observation posts. Before returning, I stopped at the company command post and was shocked to find that the company commander was obviously on the verge of a nervous breakdown. He babbled continuously and incoherently about the trials and tribulations his company had experienced in the advance. He never stopped talking or staring. I began to feel strange and got out as soon as possible and made excuses before his condition proved contagious.

As I hustled away, a tired, bearded sergeant followed me.

"Don't hold that against him, lieutenant," the sergeant said. "He's a fine officer. I swear he is. But none of us has had much sleep lately, and he takes his responsibilities too much to heart."

Back at the position I had chosen, there was little sleep that night for us either. We had too much to do to be ready for the next morning's attack; besides, it was hard to sleep at any time in the holes we dug around Brest. It was impossible to tell what made our teeth chatter so much—the intense cold of the nights, the foggy, clammy atmosphere, or the unearthly noise of the incoming artillery. At least the unusually low temperature of the French summer gave us an excuse for shivering that spared embarrassing explanations.

When morning came our artillery began a preparatory barrage. It was a ticklish problem of accuracy for the artillery because the shells had to clear our ridge and drop into the gully just ahead of us. It took exceptionally close figuring to accomplish this delicate adjustment. The noise of the onrushing shells rose from a whisper to a shout. It was the biggest preparatory barrage we had seen thus far in the war.

From our positions it seemed that the shells must be only a few inches above our heads. Though we sat on the edges of our foxholes at first and watched the thundering spectacle in awe, gradually we slumped into our holes until eventually we were lying flat on our faces, fully believing we were about to be blasted into eternity by our own artillery .We had the feeling that if we stood up, the shells would slice us in half. The smoke and dust from the explosions drifted back over the trembling earth toward us and was choking, smothering, terrifying.

Then, as swiftly as it had begun, the shelling stopped and the ground stood still. With a cautious, uncertain look over our shoulders to make sure no more shells were coming, we got off our bellies and moved to our guns.

# 8

Our first look at the gully was heart breaking. Hanging over it was a long, low cloud of dust and smoke that obscured everything. We held our fire. I knew our riflemen were advancing through the gully, but I dared not fire for fear of hitting them. I sent my messenger, Hugh Perkins, to find the commander of Company F, whose company we were supporting, for additional instructions, but Perkins came back with word that Fox Company had run into no opposition and the company commander wanted us to wait where we were until he sent for us.

In a few moments the air became almost as full of Big Brass as it had been of shells a short while before. The regimental commander, Colonel Jeter, and the assistant division commander, Brigadier General Charles W. Canham, came to our position in hope of using it as an observation post to watch the progress of the attack. Reporting to them in snappy fashion, I told them what I knew of the advance up to that point, since they obviously could see nothing until the dust settled.

"Take your men and move along with the others," Colonel Jeter ordered, with never a glance, I thought to myself, to see if any of us were wearing German belts.

"Yes, sir!" I responded, realizing that his orders superseded any I had received from Company F's commander and, what is more, made better sense. Turning, I gave a short command to my men. Within an instant they were on their feet and on the move. I caught a slight gleam of astonishment in Colonel Jeter's eyes at the speed with which we made ready to go. There was no point in telling him we had just finished extensive preparations for just such a contingency.

As we moved down the ridge onto a road leading into the gully, everything was strangely quiet. Not a vehicle or a soldier was to be seen along the whole stretch of road that only a short time before had been teeming with traffic.

We continued down the road with a file on either side when a plane bore down on us savagely, with machine guns chattering. It was a "friendly" plane, a P-47, but that made no difference— it was shooting at us. The bullets bounced off the road, sending up chips of asphalt, and as the pilot banked to make another run, we fled from the road into the fields. God bless our Air Corps, but . . .

For the rest of our journey, we stayed well concealed, as far from the road as possible.

The day our 2nd Battalion made the sudden wheeling movement in front of the Lambezellec ridge was one day when every GI in our outfit admitted the generals earned their pay. All the German positions—and they were both numerous and formidable—were facing toward the ridge where, their well-placed weapons had stopped the 13th Infantry. But as we came on the German flanks, none of the guns was able to cover us. The Jerries had to abandon their positions and fall back. We moved cautiously but steadily toward the town of Lambezellec with comparatively few casualties.

Most of our advance that day consisted of searching evil-smelling Jerry dugouts for stray prisoners and souvenirs. We found a little of both, but in the process we lost a lot of respect for the German as a soldier. We saw evidence everywhere of his lack of training in simple sanitation and field discipline. Though we could appreciate that our artillery and planes had kept him in constant fear and danger, we could not understand how any man could defecate in the very hole in which he had to live. Nowhere did we see a common latrine, something which was normal practice with American troops. Nor did we see any evidence that Jerry had learned to dig a small hole to bury his personal filth.

As we entered Lambellezec, the undivided attention our artillery and aircraft had been giving the town for some time was apparent. The streets were pockmarked with holes and cluttered with the debris of ruined buildings. Broken trees further blocked the streets. The center of the town was particularly badly damaged, almost flattened.

When men ahead of us came to a halt, we set up our guns in the middle of a fallen building at the intersection of the town's main streets. Here we might be ready for danger from any direction. We had crouched behind broken walls to relax and catch our breath for the next jog ahead when suddenly we heard the clatter of horses' hooves on the road. Two beautiful animals came into view. How they had escaped harm in the shelling amazed us. The fact is, they were totally oblivious of the war, for the male of the pair was engaged in a pursuit of a far more interesting and amorous nature. With a wild and anxious neigh, he tried to mount his companion, but either his anxiety or her coyness spoiled the effort.

We forgot the war momentarily to give full attention to this equine diversion. As The horse whinnied in frustration, we cheered them on. When the male failed again, we groaned in sympathy.

It was the best show of the war to a bunch of men who for months had been forced to keep sex well in the back of their minds, and we admired the animal's determination to get on with his pleasure despite the efforts of war to interfere. In espousing his cause, perhaps we were seeking a measure of vicarious satisfaction. But to no avail. Though the stallion's efforts became increasingly furious, though his neighs fairly reeked of frustration, his aim failed to improve.

In time, the amorous exertions of the pair carried them away from our positions to a spot obscured from our view. Yet for a long time we still could hear the male whinny and snort and knew that the mare was standing faithfully but impatiently, waiting for him. In the end, one of the men thought he detected a note of triumph and proudly announced that the stallion had won. But it was pure conjecture, really, and was probably fathered by wishful thinking. We had no proof, and we never saw the horses again, though we continued to hope that they, at least, had overcome this basic frustration which war had imposed on millions of people.

As we waited for orders to resume the advance, our area became filled with visitors, one of them a cameraman from a British newspaper. He wanted some "real action pictures" and asked to borrow some of my men for the shots. Knowing that we might have to move out at any moment, I was reluctant to comply until I saw that several had already begun to primp for the camera, and I didn't have the heart to refuse them.

Never did a cameraman have more willing subjects. The men crept and crawled and ran with their weapons through mountainous piles of rubble until their tongues were dragging. The cameraman got his "action pictures" and was happy, but later I had doubts as to whether or not I had done the right thing. Many of the men wrote home with instructions to their families to be on the lookout for the photographs, and return letters indicated that relatives were poring over every publication with infinite care. Their chance of seeing the photographs even if they were used were slim indeed, for they were taken for a British publication.

The sudden influx of visitors gave us the impression we were rear echelon. We felt especially so when Military Police arrived and, despite the razzing, nailed up a huge sign: "This Town Is Off Limits." One of my men insisted that if the town was off limits, we were trespassing and the MP's should cart us all off to some rear stockade. Surely this must have been some kind of record for putting a town off limits after capture.

When word did at last come to move forward we got only as far as a cemetery on the far edge of town before again being told to halt. A cemetery is an undesirable place to be under almost any circumstances, but despite the danger, we were naturally reluctant to dig in.

"I wonder if we have to belong to the grave digger's union to dig a foxhole here," said Jerry Schwartz.

"No," retaliated Vince Gulazza, "but you dig and you're liable to contact the French underground."

With a slight disrespect for the dead but a healthy regard for the living, we turned to the deep vaults for protection.

Just before dark we moved forward again to occupy a hill that was studded with Jerry defenses—deep trenches, pillboxes, foxholes, and antiaircraft guns. As we scrambled over the positions, weapons ready for action, we were delighted to see that the 88's which were to have stopped us already had been put out of commission by our planes. Nearby were piles of shells that had not been fired. The guns and the pillboxes had been prepared for demolition, but whoever job it was had either run or been killed.

After making a quick inspection for booby traps, we crawled into the big shelters for protection. When night came, we found out how Jerry had been able to withstand so much of our artillery bombardment, for even though the Germans shelled the hill all night with their heaviest weapons, we were hardly disturbed.

In the morning I was ordered to transfer my platoon to support of Company E in a resumption of the attack. Moving to Easy Company's area, I found the company commander, Captain Ben Inman, in a cellar alongside a road which ran parallel to wide open fields which the attack would have to cross. I gave him an idea of what my guns could do to help, then set about the task of finding good firing positions.

I managed to find several good positions, but when the attack started the riflemen needed more support than we could provide. Thus, the attack bogged down in front of one of the bulwarks of the Brest defenses, Fort Bougan, an old French fortification built originally in 1680. It was old, but it was massive and virtually impregnable.

Among the wounded who drifted back from the direction of the fort was Lieutenant Lee^Norman. Bandages covered his head.

"One of those damned mortar shells got me in one eye," Lee said in a matter-of-fact tone. "I guess I won't use that one any more."

Lee went on to tell us about the fort. He said he got a look at it before they put his eye out, and the way he figured it, we were in for a tough job.

Lee was right. Even in the face of modem weapons, Fort Bougan was formidable. The walls were 25 to 35 feet high, and a dry moat 15 to 20 feet deep surrounded the entire structure. The walls were of such incredible thickness that shells tossed at them bounced off like marbles on a floor. Even later when our artillery brought up big 240mm pieces and fired almost point-blank, the effect was scarcely noticeable.

We were stopped cold.

Still unconvinced that we could not take Fort Bougan, my battalion commander, Lieutenant Colonel James Casey, suggested that my platoon might be able to help by firing our machine guns over the heads of the riflemen and over the walls into the fort. I set out to reconnoiter for positions. Eventually we came across a lieutenant who suggested we go with him to a spot from which we might get an unobstructed view across the dry moat.

Following him, we crawled into a crevice behind a small parapet of earth. I cautiously raised my head to look around.

*C-r-r-ack!*

I ducked in the day's fastest move. So close had a bullet come to my ear that I thought at first it must have injured the drum. For days afterwards I was to have a perpetual ringing in my ear and a small shiver up my spine every time I thought of how close that one came. This, I was convinced, was as close as a bullet could come without ending a man's military career.

Completing my survey, I returned to battalion headquarters where Colonel Casey was awaiting my report.

"I might as well throw a handful of rocks up there as use my machine guns," I told him.

He wanted to know what I would suggest now that I had had a close look at the fort. I replied that direct-fire weapons like tanks and tank destroyers appeared to be our only chance.

At Colonel Casey's suggestion, I waited around the headquarters until he could send for a tank company commander. Having already conducted a careful study of the best firing positions for my own guns, I had no trouble pointing out to the tank commander the best positions for him. The rub came when he chose the very spots where I had located my guns. My men had to move.

Backing, turning, twisting to take advantage of all possible concealment and cover, the tanks rumbled noisily and slowly into position. Though the Germans threw round after round of artillery fire after them, the tanks pulled in close to a group of houses before the fire found them. On the other hand, their own fire turned out to be almost as ineffective. One tank knocked out a poorly camouflaged 88mm gun that was outside the fort, but the rounds directed at the fort itself did almost no damage.

Under cover of the fire from the tanks, a group of men from Company G under First Lieutenant Gordon Arnold, whom I had known back at Camp Van Dorn, managed to get into the moat and tried to scale the walls with ladders, but to no avail. The Germans quickly picked up the movement and poured such heavy fire into the moat that the men had to withdraw.

There could be no question about it, our attack was stopped. Orders came down to contain the fort while the 2nd and 29th Divisions continued to fight forward in other sectors.

The comparative lull in operations gave us time to get better acquainted with the men of the tank units and to take advantage of some of the extra comforts they carried on their big vehicles. It also gave me an opportunity to straighten out a small problem within my platoon which had been created without my knowledge by my company commander.

Unknown to me, technical sergeant Albert Lawrence, who had been platoon sergeant before I joined the platoon, had recovered from earlier wounds and returned to the company. Assuming I did not want my platoon organization upset, the captain had failed to notify me of Sergeant Lawrence's return. He had held him back at the company command post while Lawrence fumed and fretted and blamed the whole unfortunate episode on me.

After two weeks the captain at last confided to me what he was doing. It seemed obvious that the sergeant had been getting rotten treatment, and I took it upon myself to ask him personally to come up to the platoon. I had never been certain that Clarke was the man to be my platoon sergeant, even though he had held the post for several weeks and was an excellent soldier. I thought I would see how Lawrence worked out.

It took little time to see that Sergeant Lawrence was the man I was looking for. He was not only capable, but he took over the platoon in a quiet, confident way that made the men like him immediately. It was a pleasure to have him with us. Though I regretted having to shift Sergeant Clarke back to his former job as section leader, I considered that arrangement best.

Not all was so serious and somber during our stay opposite Fort Bougan. There was, for example, the experience of two of my men, Bill Fisher and Bob Osterberg, when they took refuge in a Jerry sentry box one day during a heavy shelling.

The sentry box was ostensibly constructed of concrete and looked like one of those old-fashioned sentry posts that always appear in story books at the entrance to the king's estates. The space inside was just enough for the two men to sit, facing each other, on steps no doubt built for the sentry to stand on when looking out the observation slits. The men's faces were only a foot apart. Although the shelling was heavy, the men passed the time in comparative comfort and apparent safety while talking of other, better days.

Suddenly their calm was rudely interrupted by an ugly piece of hot steel which ripped through one wall, went right between their heads, and pierced the other side of the sentry box. What they thought was concrete was nothing more than hollow tile blocks faced with plaster! The two men stumbled out of their falsely secure hiding place, shaken, and trembling.

The story had a sequel which I learned from one of the letters I censored. Since I never divulged the contents of any letter, no matter how trivial it might seem, I had to resist the impulse to tell the others.

At the first chance to write home after the incident in the sentry box, Fisher wrote both his wife and his mother.

"I want you to go out right away," he implored each of them, "and give some money to a worthwhile charity. Don't ask me why—just do it. Perhaps some day I'll be able to explain."

In the meantime, Fort Bougan refused to budge. News spread that they were bringing the 240's forward to blast at the walls point-blank, but on the same day these big pieces were scheduled to arrive, men appeared in our area wearing the big Indianhead shoulder patch of the 2d Division. Rumor quickly had it that we were to be relieved.

It didn't take long for the rumor to be confirmed. As soon as night came, the 121st Infantry picked up its weapons and gear and silently stole away. At the same time the 2nd Division's 9th Regiment moved in.

Over rough trails lighted at intervals by burning buildings we stumbled and cursed our way to a spot where a big hill shielded us from observation. There was a long column of trucks waiting for us.

"Uh-oh," said one man, "they must have dirty work ahead. They wouldn't be nice enough to give us a ride if they didn't have a lousy job in mind."

He was right. They had another job for us.

## 9

The trucks, creaking and rumbling, took us back to the vicinity of the farm from which we had jumped into the battle for Brest. Wearily we unloaded to try to find a comfortable spot in the cold, damp fields. In the morning we moved, again by truck, to another assembly area even farther to the rear, but instead of enjoying the ride, we were justifiably suspicious. We could detect a tough assignment ahead.

When we reached the assembly area and gathered around the briefing officer, our suspicions grew stronger. Hot showers, the officer told us, were ready, and we would have steak for dinner that night. It would be the first fresh meat I had eaten since landing in France.

"Steak?" Jerry Schwartz muttered to Johnny Pavlick. "What the hell is steak?"

"Steak," said Johnny solemnly, "is what they give prisoners in the death row for their last sumptuous meal."

"I see what you mean," returned Jerry dryly. "I see just what you mean."

We didn't have long to wait to find out exactly what it really did mean. The 8th Division's next mission, our briefing officer told us, was to clear the Crozon Peninsula.

The Crozon Peninsula is a small finger of land south of Brest. It was the big guns of Crozon which dominated the entrance to the Brest harbor. No matter who held Brest itself, the harbor would be useless unless he also commanded the harbor entrance, and that meant holding the Crozon Peninsula. Also, since many of the big artillery pieces that had been making the attack on Brest so difficult were located on the peninsula, clearing it would contribute directly to capture of the city.

Reducing the peninsula was to be primarily an 8th Division assignment but with help from a task force of tank destroyers, armor, field artillery and members of the French Forces of the Interior, the FFI. The latter were men of the French underground resistance movement who had been armed by the Allies before the invasion and who had made life miserable for Jerry all over Brittany. They had no uniforms but wore identifying arm bands with the letters FFI scrawled on them. Most of the men were poorly trained, but what they lacked in military instruction, they made up for in hatred for the Germans and enthusiasm for the battle to liberate their homeland.

Before being committed to this engagement, however, our men were to be paid. Designated as company finance officer, I was to make a trip back to Division Rear headquarters to pick up the money and the payroll.

In combat a division headquarters is divided into two sections. A forward echelon, which follows comparatively close to the fighting, is the tactical nerve center; the other portion farther to the rear is the housekeeping establishment, a place where men do paper work and keep the vast records required by the 15,000 men assigned to the division. To the fighting man, both sections appear far from danger, but even the men in the forward echelon of the headquarters look on those at Division Rear as a bunch of school boys with safe, easy jobs.

With a jeep and driver, I set out. The day was delightful and the countryside beautiful. I relaxed completely, the noise and stress of battle almost forgotten. The woods and fields, little damaged by the war, were lush and green with the full bloom of late summer. It might have been Virginia in the spring, New Jersey when the fruit trees are in bloom, or Southern California almost any time of the year.

Division Rear was situated on the north shore of Brittany in a lovely little town whose name escapes me, but I can well remember that we drove along the coast past numerous little coves where inviting blue-green water lapped up on clean white sand. The town itself was perched on the very edge of the sea, peaceful, quiet, delightful.

Though the setting was pleasant, a strong feeling of resentment grew within me. These soldiers moving about the town wore the same shoulder patch as my own men, received the same pay, the same promotions, and when they got back home they would be acclaimed as rugged fighting men of a combat division. Yet most of them had never heard a shot fired except on a rifle range. They were clean-shaven, freshly washed, their uniforms pressed. And some of them wore overcoats! I thought of how my men had slept on the ground the night before with wet, clammy raincoats wrapped around them, clad only in field jackets, trying to sleep while they shivered and their teeth chattered. These men lived in squad tents with cots and blankets. They ate good hot food on a three-meals-a-day basis and worked regular office hours with the rest of the time off.

"Guess there's more than one way to fight a war," I thought bitterly.

I did see one man though I did not envy. He was Lieutenant Macon Roberts, of my own company. Just before we moved into the Brest fight, Robby had been selected to return to Division Rear to orient new replacements coming to the division. Though he was enjoying his job and the excellent rest he was getting, he could not forget that it was temporary.

"It's going to be tough to get back in a foxhole after this," he told me, "especially after you've seen how these guys back here are fighting the war and still getting paid for it."

Finishing my business, I enjoyed another relaxing ride back to the company. Once there, I turned the money over to the other officers so they could be paying the men while I sought a bath. Rather than take the time required for a trip to the showers, I decided to go to the nearby community watering place, where the French had dammed a creek and used the stream for both washing and drinking. It seemed to me that they used it also as a community meeting place, for just as I became fully involved in my bath, the local housewives began arriving with jugs and buckets. I had to duck behind bushes in order to preserve my modesty.

Escaping at last with my modesty virtually intact, I found that a considerable sum of money remained for return to Division Rear. This was because the payroll had been made for all men who were in the company before the attacks on Dinard and Brest. Many of these men had become casualties, some were in the hospitals, some beyond the need of money forever.

The second trip to Division Rear was even more enjoyable than the first because Jack got permission to go with me. We naturally talked a lot of home and made constant comparisons with other journeys we had taken together in the States. Sometimes we stopped along the highway in response to the shouts of French kids and traded cigarettes and candy for fresh eggs, though we generally lost out in the swap.

While I was turning in the cash, Jack had a thorough look at life in the rear echelon.

"It's wonderful," he said. "Just like a great big plush-lined foxhole."

In the morning we climbed into trucks for the ride to the Crozon Peninsula, some 90 miles from our assembly area. The weather was as beautiful as only a French summer can be, and having the tops of the trucks down enabled us to enjoy it thoroughly. Most of the men acted more like they were headed for a picnic than a fight. Everywhere the French people gave us rousing receptions. They lined the roads, crowded the intersections, jammed the villages. At the farm houses whole families would run out to wave vigorously and shout, "Vive les Americains!"

From all sides we received the universal salute of victory started by Prime Minister Churchill of Britain, the upraised hand with fingers outstretched in a symbolic V for Victory. But the happy farmers of Brittany added another gesture Mr. Churchill never thought of. They began to throw apples at us!

It became an enjoyable—but dangerous—game. When added to the speed of our trucks, the apples came like bullets. Sitting on the front seat alongside the river, the windshield open, I had no place to hide from the wild pitches. Sometimes the apples came two or three at a time.

"Reach behind the seat, Lieutenant," the driver said.

I did, and came up with a baseball glove!

From then it was pitcher to catcher to the men in the rear of the truck for the full 90 miles as farmer after farmer tested his marksmanship. War was something far away, almost forgotten.

But it came back with a rush when the trucks came to a halt beside an open field and we disembarked with orders to dig in and await further instructions for an attack. We were still awaiting orders when word came that religious services were to be held in the next field. It was a Wednesday, but church was something we could not afford to reserve for Sundays—we had to take it whenever we could.

It seemed strange to attend church in an open field with a carbine across my lap and a steel helmet for a pew. On the other hand, this took nothing away from the solemnity of the service. The prayers raised from the fields and foxholes of France that summer could have had no equals in earnestness among all the glorious churches of the world.

We had three chaplains in the regiment, two Protestant and one Catholic. This was according to statistics showing that of a given number of men in a unit, so many would be Protestant, so many others Catholic. Our Protestant chaplains were Captain Neil H. McGeachy, of Fayetteville, N.C., and Captain Maxwell Pullen, a Georgian. Our Catholic chaplain was Captain Peter Wiktor, of Detroit. We lacked a Rabbi, but there again the percentage was the factor that decided whether one was assigned our regiment or not. Yet each division and corps had a certain number of Hebrew chaplains who travelled from unit to unit. Whenever a Rabbi visited our regiment, Jack gathered the Jewish boys together and took them to the services.

The same religious spirit prevailed that had impressed me in the foxholes outside Dinard. It was a common sight to see a long line of men waiting to approach a priest for confession in a quiet end of a field while others of us went about our jobs. Many of my men continued to be engrossed with their prayer books and doing Novenas for the end of the war, although the latter were conspicuously without success. I still prayed for Jack and for myself, while he prayed for me. Thus I felt protected on two sides. It was about this time that something prompted me to look for more complete protection. I wrote to Eleonore, who is Catholic, to send me a small religious medal to wear. I assumed that since my prayers were Protestant, Jack's Hebrew, and Eleonore's Catholic, one of us would be sure to have the right approach.

Elsewhere, preparations were moving rapidly for the attack. The fact was, higher headquarters was pushing the jump-off time right down our throats. At the start, the 28th Infantry and the One-Two-One were to attack together along parallel ridges while the gaps between us and on either flank were to be filled by the cavalry and the FFI. My machine gun platoon drew the assignment of protecting the left flank of our battalion. We were to be attached again to Company G, whose commander was still my old friend, Captain Black. The fine job he had done at Dinard had earned Black a promotion.

Just after dark we moved to another assembly area while waiting for Company E to send patrols to secure our line of departure. The patrols ran into trouble almost from the first—one was ambushed and its leader, Second Lieutenant Robert LaPreze, killed. The platoon sergeant also was killed, but a squad leader, Staff Sergeant William

F. Hobbs, whom I was to get to know well in subsequent days, reorganized the survivors and completed the mission.

A night move through unfamiliar terrain is always difficult and requires full cooperation from everyone. Unfortunately, on this night Jerry simply would not cooperate. The contact he made with Easy Company's patrols made him trigger-happy, and bursts of machine gun fire swept the fields intermittently. Only after considerable delay did we finally arrive at the line of departure and lie down to sleep in a cold, drizzling rain.

It stayed cold and foggy all night, so that when morning came only our watches could really tell us when the night had given way to dawn. At 7 a.m. we moved quickly to Company G's left flank and started forward with the rifle platoons, but within two minutes the Germans opened up with a savage, accurate artillery barrage.

Crawling close to a hedgerow, I pressed as close to the ground as the buttons on my field jacket would allow. I tensed the muscles in my rear end in an attempt to make it as small as possible, for it always seemed that this portion of my anatomy was protruding more than any other. As each shell exploded and the sickening whine of steel fragments filled the air, my stomach seemed to reach up past my head, take hold of my helmet and pull it down over my ears.

But as fierce and concentrated as the artillery attack was, it lasted but five minutes—and we all came through unscathed. I gave the signal to move forward again.

As soon as we came to a place on the flank where our guns could cover a wide stretch of territory, I left one section in place and moved ahead with the rest. As soon as we found another spot with good observation and field of fire, we set up, then sent back for the first. This leap-frog technique guaranteed one section in place and ready to fire at all times.

The only thing that slowed our advance was artillery fire. Once when I happened to look well to our left front, I actually spotted some of the enemy's big guns firing from a finger of land that jutted out into the ocean. I counted the number of flashes, then dived into a deep foxhole to wait for the shells to hit. Certain that I had detected a profitable target for our air and artillery, I hunted an artillery forward observer and pointed out the guns to him. He checked the location on his map and made a few rapid calculations. He finally said that the enemy pieces were out of range of his guns, but he promised to get artillery of longer range to take care of them. They'd be eliminated, he said, before we could say Crozon Peninsula.

We might have said Crozon Peninsula or Wooloomooloo until we were tongue tied if we had waited for either air or artillery to knock out these particular enemy pieces. They were to continue to plague and pepper us all through the battle. They were naval guns, installed by the French before the war in deep concrete casements. They would rise out of the ground to fire, then disappear. Our planes and later our biggest artillery worked to knock them out without success. It remained for the doughboys to dig them out in close combat in what amounted to the last bit of fighting on the peninsula.

Company G meanwhile ran into something more than artillery — intense small-arms fire from automatic weapons, backed up by accurate mortars. To the right of George Company, Easy Company joined the attack but was stopped cold with heavy losses. That meant the entire 2nd Battalion was butting against a solid Jerry line.

Leaving one section of guns to guard our flank, I brought the other two squads up to help Company G's attempts to advance. The big obstacle was a hill to our front that commanded all the ground around. As the day drew on, we added the fire of our machine guns to the pounding of our artillery on this hill; but each time our riflemen tried to move, Jerry loosed a withering blast of fire. Gradually there built up all around us the inevitable evidences of struggle—wounded men, wrecked equipment, battered buildings.

Determined somehow to break the impasse, I kept a constant vigil on the hill ahead. My efforts finally paid off when I saw the sun glisten on German helmets in a communications trench. Alerting my men quickly, we fired a series of deadly and accurate bursts on the trench. I was crouching close to one of our guns directing the fire of Jerry Schwartz, the gunner.

Suddenly: *whoooompff!*

The terrific explosion blasted me flat on my back. A mortar shell had landed within two feet of us, directly on the other side of the low hedgerow we were hiding behind. It was almost unbelievable that none of us was hurt. Had the shell landed a foot closer it would have cleared the hedgerow and been in our hip pockets, a foot farther away and the nasty, deadly bits of broken metal would have flown over the hedgerow to hit us full in the face.

"That sonofabitch had an eye like an eagle," said Jerry Schwartz. "A few inches closer and they'd be picking up our dog tags right now."

The German mortar fire had also come close to the other three guns, but the accuracy that had amazed Schwartz and me was not quite so evident at the other weapons. The best the Germans could claim was a small thigh wound on Sergeant Edwards.

But it was only a small sliver of metal, easily extracted, and Edwards stayed with us.

Suddenly we realized Jerry's mortar fire had been a parting gesture. The Germans came streaming down the hill, flying a white flag. Captain Black quickly took command of the situation and sent a platoon of riflemen ahead to occupy the hill. Since darkness was rapidly approaching, he decided not to risk sending his entire company or my machine gun platoon forward, for Easy Company on our right still had been unable to advance.

In the early gloom that night, as I made my way about while checking on various details, I saw a man on his knees praying. I carefully detoured past him, but as I passed again on the way back, I noted the man was still there in the same position, bent over at the waist with his hands flat against his face. This time I looked more closely. To my horror I discovered that a piece of shell had torn off a side of the man's skull.

I could only hope that he really had been praying when the shell had come from out of nowhere to end his life.

This experience was a forerunner of a hectic night to come. The fierce routine noises of battle were nerve-wracking enough, but to add to these, somewhere near us a wounded German began to call out. For what seemed like interminable hours he filled the air with pitiful howls for help. "Herr Oberst!" he called. "Herr Oberst!" We could not help but feel sympathetic after all, he was a human, and he was hurt, but we dared not go to his assistance for fear it just might be a trap.

Herr Oberst never came. The sounds grew weaker and eventually died out.

Near midnight the Germans swiftly and furiously counterattacked the platoon of Company G which had occupied that part of the hill which they had surrendered in late afternoon. But there was nothing we could do to help. The men were kicked off the position and were back with the bulk of the company almost before anyone else knew what was happening.

As one might expect, however, out of some of the most serious situations come some of the drollest experiences. The Jerry counterattack that night provided us with one of these—pathetic, yet not without humor.

Sometime during the noisy night I dropped off into a shivering sleep when Perkins, my messenger, touched me on the shoulder. I awoke with a start.

"Shhhhhh," Perkins cautioned. "You hear anything?"

I tried to listen even as I adjusted myself to the sudden shock of waking. Finally I made out a weak, plaintive voice.

"Pat!" the voice called. "Hey, Pat! Where are you, Pat?"

We listened intently, holding our breaths so we might hear every word.

"Hey, fellas, wait for me!" the voice continued, almost in a sob. "Wait for me! Please don't leave me! Hey, Pat!"

The voice drew slowly closer. It trembled, it pleaded, it broke, it almost seemed to weep.

"Hey, Pat! Wait for me. Hey, fellas!"

Cautioning my men against shooting, I crept slowly toward the sound. I waited until I was close on the man before I commanded him to halt. When he came to an excited, jittery stop, I could see that he was wearing our uniform, but when asked the password, he was too nervous to remember.

I finally made out that the man was from Company G's first platoon which had been on the hill, and he had lost his squad and his squad leader, Pat Riley. Satisfied at last that he was a GI, I led him back to our positions. He shook and trembled so we put him in a foxhole and covered the entire hole with a raincoat to enable him to have a smoke and go to sleep. When morning came, he was better and made his way to his platoon.

For weeks after that, my platoon's watchword was, "Hey, fellas! Wait for me!"

I could hear it almost everywhere I went, sometimes even in the thick of battle rising above all other sounds, and never did it fail to amuse me. Perhaps it was cruel to laugh at the plight of another soldier, but this never entered our minds.

"Hey, fellas! Hey, Pat! Wait for me!"

# 10

We were getting ready to renew the attack against the hill the next morning when we took a prisoner. Perhaps took is not exactly the word, since he came in voluntarily and surrendered. Hasty interrogation revealed that the other men in his outfit on the hill also wanted to surrender. The man offered to act as a guide if we would send an emissary to talk terms.

Captain Black selected one of his new platoon leaders, First Lieutenant Chauncey E. Barney, of Lincoln, Neb., and his communications sergeant, Rudy Greiss, Jersey City, N.J. Greiss spoke fluent German.

The surrender parley served to convince us more than ever that these Germans had strange minds. After spending the entire night fighting to regain the hill, they had sent out a decoy to see how we would react to a surrender offer. When Barney and Greiss reached them, the officer in charge insisted that he could not surrender unless he and his men were under fire, otherwise they would be classed as deserters. Quick-thinking Barney pointed his carbine into the air and fired several shots in rapid succession. Every one of the Jerries raised his hands in surrender. They marched down the hill—40 of them— honorable prisoners of war.

We moved out this time with all of Company G to occupy the hill, but Company E continued to have trouble, much of it from a village, Tal-ar-Groas. In the pocket of a dead Jerry on the hill I found a paper showing the fire plan for the entire area, including the village in front of Company E. When I sent this back to battalion, the C.O., Colonel Casey, decided to move Company F to our hill for commitment against the undefended flank of the enemy at Tal-ar-Groas.

From our hill we were able to aid Company F's advance with Company G's 6omm mortars. Barney and I spotted targets while the mortarmen plastered them. Because of the nature of the mortar which is a high trajectory weapon, mortarmen seldom get to witness the immediate results of their fire. Therefore, when one round landed just behind a hedgerow and blew a body high in the air, every man cheered.

Even after Company F cleaned out the village, some isolated dyed-in-the-swastika Nazis continued to hold out. Sometimes they opened fire on columns of prisoners which our men were leading to the rear, not, it seems, to get our men but to kill their own comrades, who had surrendered. In several cases they found their mark.

In the end Colonel Casey left Company E to clean out these remaining pockets and sent Companies F and G racing forward to exploit the advantage gained in taking the hill and the village. But hardly had we begun to move when I became aware that a hundred yards ahead of us the ground sloped sharply to a hill dotted with concrete emplacements. Properly defended, this could be an obstacle almost as difficult as Fort Bougan.

As Captain Black radioed back to battalion to warn of what we were approaching, I could make out the men of Company F, well off to our right, continuing forward, oblivious to the danger on their flank. Our job, it seemed to me, was as much to protect Company F as it was to advance ourselves. It was obvious that we should put every bit of our firepower against the fortified hill to forestall the enemy opening fire.

A cobblestone wall six feet high along the forward slope of the hill ruled out using machine guns, so I quickly contacted the leader of the rifle platoon we were accompanying. He was a slim, moustached second lieutenant whom I was destined to look on with derision not only in the hours ahead but months later. I asked him to do the job with his riflemen.

"We can't do that," the lieutenant answered in alarm. "If we start firing, they might bring mortar fire down on us."

I looked at him in amazement.

"Well, goddamnit," I practically shouted, "if we sit here and do nothing, F Company is going to get shot to hell and we'll get it too."

But the lieutenant would not budge. I turned away from him in disgust, rounded up my own men, and moved to the wall. From this point we found we could fire with our carbines and rifles at the embrasures of most of the emplacements. We also fired several bazooka rounds yet not a round of answering fire came from the German positions.

I was relieved, but nevertheless still concerned that the Germans were waiting for the men of Company F who would present a much more profitable target. Leaving most of my men as a base of fire, I took Sergeant Lawrence, Sergeant Mazza, and First Lieutenant Robert Armstrong, who had recently joined us as a mortar observer, to go forward and investigate the emplacements. Scaling the cobblestone wall, we picked our way through roll after roll of barbed wire, but still no fire came from the enemy positions. When the first few emplacements proved to be empty, we breathed somewhat easier, but continued to approach each position cautiously. At last I called the rest of my platoon forward to join the search.

As I moved down a narrow path joining two dugouts, I heard a small voice calling:

"Kamerad! Kamerad!"

I looked around. All I could see at first was a pile of broken branches, but as I watched a hand reached up through the branches and waved a dirty handkerchief. I rushed over, kicking the branches aside. There in a deep foxhole, cringing and crying, was a pair of Hitler's supermen.

One was an old fellow about 55 who had no stomach for war, for Adolph Hitler, or for his dirty foxhole. He pleaded to be allowed to take his personal belongings with him, to which I agreed providing he would tell where the rest of his unit was located. He unhesitatingly pointed to a bend in the road and emitted a stream of German. Satisfied that he had given us a good clue even though we could not understand all he said, I allowed him to scrape together his dirty belongings.

When the men from the rifle platoon joined us, we swept across the hill to find the rest of the German unit exactly where the old man said we would. They were crouched abjectly around a 40mm anti-aircraft gun. They raised their hands as we approached.

We continued forward, picking up an occasional prisoner here and there. By this time the slim, moustached young lieutenant had virtually abdicated as rifle platoon leader in my favor, so that I found myself directing both riflemen and machine gunners. But darkness was coming and we had not gone far beyond the anti-aircraft gun when word came to halt and pull back several hundred yards in order to straighten our lines for the night. On the way back we took apart the anti-aircraft gun, and carried pieces of it with us.

As the men began to dig in, I started for the rear to do something about getting chow and ammunition. I had gone less than a hundred yards when the Germans opened up with a tremendous artillery barrage. The huge shells came in a seemingly endless stream, the first time, it seemed to us, that Jerry had thrown artillery with the same ferocity and in the same quantity which we customarily threw at him. Some of the shells struck a cache of German mortar shells which I had noted during our advance that afternoon, and the whole pile exploded with a deafening roar.

Being caught in the open, I began to feel panicky, naked, afraid.

I looked at Sergeant Lawrence, and he looked at me.

"Time to be somewhere else, Lieutenant," Lawrence observed wryly.

I agreed. Together we ran to the nearest ditch.

Back at Tal-ar-Groas where Easy Company still was fighting to reduce bitterly resisting pockets of Germans, the shells had come in with much the same intensity. The Germans were just beginning to surrender and were emerging from their holes with hands high when the terrifying barrage started. GI's and Jerries, officers and men alike, dived for the same holes.

Sergeant Hobbs later told me of his experience.

"I jumped in a hole with five tough looking Jerries. They were armed like pirates, hand grenades hanging all over them. I didn't even have time to take their rifles. They looked scared to me, and I wasn't interested in looking brave to them either. All I wanted to do was get as low as I could in that hole."

When the shelling stopped, everybody crawled out of the holes to take up where he had been when the barrage started. The Jerries put their hands over their heads and our boys dusted themselves off and accepted their surrender as though nothing had happened.

That night was a cold one. It rained intermittently between periods of thick fog. In a vain effort to ward off the chill, we even stooped to covering ourselves with Jerry blankets. This was quite a departure for most of us, for we usually avoided using any enemy equipment since it was almost always indescribably filthy and smelled to high heaven.

When morning came and the fog lifted, we looked to our rear at a spectacular sight. From our position we could make out our artillery pieces, stretched, it seemed, as far as the eye could see. As each piece barked, we watched the puff of smoke and flame, in awe at the power of it all. But aside from the military aspects, our view from the hill that morning impressed even the least poetic among us. On one side lay the clear blue ocean with a brilliant sun highlighting sparkling ripples that followed the contour of long, graceful waves. On the other side the verdant green of an undulating landscape extending uninterrupted for miles. It seemed sacrilegious for men to be fighting in such a glorious setting.

But fighting was our business, and again we moved forward, this time paralleling the ocean.

Between us and the sea were men of the FFI. Looking down on them from higher ground, it was easy for us to see how their lack of military training led them into numerous tactical errors which, against a determined enemy, could prove disastrous.

Rather than using the hedgerows for concealment, for example, they exposed themselves unnecessarily in the middle of the open fields.

Later in the day when we took a Jerry supply depot, I turned it over to the leader of the French outfit. Though the French naturally refused to use any portion of the German uniform, they were obviously grateful for the boots, packs, and other equipment. We regretted that language differences kept us from becoming genuinely acquainted with these men. We could indicate our friendship only by gestures, supplemented on occasion by a French word or phrase we had picked up.

As the Frenchmen swarmed about the supply depot, I heard two of my men discussing them.

The first one was almost arrogant in his appraisal.

"They sure look like hell, don't they?" he said.

The other man looked at the Frenchmen, then eyed his partner up and down.

"You don't look so goddamned hot yourself, fella," he said.


As we continued to advance, I rounded a bend in the road and came upon the moustached rifle platoon leader. He was sitting by the road with a field telephone in his hand.

"You in touch with Captain Black?" I asked.

"No," the lieutenant said. "I'm in touch with my first squad. It's out in front."

I almost fell over. The man was directing his platoon by telephone!

It may be the privilege of officers of higher rank who command great numbers of troops to direct units by telephone, but a platoon leader is supposed to lead his men, not send them. It's his job to set an example of aggressiveness, to see that the job is done by doing it himself along with his men.

For the second time since I had known this lieutenant, I turned away from him with no effort to hide my disgust.

Impatient, I hurried forward to join the lieutenant's riflemen. They were approaching a group of imposing farm buildings.

With their permission I joined forces with them and for the rest of the day led the rifle platoon along with my own men.

At the farm we found evidence of Germans, but none were to be seen. They obviously had fled in haste, leaving vast amounts of equipment and personal effects behind. Finding a wallet filled with French money on a table I stuck it in my pocket. The place must have been a supply establishment of some sort, for we came across large stores of jam and tinned meats and a wagon load of freshly baked bread. Though most of the men tried to carry several cans of the food with them for a welcome change in diet, the extra weight soon prompted them to drop the cans by the way. The Infantry can't afford luxuries, even for the stomach it allegedly travels on.

Determined enemy resistance, it developed, became a stranger to us that day. So far and so fast did we travel that we outdistanced the other battalions of our regiment which had not shared our good fortune. Thus, eventually, we had to halt so we wouldn't get too far in front of the others.

From where we stopped and began to dig in, I could see another group of farm buildings about 600 yards beyond a broad, open field. Since nobody knew how long we might have to stay, these buildings were a danger until we could determine whether or not the Jerries occupied them. With Sergeant Lawrence and Sergeant Mazza, I set out to investigate.

As we approached the buildings, I could make out human forms at some of the windows, but couldn't be sure whether they were soldiers or civilians. Not until we cautiously entered the courtyard, could we be certain they were civilians. I called to them in my best French to come out, and, despite my French, they obeyed. They moved slowly and suspiciously until it occurred to me they were farm people and did not understand who we were.

I called out, "Americains!"

The magic word produced instant pandemonium! People ran around shouting the word at various doors and windows, whereupon the group expanded considerably. The people crowded around us, all talking at once with no one listening to anything anyone else said. They embraced us, shook our hands, hugged each other.

It was only with considerable effort that I managed to make myself heard.

"Beaucoup Boches ici?" I asked haltingly with appropriate gestures.

One of the Frenchmen grabbed me by the arm and beckoned for me to follow. Passing between two houses, we came to the rear of a large barn. He pointed to a huge haystack in which someone had carved out a shelter. At the opening sat an old lady much in the manner of a sentry. As we came forward, she put a finger to her lips and with a bony forefinger she pointed to the interior of the haystack. There, sleeping with rifles tucked in their arms lay two dirty, disheveled Jerries.

I reached over and stuck the muzzle of my carbine directly under the nose of one of the men. Sergeant Lawrence rammed the other in the rear end with the butt of his rifle. The two Germans bounded awake. The one facing my carbine appeared hypnotized —his hair seemed literally to stand on end and so fixedly did he stare at the muzzle of my weapon that his eyes crossed.

The French civilians roared with many years of pent up laughter.

The halt near the farm proved to be less lengthy than I had anticipated. Word came later the same day that the other units of the regiment were catching up and we were to continue to advance, this time on the town of Crozon itself.

The Germans we met on the way obviously were rear echelon troops who had little taste for fighting—men who were more at home behind a desk than in a foxhole. They were scared and confused and preferred quick surrender to the prospect of close combat.

Crozon itself fell quickly, yielding at least a hundred Germans who could have made it rough for us had they chosen to fight. It had been a long, wearisome day, but the tactics of moving ahead swiftly despite fatigue had paid off in long advances and virtually no casualties.

More supplies fell into our hands in Crozon, and we feasted on pumpernickel and salami.

"Gastronomically speaking," said Bob Osterberg, munching on a thick sandwich, "this has been an excellent day."

"I don't know what that means," gurgled Jimmy Hearld with his mouth full, "but we sure been eatin' good."

We were still feasting when orders came to move out at once and occupy Hill X, just beyond the town.

"Goddamn those bastards," growled Johnny Tardibuono, "don't they think we ever get tired?"

I was inclined to agree with Johnny, though I was aware it would do no good for morale if I did. My men were thoroughly exhausted. They had matched the riflemen stride for stride all day, while at the same time had carried heavy machine guns, tripods, and ammunition in addition to personal arms and equipment.

But for all their grumbling, the men shouldered their equipment and moved out through the outer streets of the town toward Hill X. We were passing through a small woods on the slope of the hill when somewhere, someone let loose a wild burst of machine gun fire. I hit the ground, spotted a long narrow hole to my left, got up and made a dash for it. One of my squad leaders, Sergeant Gerald D. Smith, ran faster than I did and with a bold rush leaped past me and landed feet first in the hole.

Hardly a moment passed though before he dejectedly crawled out. It didn't require close observation to make Smith's embarrassing plight apparent. He had discovered the only German latrine we came upon in all of France!


When at last we got to the top of Hill X our tongues were dragging. Too exhausted to dig in, we looked for protective obstacles along a line of houses bordering a road which ran across the top of the hill. Even though French civilians ran from the houses to welcome us, most of the men were soon asleep, dead to the world and oblivious of the joy our arrival had wrought. There was no thought of bringing up rations—no one wanted anything to eat. All we wanted was to be able to rest without a thought of carrying a machine gun or a tripod or an ammunition box another blessed step.

The next morning a distant rumble of heavy artillery told us that the war had passed by us as we slept. The 13th Infantry had passed through to complete mop up of the peninsula while the One-Two-One shifted back to division reserve. But our job was not over by a long shot as we still had to round up German stragglers. Some still occupied their defensive positions, but generally they had lost the will to fight.

The rapid conquest of the peninsula eventually brought a piece of good news; the two companies which Jerry had captured when we had been on our way to Brest were rescued. The men were all in good health, though clearly not overfed. They hadn't been mistreated, but we attributed this less to a change of German heart than to the realization on his part that he was bottled up and would soon be playing the role of prisoner.

The parade of returned prisoners brought back a lot of tales, but few in the entire war equalled the incident which happened in the last violent action to clear the Crozon peninsula. As the 13th Infantry swept forward to take a finger of land overlooking the harbor of Brest, the men swarmed all over the command post of the German general who had commanded the defense of Brest, the paratrooper, Herman Bernhard Ramcke.

Ramcke stayed deep in his protective dugout while sending an emissary to meet his conquerors.

"General Ramcke is below," said the stiff-backed Nazi with a supercilious look at the GI's on all sides of him, "but he will surrender only to an officer of equal rank."

Since the assistant division commander of the 8th Division, General Canham, was closely following the attack, a message got to him quickly. Arriving at the scene, he descended to the bottom of Ramcke's deep, concrete shelter.

Arrogant, a monocle in one eye, looking for all the world like Eric von Stroheim in the movies, Ramcke glared at General Canham with condescension.

"Let me see your credentials," the German demanded. General Canham stared at him for a moment. Then he glanced at the tough, battle-proven troops standing all about him.

"These," General Canham announced with a sweep of his hand, "are my credentials."

# 11

When it became clear beyond any doubt that Brest and the Crozon peninsula were both in hand, we moved to bivouac areas near the town of Morgat, close to the sea, where hot food awaited us. That night we had blankets to keep our teeth from chattering and pup tents to keep us dry. It was warm and good to relax, to rest, to feel reasonably sure we would see the sun rise.

Our first morning in the bivouac area, a group of men asked if we could make up a swimming party. The battalion commander, Colonel Casey, was reluctant at first, hesitant to risk losing men by drowning, but I assured him I had been a lifeguard most of my life and would make sure nothing happened.

"I've been responsible for their safety for the past two months in some pretty tight spots, so I guess I can be responsible for them when they're having fun," I said. The Colonel agreed.

I rushed back with the good news but they had anticipated me and were ready to go. We walked down to the water and then along a sandy beach until we came to a particularly pleasant spot. The men stayed out of the water while I dived in to make a preliminary search, for the entire strip of beach was studded with German defenses against attack from the sea, tall poles with land mines and shells attached to them, great iron tetrahedrons, and other obstacles. But in this spot there were no mines or obstacles other than those above water which we could see. The men quickly skinned out of their uniforms and plunged in with a raucous chorus of whoops and yells.

Though the sun was warm, the water was brisk, for now it was September. We ran in and out of the water, as naked as the day we were born. All along the beach men from other units began following our example, piling their uniforms on the sand and taking advantage of the water and the magnificent day.

The taste of salt water in my mouth and the fresh feel of the breeze on my face created an overwhelming case of homesickness within me. Staring out across the endless ocean, I wishfully believed I could see Eleonore far away at the water's edge in Long Beach, looking toward me. I had a tremendous desire to become the first soldier ever to go AWOL by swimming the Atlantic Ocean.

Our antics in the surf meanwhile drew a gallery of French civilian sightseers. Though our spectators were of all ages and both sexes, they all seemed equally oblivious of our somewhat exposed condition. Realizing that they were some little distance from us, I excused their disregard, but I never could understand the motives of one young Frenchman who walked along the beach with a pretty young mademoiselle. Hand in hand, they strolled right among us. The only explanation I could hit upon was that the Frenchman must have been sure of his own physical proportions and was trying to prove to his companion that he was quite a man by comparison.

The peace of our spot gradually disappeared as more and more men arrived for a swim or a stroll. Nor did it help when some of our artillery units began using a small strip of land out in the water as a target for zeroing their weapons. That kind of spoiled it, so somewhat reluctantly we put on our clothes and headed back toward the bivouac area.

For the next few days we were able to return to the beach every day. Entertainment units also visited us, and in a nearby town movies were shown. One night Jack and I made the long hike into Morgat for a movie. As we waited for the film to begin, a happy buzz of conversation filled the building. Gradually, as the makeshift theatre became jammed with men and the show still failed to begin, the buzz changed to wisecracks, then to whistles, catcalls, and stomping of feet.

A hapless Special Services officer finally responded.

"Men," he announced apologetically, "I'm sorry to keep you waiting, but we're having trouble with our generator. We'll start the show just as soon as we can."

By this time night had fallen. We sat in pitch darkness, shifting restlessly in our seats, eager for the film to begin, when off in a corner somebody began to sing. Here and there over the hall lusty voices joined in until the air vibrated with song. There was no leader, and even had there been one, we could not have seen him, for the only light in the building came from myriad cigarettes glowing and subsiding—but no sooner did one song end than another began.

We ran through a vast repertoire of familiar songs, some from World War I, others from World War II, some with no wartime connotation. Then from somewhere rose a clear, resonant voice—

*"God Bless America! Land that I love"*

Others joined in. The volume swelled, loudly, proudly, confidently.

*"Stand beside her, and guide her ..."*

Warm little prickles ran along the back of my neck.

*"God Bless America! My home, sweet home!"*

When it was over, no one spoke. The faintest whisper would have sounded like thunder in the silence which settled over the hall—a deep, penetrating, reflective silence.

At long last a brazen, raucous voice piped up with a shout.

"To hell with France! Give me Brooklyn!"

The audience broke into a spontaneous cheer.

For two hours we sat in the building waiting for the film to begin, but in the end the Special Services officer had to return and confess failure. We drifted out into a dark street and slowly picked our way along the road back to our tents.

We had seen no movie, but the evening had not been wasted.

I got paid during this interval of rest, my first pay in several months. Before leaving the States, I had arranged for Eleonore to receive the majority of my pay in the form of a monthly allotment, but despite this, I had managed to accumulate about 9,600 francs. This amounted to approximately $196. Yet when you have nothing to spend it for, money means nothing. I sent the entire amount home.

I used the francs from the Jerry wallet I had picked up to buy a Post Exchange (PX) ration for my platoon. This paid for plenty of candy, cigars, and the like. While visiting regimental headquarters, I also managed to liberate a number of cans of sardines and a few bottles of wine. I took these back concealed under my field jacket and we had a feast.

We had no way of knowing as we ate, but this was in the way of a farewell ceremony for me. Word came shortly after we finished that I was to be transferred from the platoon to become executive officer of Company E!

If my men were not genuinely upset, they put on an excellent show to that effect. They even got up a petition to the battalion commander, asking him to rescind the order, but I talked them out of it. I knew the reason for the order. In the fighting at Tal-ar-Groas, Easy Company had lost all its officers. Colonel Casey had taken Bob Fay from his job as S-2 on the battalion staff to take command of the company. In looking around for an executive officer he had settled on me because he was aware that most of my training experience had been with a rifle company. Besides, the appointment was somewhat of a promotion since the executive officer takes over as company commander if the occasion demands.

I was naturally touched at the efforts of the men in the platoon to keep me, but I did not kid myself that it was all personal attachment. We had been through a lot together and, in the process, had suffered fewer casualties than any other platoon in the battalion. Every man likes to stay with a lucky combination; my men were no exception. As a parting gift they presented me a tiny pair of wooden shoes which each man autographed.

I never received a finer gift from a finer bunch of men.

About the same time I shifted to Company E, the entire regiment moved back to the heart of the Brittany peninsula near Landernau. This brought an end to the swimming and produced an increase in the work that came my way as Executive Officer of the company. With the lull in combat, we naturally had to catch up on the small mountain of paper work that had been piling up steadily. My unfamiliarity with the men of the company added to the problem. Fortunately, I had the whole-hearted assistance of the best first sergeant I ever met in the Army, Fred E. Foy, a North Carolinian. Sergeant Foy was a little older than most of us. He had seen years of service, knew his job, and did not have to be prompted to carry it out. It would be a long time before I lost the feeling that I was merely a novice in many respects in comparison with Sergeant Foy.

Rest and relaxation were over; rules and regulations took their place. We had a definite time for reveille each morning. Training schedules went into the planning stage and were to include such comparatively dull subjects as "Military Courtesy and Discipline." Rumors began to percolate throughout the regiment that the 8th Division was to see no more combat but was to train for a role in the Army of Occupation. The rumor sounded so good that we embellished it with each new day and passed it along to anyone who would listen.

The emphasis on garrison soldiering reached a climax when we polished up for a regimental parade and review. Though the very thought of a parade was abhorrent, we tempered it with the feeling that things could be a lot worse. Then we learned we had to make a 2-1/2 hour march to the parade ground. By the time we arrived and put in an hour of practice, we might have welcomed a few big artillery shells to bring the thing to a halt. To make matters worse, it rained hard most of the day. Yet we did get a certain amount of satisfaction out of it all when our new company commander, Lieutenant Fay, was awarded a Silver Star. We felt the company was in good hands when we saw the division commander pin this medal on him for gallantry in action back in Normandy.

A minor miracle took place when someone authorized passes to visit the town of Landernau. Jack and I got on the pass list, determined to see what a French town looks like when you don't have to fight your way into it first. But when we got there all we saw were long rows of olive-drab clad soldiers lonesomely wandering the streets or sitting around talking and trading with hopelessly-outnumbered Frenchmen. Here and there a lucky GI passed with a girl on his arm, but usually he came in for merciless razzing because his date's entire family brought up the rear as chaperones.

Hardly had we returned to our bivouac when we learned that the wishful rumors of the past few days had been no more than just that. Orders had come that we were to prepare for another move, this time by train across France, and get back in the fighting.

In preparation for the move and approaching winter we drew warm clothing, and I even managed to find an overcoat to fit me —a notable achievement. Service Company also sent our barracks bags forward. This proved to be for many a cruel, disheartening experience. First we had to cull out the bags of those who had been killed or wounded. Then when we arrived at our own, many found that their bags had been rifled. Since the bags had been held in our own regiment's care all the time, this meant that our own men were guilty of stealing. The bitterness felt toward whoever was guilty exceeded anything we might have demonstrated toward an ordinary thief, for we felt that the men of Service Company, privileged to have comparatively safe jobs, should have shown some respect for those who were doing the actual fighting. Some of the men lost genuinely valuable articles. Jack, for example, lost an expensive wrist watch. My own belongings arrived intact, probably because nothing of mine would fit anybody else.

Thus, with mixed feelings we packed our belongings and prepared to move to the railroad marshalling yard. It was a long hike over rough roads, and because the regiment's vehicles had already left in convoy for the journey across France, we had to carry all our equipment—sweating, swearing and stumbling every foot of the way.

When we struggled into the railroad yard and got our first look at our transportation, it was quite a shock. We were to travel in small, battered, dirty freight cars. On the sides of them were the words that had become so familiar a generation before during World War I:

40 Hommes
8 Chevaux

Translated: 40 men; 8 horses!

# 12

Little of our speculations about our projected trip across France had centered around accommodations. Probably all of us had the preconceived notion that train travel in the States meant simple luxury of some sort. Subconsciously we had expected similar treatment in France. But when we saw the little box cars, we knew with one sudden jolt that we were in for a rough ride.

"It ain't exactly first class, is it, Lootenant?" asked one man as we stood near a long line of cars waiting to be assigned.

"It's considered first class for horses," was all I could reply.

It must have been an incorrigible optimist who devised the theory that 40 men could fit into one of those little French freight wagons. I certainly doubt that he ever tested his theory personally with a ride across the bosom of France from Brest to Luxembourg. I have no data on the manner in which the eight horses could make out, but as for 40 dogfaces, complete with barracks bags, packs, rifles, rations, and miscellaneous gear, I can state without equivocation that the sign "40 Hommes" is a gross exaggeration.

GI humor was at its loud best as we surveyed our transportation and awaited orders to climb aboard. Meanwhile, I checked the rations and water in each of Easy Company's cars and reported to Battalion that our cars were ready. An officer at Battalion told us to crawl aboard and make ourselves comfortable.

"Are you kidding?" I asked. "Let's just amend that to read we climb aboard."

"Well," said the officer, "comfortable or not you're stuck with it, so you might as well like it." He said it with the air of a man who had brought along an air mattress for just such an emergency.

The night was pitch black. There were no lights at the station, and few of us had flashlights. We scrambled aboard somehow and milled around in the darkness trying to get settled, but it was no use. No matter how we tried, we always wound up with several men standing with no place to lie or even sit. Fortunately, almost everybody was in a holiday mood, so that we still could make jokes even as the string of cars with their cramped human burden pulled out of the freight yards.

I bunked with the weapons platoon, a group that remained full of high spirits through the night even though we soon became convinced we were travelling over the roughest roadbed in France. We were jostled interminably around the floor of the car on hard boards that refused to give even the slightest with our weight. When dawn finally came, we met it with bloodshot, sleepy eyes and stiff, aching bodies. They say that soldiers are happy only when they have something to gripe about. If this is true, we were without doubt the world's happiest troops.

The train made numerous stops. Some were because of bomb damage to the line, others were for refueling, and still others, it seemed to us, simply because the patched, wheezing little engine got tired. At every stop groups of French civilians traded with us—long loaves of French bread in exchange for candy, chewing gum, and cigarettes. Sometimes they also bartered various kinds of wine and cognac, which helped to make our K-ration diet more palatable.

Sanitation was one of our more major problems. Each car carried a large pail which we promptly christened the "honey bucket," but to designate a pail a latrine and to get the men to use it were two different things. The pail remained unspoiled through the entire trip while the men adjusted to their personal emergencies as best they could. When the train was in motion, the accepted method—when you simply could not wait—was to use the wide, open door with a trusted comrade holding you tight. But for needs requiring more preparation the men generally gritted their teeth until the train stopped. Then a general exodus began from every car, each man with shovel in hand.

Since we could never know how long any stop would be, it took considerable courage to dig a hole and undo your pants. The engineer operating the train obviously took diabolical delight in starting up just at the most crucial times. It became a common sight to see a man running full speed after his car, his shovel in one hand, his pants held up with the other. Cheers and jeers urged him on to greater speed.

When he finally reached his goal, helping hands reached out to pull him aboard, and he received an ovation from every car in sight.

Meals aboard the train were less of a problem. We had loaded enough K-rations for the entire journey into each car, and at mealtime we simply doled them out. Though we ate perfunctorily and with little relish, at least we ate. The roadbed all the way from Brittany was strewn with the trash of ration tins and boxes. We had no alternative but to throw them out, for we could not afford to take up space in our cramped quarters with garbage. Though the company kitchens were set up and ready to operate in some of the cars, feeding hot meals proved to be impossible, primarily because we never knew how long we were going to stop and because we had no way of passing between cars. The kitchens did make an effort to provide hot water on occasion so we could make coffee or bouillon, but the unscheduled nature of our stops usually precluded even this.

In checking with the kitchen for hot water during one of the stops, I became marooned in the kitchen car. At first I resigned myself to a prolonged, boring wait but soon came to realize that in reality it was considerably less than a hardship. The cooks in the kitchen car were from Company H, my old outfit, and they insisted on preparing me something hot to eat. There was no use protesting! Mess sergeants are a race apart; their kitchens are their domain and their word is unquestioned law. With a typical desire to please, the cooks dug deep into stocks they may have been saving for themselves and came up with a new type C-ration I had not seen. One consisted of spaghetti, another of frankfurters, a third chicken—all made my mouth water after the monotony of K-rations. Though C-rations themselves could become as banal as K's if you had them all the time, to those of us more accustomed to K-rations, the C's were a delicacy.

K-rations—God love 'em—came in three types: breakfast, dinner, and supper. Each was packed inside a cardboard box, heavily waxed to make it waterproof. We burned the boxes whenever possible to heat the rations, but often the situation wouldn't permit this. Nor could we heat them on the train for fear of setting the wooden freight cars afire.

Breakfast was by far the most popular meal. It contained a can of ham and eggs or pork and egg yolks, four cigarettes, a bar of concentrated dried fruit, soluble coffee, sugar, and hard biscuits. Coffee was one reason the breakfast package was so popular. No one ever understood why the Army did not see fit to put coffee in all three meals.

The dinner ration was the least popular, and justly so. It contained a can of processed cheese, the inevitable hard biscuits, lemonade powder, cigarettes, a roll of malted milk tablets that hardly anyone ever ate, and sometimes a pack of lifesavers.

The supper meal was more popular than the dinner only in the sense that it was less unpopular. Personally, I never minded it too much. When we were able to supplement it with white bread, it made an acceptable meal. Supper was either a can of beef or pork, bouillon powder, cigarettes, candies, the same damned hard biscuits, and—precious commodity—toilet paper.

We always had to supervise handing out the rations, for if left to his own devices, every man would unashamedly take three breakfast rations. That would mean that the man to be fed last— the hapless lieutenant—would get three despised dinner boxes. I saw times during the course of the war when we would reach over and relieve a dead man of his breakfast ration, whereas we would not disturb his dinner or supper.

C-rations came in small round tin cans. Two cans made a meal. But carrying C-rations in combat was awkward because of their shape, which is probably why the Infantry got few of them.

Another ration which made a big hit with us was 10-in-1. This also was boxed, but one big carton contained a full meal for 10 men. The food was better and in greater variety and contained margarine, jam, and powdered eggs. We got this only when it was possible to prepare hot food. The cooks usually prepared this ration and brought it forward in cans.

Prior to our second night on the train we decided on a scientific approach to the problem of finding enough space for everybody to sleep. Before it got dark, everybody got to his feet. Stowing all non-essential equipment in one end of the car we prepared a huge bed by spreading all our blankets on the floor. With infinite care we put several thicknesses of blankets over the roughest boards.

I directed one man to lie in a comer of the car with his face to the wall, then another to lie in the opposite corner so that their feet were together.

"So far," I thought, "so good."

One by one I called forward each of the other men to lie with his face toward the back of the man ahead of him. As a neat, orderly pattern of prostrate men began to take shape, I was proud that it was I who had fathered such a scientific approach. But as we neared the far end of the car, I began to have my doubts.

These doubts proved justified. We ran out of floor space, but not out of people. We still had two men left over!

I signaled everyone to his feet again. This time we tried it another way, the men lying head to foot lengthwise in the car. At first, this too looked like the solution, but again when we reached the far end of the car, the result was the same.

Two men left over!

Two more times we tried it, once each way. But each time the same. Two men left over. Somebody then suggested a diagonal approach, but this seemed to offer no real possibility of success—particularly at the corners.

By this time it was dark, and we had no choice but to give up. The solution we had to accept was a rotation system whereby the two men left over acted as guards—not that we really needed guards. Dividing the remaining hours of darkness, we posted a list which showed how long each pair was to stay awake and whom they were to tap when it came their turn to lie down and sleep.

The system was just as uncomfortable in practice as it may sound in the telling. We were so tightly packed that if one man insisted on turning over or otherwise altering his position, everybody else had to follow suit. And the man with the weakest kidneys was invariably the one in the farthest corner from the door. His efforts to find his way to the door inevitably led to much shouting and confusion.

One night of this arrangement was enough to prompt us to try more rehearsals the next day in an effort somehow to find a place for those two men. But to no avail. As a matter of fact, we tried throughout the entire trip, but no matter how much we studied by day, drawing intricate diagrams, practicing time after time, the result was always the same.

Two men left over.


As we lurched along on our uncomfortable way, the scenery provided refreshing changes, from the closely-walled hedgerow country of Brittany to the great open fields of the interior of France where waving grass beckoned from long, gently sloping hills. Picturesque villages, built usually around churches, nestled along rivers or at the foot of the verdant hills. Stretches of open country, patches of forest, gentle rivers, and people who never seemed to tire of waving friendly greetings.

"It sure looks good," said Sergeant Dixon, "but I'm waiting for this contraption to go through Paris. All my life I've wanted to see Paree, and I got a feeling it's gonna be now."

"Don't be crazy," replied Sergeant Archie Champion. "If this train gets anywhere near Paris, they'll be looking for the One-Two-One for the next two years."

I had no way of knowing whether we would go through Paris, but I silently agreed with Sergeant Champion that we would have quite a problem if we did. The results, I could well imagine, would be catastrophic. In fact, even while we were still conjecturing about Paris, our train stopped in the station of a fairly large town, and we had our first AWOL. What made it worse, the man was from my own car.

As we finally learned the story, the man missed the train for a fundamental physical reason. He let a thing called sex get the better of him. The guilty man—who in the end drew less censure than envy from the others—was a little fellow with a long, hard-to-pronounce Polish name that escapes me, but he eventually arrived at our destination by catching the next section of our train, which ran a few hours behind us.

The man's explanation was fairly simple and easy to believe. He had gotten off the train to stretch his legs and had walked behind the station platform to the latrine. As he emerged, a beautiful (to hear him tell it) mademoiselle accosted him with an offer of an attractive way to spend some of the otherwise useless francs that were bulging his pockets. They retired to the nearest place of rendezvous which was a dark hallway, but in his quest, our hero lost all track of time. By the time he finally completed his business transaction, our train had left. Even though he caught the next train, the episode eventually cost him not only what he had paid the young lady, but two-thirds of his pay for six months.

But he appeared not to mind the punishment.

"It was worth it," he contorted. "Oo-la-la!"

## 13

Our trip through Paris never got beyond speculation. Our train did pass on the outskirts of the city, but it was at night and none of us even suspected we were in the vicinity.

But we apparently could not be content unless we were speculating about something, for no sooner had we learned that we had left Paris behind than we began to guess just when and where our ride might end. At one stop a man talked a Frenchman out of a tattered road map, and by plotting on the map the names of the stations we passed through, we managed to figure roughly where we were.

When we finally did crawl creakily out of our 40 & 8's, it was on the northeastern border of France near the Duchy of Luxembourg at a quaint old town called Longuyon. Waiting for us was a reception committee made up of men who had preceded us in the motor convoy. They guided us into an assembly area in a large forest several miles from town where we went into bivouac while awaiting the rest of the regiment. As night came, word spread that we would leave by truck the next morning for our new assignment at the front.

From France we passed into Luxembourg, then into a corner of Belgium. Following our course on our tattered map, it seemed for a while as if we were going in circles, and we began to wonder if anybody actually knew where we were headed. Yet we didn't mind for the weather was delightful, we had the covers off the trucks, and the roads were lined with people who shouted and waved Allied flags at us. Gay signs of welcome, and pictures of the Grand Duchess of Luxembourg covered every house and store front.

At long last we came to the pleasant city of Diekirch, ostensibly undamaged by war. It felt good to see a place that size without the destruction we had come to expect in France. But beyond the outskirts of the city our trucks finally stopped and we piled off. We were getting close. We were to walk the rest of the way.

Lieutenant Fay briefed me as we marched along a tree-shaded road paralleling the little Sauer River.

"Paul," he said, "we relieve units of the 5th Armored Division. Our company will be stationed in Bettendorf, just a few miles ahead. I won't make any definite plans until I see the terrain, but while I go ahead with the non-coms to reconnoiter, you take care of the rear. Find us a good CP in Bettendorf and keep everybody ready to move just as soon as you get word from me."

Bettendorf proved to be a quiet little rural town with several beer parlors—the sight of which brought whoops of joy as we marched along. Passing through the town quickly, I found a deserted chateau on the far edge, the side closest to where I thought our positions would be. After a cursory inspection, I decided it would make an ideal CP. The men quickly nicknamed it "the Castle." I set up the company headquarters in a room dominated by a huge fireplace.

After completing all that I thought necessary for the moment, I went up the hill to look for Lieutenant Fay. I found him talking with a group of men from the 5th Armored and for the first time got some idea of where we were and what we were to do.

The hill we were on ran parallel to the Our River, the dividing line between Luxembourg and Germany. Through tall trees tinged with autumn colors I could make out the far bank of the river and beyond it parts of the German border fortifications, the Siegfried Line. The concrete pillboxes and a curving line of concrete antitank obstacles looked unreal against the rural setting. Seeing the defenses for the first time sent little chills up my back. I could not help but shudder at the prospect of attacking it.

"If they had just given us some gasoline and some infantry," said a bearded sergeant from the 5th Armored, "you guys wouldn't have had to worry about going through them dragon's teeth or nothing else. Our whole company was ten miles through that line and never met no opposition to speak of. We just rolled past pillbox after pillbox. All of them empty."

"Yeah," a tank driver put in, "then we ran outa gas. We begged for it, but we couldn't get it. Somebody else had a higher priority, they said. Who shoulda had more right than us? We were right through the toughest part of Germany like a dose of salts." "What made you pull back?" I asked.

"Orders," spat out one man.

"Yeah, orders," said the sergeant. "Orders and the fact a few Krauts begun to sneak in behind us and cut our supply lines. We couldn't even get no ammunition, so they told us to fall back. We didn't have enough infantry to hold the pillboxes, and we didn't have no TNT to blow 'em to hell. We didn't even have enough gas to bring all our tanks back. We didn't have nothing." The withdrawal had obviously affected these men deeply. They had been in the vanguard of a bold, rapid sweep across France and into Germany. They were proud, and the sting of defeat, no matter what the excuse, was hard to take.

"A lotta guys gonna have to die to take that ground back again," said a man softly who had been standing quietly while the others talked. "A lotta guys gonna have to die."

He was right. A lot of men would die here, for this was a part of the front which Hitler would choose for launching his big counter-offensive in December—the "Battle of the Bulge."

Lieutenant Fay and I surveyed the long hill and the positions occupied by the 5th Armored.

"Well, we're going to get a taste of a defensive situation," Bob said as though thinking out loud, "but it's going to be a helluva defense. We couldn't stop a company of boy scouts if they wanted to take the time to walk around us. The closest company to us will be more than a mile away. Looks like our platoons will be so far apart they won't be able to see each other, even in daylight." Bob's concern was well founded, for the 8th Division had drawn a sector 28 miles wide, a width normally accorded three divisions even in less compartmented terrain.

"Our job will be to hold key terrain features. We'll have to send out plenty of patrols, and we'll have to keep German patrols the hell out of our lines. We've got to see they stay on their side of the river—and we're under strict orders to stay on ours."

"That last part shouldn't be too hard to manage," I grinned.

Completing our reconnaissance, we selected tentative positions for the platoons, and I went down the hill to bring the company forward.

With the thought that we might be here a long time, we told the men to dig in solidly, not small foxholes or prone shelters but dugouts big enough to hold three men comfortably, covered with logs and tarpaulins to keep out the weather. We put two platoons in position on the hill and kept the third in Bettendorf as a reserve that could move quickly to either forward position if the situation demanded. Battalion headquarters in turn set up a rotation plan whereby each company was to spend six days on the line, then three in reserve. When our first stay in reserve ended, we moved to the opposite end of the long battalion position so that we could become acquainted with the length of the entire front.

The first few days in these positions we knew little of what to expect, so everybody was jittery. The attitude of the men went to two extremes; some acted as though Jerry was a thousand miles away while others could see him lurking behind every tree. But it was not long before all became convinced that caution was essential, for as men of Fox Company were adjusting their positions one night, the Germans skillfully ambushed an entire rifle squad.

Since the day we arrived in Luxembourg was October 2nd, my birthday, I considered it fitting that I should sleep that night on a bed, my first time since landing in France. I spread my blankets and bedroll with great ceremony across the bed in one of the rooms of the chateau and then luxuriated in the delightful softness of it. Of course, there were two other men in the bed with me which made it a trifle crowded, but it was a bed.

Early in our stay in Luxembourg, a miracle happened. Jack was assigned to company E.

It was not the permanent assignment both of us had hoped for. I had been pressing Bob Fay to get Jack in the company ever since I had been transferred, and Bob was sympathetic enough to put pressure on battalion. At last Colonel Casey agreed that since Company E temporarily had fewer officers than any other company, he would let us have Jack, but only until replacement officers arrived. We considered we had accomplished the first step and that making the transfer permanent would be easier now than it would have been otherwise.

When the company completed its six days in the line and came back to the chateau in Bettendorf, every man got a hot shower or bath in a big brewery, converted for the purpose, in Diekirch. Because the weather had begun to turn cold, few of us had elected to take *al fresco* baths in our helmets. Thus, these baths were not a luxury but a prime necessity.

The fact that beer—watered, to be sure—was available in Diekirch did not make the visit any more unpleasant.

When our three days in reserve were over, we moved to the position on the right of the battalion front, and I shifted the company CP to the little town of Mostroff. The forward platoons were in and around the village of Reisdorf, near the junction of the Our and Sauer Rivers.

We had only been there overnight when we received a rude shock. Orders arrived for Bob Fay to report to headquarters of the Ninth Army for duty. He was to leave immediately.

We hated to lose Bob, and he disliked going, but all of us realized that men live longer in a rear headquarters, and we were glad to see him get the break. He had already proven his ability and courage in combat so that a rear echelon job was something he could wear with dignity. He packed his gear and was gone almost before we could realize it had happened.

I took over command of the company and left immediately to have a look at the front line positions, but when I got back to Mostroff at nightfall I found my command had been short-lived. Regimental headquarters had sent down Captain William McKenna, of Macon, Ga., to fill the vacancy. Captain McKenna was an experienced officer who, a month or so earlier, had been wounded by a hand grenade. He had only recently returned from the hospital.

Until late that night Captain McKenna and I hunched over a map while I told him what I knew of the company's positions. Hardly had we turned in and fallen asleep when the field telephone beside my bed jangled nervously. The Jerries had attacked one of our positions, a voice on the other end of the wire told me excitedly, and wiped it out.

Hurriedly, Captain McKenna and I dressed and started forward to determine for ourselves just what had happened. We reached the position just at daylight and there heard a strange story of coincidences that can and often do cause tragedy in war.

The position that had come under attack was located at a bend in a road where a machine gun crew from Company H was covering the road with fire. A half squad of riflemen had dug in on either side of the road to protect the gun so the position constituted a fairly strong outpost. The men manning the position had been anticipating return of one of our patrols which had gone out earlier. Unknown to them, though, the patrol had gotten lost in the darkness and had come through our lines at another location.

Word of the patrol's return didn't reach the outpost, and about two hours before daylight the men at the outpost heard a noise to their front. They ordinarily would have fired immediately, but suspecting it was our patrol, they called out, "Halt!" and demanded the password. The only answer was a scuffling noise on the road.

Still concerned lest they fire on our own men, they repeated the challenge. A hand grenade was the answer. For the Germans it was a lucky toss for the grenade landed directly in front of the machine gun, wounding both men behind the gun and putting the weapon out of commission. Alerted, the nearby riflemen opened fire, but a burst from a Jerry machine pistol killed two of them.

The report I received that the position had been wiped out was exaggerated, but losing two killed and two wounded in this manner was bad enough.

During the next few days Captain McKenna directed minor adjustments in our positions. He was, I soon learned, a thoroughly capable and conscientious officer, firm but fair in everything he did. He never took anything for granted, going into the smallest details to make sure everything was just right and everybody understood. I admired him and learned a lot by watching him.

When we became accustomed to the way the Captain wanted things, the company functioned smoothly. First Sergeant Foy easily handled details that other non-coms might have overlooked, thus enabling me to spend a number of nights up forward with the platoons and to go on numerous patrols.

One night I got a call from Jack to send someone to his platoon to bring back three prisoners. I decided to go myself.

At Jack's command post I looked the three men over critically. They were typical Jerries, unkempt and dirty. All three had been wounded and returned to duty before being completely recovered.

The prisoners protested that they had come across the river with the sole object of surrendering. Yet all three had been armed when captured and were heading back toward Germany with chickens under their arms.

"If you were going to surrender," the interpreter asked, "why did you have the chickens?"

"We had no white flags to wave for surrender," one of the Germans replied, matter-of-factly. "We were going to wave the chickens."

"I suppose," the interpreter rejoined, "you brought along your rifles so you could give them to us because we are short of weapons."

"Yah, yah," the German answered eagerly.

Brushing aside further protests, we hustled them outside for the trip to the rear.


One day the 121st Infantry commander, Colonel Jeter, and our battalion commander, Colonel Casey, made a tour of our part of the front. Hardly had they left when Lieutenant Joseph Kowalewski, who had taken over Bob Fay's old job as Battalion S-2, toured the same route with a messenger and an artillery liaison officer. After passing through one of our outposts and going less than a hundred yards, a Jerry armed with a machine pistol rose from a pile of leaves and motioned them to surrender. With the muzzle of the weapon staring at them, the three men needed little urging.

Though our men in the outposts could see what was happening, they dared not fire for fear of hitting the three Americans. But when the German insisted on marching his captives toward Germany, this proved too much for Joe Kowalewski. Letting out a loud shout, he threw himself to the ground. The other two men dived in opposite directions. Picking up the cue, the men in the outpost began to fire. The Jerry didn't even bother to look around. He headed post haste for Germany, leaving behind a thankful trio of escapees who considered they had spent the shortest time on record as prisoners-of-war.

As the story of this narrow escape spread through the company, none of us could help wondering what would have happened if the Jerry had chosen to rise when Colonel Jeter and Colonel Casey were passing.


One of the most maddening aspects of our stay in Luxembourg was a perpetual shortage of artillery ammunition. Each gun was rationed to a strict number of rounds per day, with the artillerymen strictly forbidden to fire more unless we were actually under attack. Utter frustration often gripped us as we spotted particularly inviting targets on the other side of the river and called back to the artillery fire control center only to learn the artillery could not fire.

"Sorry, Loo tenant. We used up our shells for today. Try again tomorrow. Maybe you'll hit the jackpot."

And while we gritted our teeth, Jerry walked about unmolested beyond the range of our rifle and machine gun fire. Eventually, they grew bolder and bolder until we almost felt like swimming the river and throwing rocks at them.

It was during this time that the mortar platoon of Company H came into its own. By hook, crook, and other connivance, the men of the platoon managed to accumulate a fairly sizeable stock of ammunition and gradually began to take over most of the fire missions which ordinarily would have been handled by the artillery. We patiently watched our enemy as he went about his daily routine, moving from pillbox to pillbox, assembling for details, digging potatoes, or perhaps going to the latrine. Then with carefully planned malice aforethought let loose with a potent mortar barrage that drove him back into cover for good.

H Company's mortar platoons were led by capable officers. Oid Wineland, comparatively new to the unit, was one of the men whom we saw constantly searching for targets of opportunity. Winey, a big man from Kansas, not only proved his ability with the mortars, but later, after recovering from a wound in a hospital in England, he returned to take over a rifle platoon composed entirely of Negro soldiers. Under his superb leadership they proved their right to glory, earned a flock of decorations and the undying admiration of a unit born in the heart of Dixie.

Our system of rotating companies eventually returned us to the old chateau in Bettendorf. I came to love this old building. Constructed originally in 1729, it was quaint and picturesque. Though many rooms contained bunks and other installations which the Germans built during their occupation, the charm of the building still shone through. In some rooms we could see evidence that Jerry had removed much of the priceless carved woodwork and the ancient trophies that once had adorned the walls. We vehemently condemned this looting, but I fear our indignation stemmed less from some high moral sense than from the fact that we were simply mad as hell he beat us to it.

In the courtyard of the chateau was a tiny chapel with a vine-covered entrance. Jerry obviously had used the chapel for sleeping quarters with his usual disdain for cleanliness, but in a short time we cleaned it up, and many a man found time for a moment of solitude or prayer at the altar.

While in Bettendorf I was lucky to find a place in nearby Diekirch to have the films developed which I had exposed at Dinard. Though I could not get prints made, since no paper was available, I cut the negatives apart and included them in small lots in my letters home.

This was contrary to regulations, but the mail was spot-censored, and fortunately the censor never spotted any of the negatives. Eleonore got them printed for me at home and sent them back. The whole process took weeks, but it was worth it.

As the weather grew colder, all of us began to think about Christmas, even though it still was October. To a large degree, our thoughts centered on whether some miracle might end the war by then, but we also had other, more personal reflections. Christmas seemed particularly important to me, for Eleonore and I had celebrated it together for 12 years and had always made it a very special day. I could see no possibility of being able to buy her a Christmas gift, but I hated for the season to pass without some reminder that I had not forgotten the special significance the holiday held for us.

One night I got the idea of writing to my sister, Margie, and making her my Santa Claus. At my first opportunity, I wrote a long letter, explaining in detail exactly what I wanted her to buy and how I wanted her to entice Eleonore from the apartment, then sneak in and fix it up just as if Santa had been there.

Once the letter was in the mail, I felt better. Now, no matter where I was or what happened to me before Christmas, Santa Claus would find Eleonore's chimney. It was a brand new chimney at that, for Eleonore and Norma had managed to find an apartment in Long Beach, N.Y., to share. Eleonore subsequently sent me a key to the door which I hung around my neck with my dog tags and vowed—and prayed—that some day I would open that door with that key.

It could not all be thoughts of Christmas, for though we were comfortable compared to most combat situations, still there was plenty to keep us on the alert.

Perhaps the most disturbing of all our chores was patrols. As Battalion S-2, it was Joe Kowalewski's job to get information about the enemy, and the primary means of accomplishing this was to send out patrols.

Joe was a big fellow, good-hearted, easy to get along with, but he was fairly excitable and had a loud voice that literally boomed. When a patrol was on his mind, he would crash into the CP and bellow:

"It's a suicide mission, that's what it is, a suicide mission. I told them bastards up in headquarters not a man would come back alive, but they say it's got to be done and it's got to be done their way. It's a suicide mission, that's what it is. We'll have to get volunteers. You got any?"

When Joe erupted in this fashion, the men around our headquarters would exchange silent glances and then slip silently away to vague duties which suddenly assumed tremendous importance. You would never get a volunteer the way Joe went about it.

Actually, Joe knew that we seldom if ever called for volunteers for patrols. Somehow in the movies men always step forward briskly to ask for dangerous missions, but in the real infantry men looked on volunteering as an easy way to end a military career. While they might be fully willing to take on any task specifically assigned them, they had no desire to ask for trouble. We solved the problem by keeping a duty roster for patrols just as we kept duty rosters for other onerous tasks. Each man took his turn.

It may sound as if we were reluctant to fight. The fact is, I cannot ever recall seeing the hero type who is supposed to champ at the bit, who cannot wait to tangle with the foe, to wrap his bare hands around his enemy's neck and hear him groan as he throttles him. As most GI's will tell you, men went into battle because that was their job. They fought because they did not want to let their buddies down, or the folks back home. They stuck it out and did what was required of them. Though they waved no flags and made no speeches, underneath they felt a surge of patriotism, a sense of duty that made it impossible to quit. They fought when orders came to fight, but when chance afforded them a period in reserve, they were exultant—this was a way to stay alive just a while longer.

From Company E's first day in combat in July until our stay in Luxembourg, this rifle company of 190 men actually had had 625 men assigned to it at one time or another. When you became aware of this tremendous turnover, attributable in almost all cases to wounds or death, you entertained unmitigated respect for any assignment which lessened your chances to be among those who came and went.

There may be some form of combat where men feel differently, where there is glory in battle and honor in death, but in the infantry where artillery guided by distant hands crashes around you and bullets fired by unseen assailants crack past you or tear into your body, this is not the case. When you see men die with their faces in the mud, when you see their raw wounds filled with flies and filth, you know there is no glamor.

An infantryman's life is strange. He comes into the army from a comparatively isolated, private civilian existence into a daily routine that makes him quickly realize that he is just one cog in a tremendous military machine. He is never alone, no matter where he turns. Always there are vast numbers around him, men in the same drab uniform, in camp, in town, in barracks, on parade. When he gets on a boat to go to war, he is crowded into an incredibly tiny space—one little speck in a gigantic, crowded movement. As he approaches the enemy he is part of another tremendous display of military power, of trucks, tanks, artillery pieces, planes. As he steps into the attack, the line thins a little, but still he has the familiar faces of his own company about him.

Then, all hell suddenly breaks loose. The noises of battle are loud and frightening, and the soldier hits the ground, scared and confused. He looks around for the reassuring sight of the men who have been with him for so long, men who have for so long usurped his privacy, men he longed to escape from any number of times in the past, but not now. But with his head close to the dirt, his rifle bulging painfully under him, his helmet falling heavily over his eyes, he can see no one. For the first time since he came into the army, he is alone, completely and dreadfully alone.

The war now belongs to one man, this man alone. He is fighting the whole German army, the entire enemy nation unassisted. Just when he needs and longs for companionship, the companions have disappeared. The fate of nations now rests solely on him.

If a man has the guts, he somehow conquers his fears and goes on to fight the war and discover that other people are present and that the other people are experiencing the same loneliness, the same fears. He shrugs it off and plunges on, but never will he lose completely that nightmare of being horribly alone.

It is men like this who realize what lies ahead and fear it, yet who somehow control their fears and go ahead to do a nasty job who are the real heroes.

Nor are there as many of them as one might presume. Few recognize what a small percentage of men in an army actually do the fighting. It takes hundreds and thousands to support the relatively few who populate the tank and rifle companies down where men do the dying. Even in a rifle company, the primary fighting unit of a division, some of the men are comparatively far removed from the direct combat which is the infantryman's basic job. During the war, a rifle company contained 190 men, but only 160 of them actually saw the enemy and knew that searing inner conflict when it came time to get up out of a hole and move toward other men who were trying to kill you.

Somebody figured out that our infantry divisions during World War II incurred 25 percent casualties. This figure in itself is astronomically high in relation to other types of units, but it takes on new and dreadful significance when one realizes that almost all these casualties occurred in the 27 rifle companies of the division and three out of four of them in the rifle platoons of those companies. This means that those rifle platoons lost 90 percent of their men.

That's where war really hurts, down in the rifle platoons, down where they do the dying.

# 14

One day when Lieutenant Kowalewski came to our company CP with an order for a patrol, he was in top form.

"It's a suicide mission, I tell you," he informed everyone within the wide range of his booming voice. "They want a night patrol to go more than two thousand yards down to that lousy river and see if the Jerries have put any bridges across. It's a suicide mission, I tell you. Suicide."

Regiment, I soon learned, wanted not only to determine if the Germans had built bridges but needed to learn if they occupied several farm houses which lay between our positions and the river. It quickly became apparent that this was hardly a job for nighttime.

"There's no moon," I said. "That means we'll have to feel our way along every inch of that river to see if they've built a bridge. Even then we won't be sure. Why not a daylight patrol? Then the men can go to some high point where they can see a great stretch of the river at once. Besides, who the hell's going to search those houses at night?"

"That's what I told you," Joe said. "It's a suicide mission. Can you get some volunteers?"

"I'll make up the patrol," I told him. "In the meantime, you see if you can't get it changed to a daylight job."

As Joe set off for battalion, I called in one of our best squad leaders, Staff Sergeant Howard Pople, of the third platoon. Sitting around a map, we discussed the job, but it soon became clear that Pople, like me, had no taste for it as a night mission. Among other things, it called for too deep a penetration beyond our own lines.

Sharing his apprehension, I gradually became conscious of a strange feeling inside. Sending men to do a tough job rather than leading them was always difficult, but this was a case where I did not even believe in the job. I felt I could not live with myself if I failed to go along.

"I'll tell you what I'll do, Sergeant," I said as I noticed Pople lick his lips in a gesture of indecision. "You and the men go on up the hill and get ready to move, either by day or night. I'll wait here to see if we can get it changed to daylight. I'll also see Captain McKenna and get permission to go with you."

Pople's face showed obvious relief.

When Captain McKenna returned, he objected at first. He had definite ideas about men sticking to their assigned jobs. Mine was executive officer of the company, not a patrol leader. Besides, we were too short of officers in the company to risk one unduly. But he did not reckon with my persistence, and at last I wore him down. Then Joe telephoned to say regiment had okayed it as a daylight assignment.

Anxious lest we run out of daylight, I took off quickly to meet Sergeant Pople in the third platoon positions at the top of the hill. Though Pople had lined up a full combat patrol, I thought we could do the job better with fewer men since we had no intention of precipitating a fight. I cut the number to four—Pople, Private Cecil Smith, Private Manuel Melgosa, and myself.

As soon as I had briefed the men on what we intended to do, we set out through the woods. We used a diamond formation. This meant that the man in front was responsible for the area straight ahead, a man out to the right and another to the left were responsible for the sides, and another in the rear was responsible for making sure we were not surprised from behind.

We traversed the small woods in front of the third platoon positions with no difficulty, then came to a dangerous open area which we had to cross before entering a dense woods through which we would move all the way to the river. Lining up along the edge of the trees we scanned the woods ahead as best we could, then set out across the open field on a dead run. Once we gained the first trees, puffing, gasping for breath, I called a halt.

Again we looked around before taking up the slack in our formation. Even though the woods was dense, it was a typical European forest with little or no underbrush so that we still were able to see for some distance. Deciding at last that our dash across the open had alerted no enemy, we continued forward.

Instead of being able to move on a direct course, we had to change direction frequently because of gullies and creeks that criss-crossed our path. We kept hoping that the high ground beyond each gully would provide us a view of the river, but each time we found only more thick woods. With haste and caution, we kept moving.

Acting as the point, I had just crossed a gully when suddenly I froze and signalled for the patrol to halt. Just ahead in a small clearing I saw what appeared to be a group of Jerries sitting around a tree. Piles of wood, neatly stacked and apparently recently sawed, stood nearby. We obviously had stumbled on a Jerry work party.

As I crawled closer for a better view, Pople came up by my side. The afternoon light was already fading. Through the thick branches of the trees above us, only a little light filtered to the ground. For almost a minute we peered intently at the group of Germans ahead, wondering what we should do.

"Let's shoot the bastards now," Pople whispered. "We can't miss from here."

"No," I hissed. "We're supposed to get information, not kill Jerries. If we fire, the only thing we can do afterwards is run. If we do anything, we'll crawl down and get some prisoners. We could send Smith back with the prisoners, then go ahead." Watching our enemy intently, I gradually became better accustomed to the dull light under the trees. Something inside me began to raise doubts about the soundness of my vision. At last I reached behind my back and pulled my field glasses into position. I muttered an oath, then handed the glasses to Pople. His face broke into a wide grin of relief. Our Jerries were nothing more than limbs of trees which had assumed human form in the fading light. The recently cut wood in neat stacks was real enough, but the Jerries were not.

My plan of finding a vantage point from which to view a long stretch of the river began to appear less and less feasible as we crossed one gully, then another, only to discover that the rise ahead provided only a view of more trees. We were all about to give up when, keeping a straight course, we at last did emerge at the edge of woods. Ahead of us stretched the Our River itself. Directly beyond, a German pillbox yawned open-mouthed at us. Watching for signs of activity but detecting none, I marked the location of the pillbox on my map, then signalled the others to follow and headed south parallel to the river.

We had passed a number of dead cows, obviously killed only recently by artillery fire, when we came upon a small herd of live ones. Seeing the cows approaching, we hid in a ditch, not for fear of the cows themselves but for fear seeing us might excite them and their excitement in turn might alert any observing Germans. Our concern proved well grounded for despite our efforts to hide, the cows spotted us and started a minor stampede. In turn, Jerry quickly began to throw rifle and machine gun fire in our general direction. Sticking to the ditch, we continued to the south while Jerry persisted with his fire, not directly at us we noted with relief, but where we had been.

Our trip parallel to the river convinced me that Jerry was building no bridges. In fact, the river was so swollen beyond its banks that it had flooded some portions of farm land on our side and some stretches of the dragon's teeth of the Siegfried Line on the other side. Tactical bridges would be difficult to keep in place in the swift current.

Satisfied at last that we had accomplished everything expected of us at the river, we headed back through the woods toward our own lines—a trip that was almost all uphill. On top of that, Sergeant Pople had a bad cold and we had to halt at intervals to permit him a rest so he would not break into a fit of loud coughing. Finally, however, we came to the edge of the woods and only the big clearing separated us from the other stretch of woods which hid our company's positions.

Under normal practice, we would have raced across the clearing to the protection of the other woods, but Sergeant Pople's condition dictated otherwise. He obviously was worn out.

"I'll never make that on the run, Lieutenant," he told me. "I'm plumb out of juice."

Surveying the situation, I decided to take the clearing at a walk but to move close to a slope on our left. This would provide some concealment from German observation, and I hoped that a single file formation with exaggerated intervals between men might discourage any enemy gunners who did happen to spot us. Since Pople was the man to whom we had to adjust our speed, he went first.

I fidgeted nervously as Pople started out with a pace that seemed incredibly slow. I thought we would never get across, but somehow we managed it without incident. I was the last to reach the woods on the other side where I found Pople and the others flopped on the ground catching their breath. I had not the heart to urge them to their feet to get moving right away.

We were sitting there puffing when we heard the sound of a big gun somewhere on the German side. We took no real notice for we had been hearing guns and listening to shells pass overhead at intervals all through the patrol.

"Sounds like somebody's going to get it," Pople remarked casually.

We heard the shell coming, whispering, whirring warning, but still we had no cause for alarm. We had heard any number of others doing the same thing all afternoon. Then suddenly this one took on a new note. It came closer and closer. We knew all at once that this one was different. It was not meant to go over.

Though I started to dive for cover the explosion caught me in mid-air. With a reverberating roar, the shell burst. The concussion forced my helmet down over my face, and threw me to the ground.

Stunned, I scrambled unsteadily to my feet. Looking about quickly, I saw none of the men was injured, at least not obviously. Then we began without ceremony to execute that well known military maneuver known as getting the hell out of there.

We had only one thought, putting as much space as possible between us and the spot where the shell had landed. Somebody on Jerry's side obviously could see us. Jerry had thrown that single shell for registration, to see if he was on his target. Now that he was sure he had the range, he would open up with all barrels.

The fusillade of shells was not long in coming, but neither had we been idle, having already put considerable distance between us and the spot where we had rested. Hearing the concentration on the way, we threw ourselves to the ground, waited for the shells to explode, then rose again to race farther and farther away.

Four times the shells roared in, seemingly about to engulf us each time, but our legs had not failed us. At long last we paused for a moment to catch our breath and take inventory. Only I had any sort of wound to show for the experience, and this only a simple cut on one hand. Wrapping a handkerchief about it to stop the blood, I motioned to the others to keep going.

We made one more stop, to check the group of farm buildings to see if we could find any signs that the Germans were using them as observation posts. They turned out to be empty with no apparent indications that Jerry ever had been there. With this accomplished, we breathed a collective sigh of relief and headed into our lines.

After thanking the men for a good job, I turned in a long report on the patrol to battalion. I ended by suggesting that it might have been easier had they sent a liaison plane aloft to observe the whole length of the river and take photographs. Somebody apparently thought not too badly of the idea, for the next time I visited battalion headquarters they showed me a group of aerial photographs of the river and stood around waiting for me to compliment them on their cleverness in thinking of this approach.

I remained stubbornly and intentionally silent.

# 15

It was about this time, in mid-October, that I lost my position as executive officer of the company. First Lieutenant Edward W. P. Zienke, one of the original officers with Easy Company, returned from the hospital after having been wounded in the foot at Dinard. Captain McKenna rightfully returned him to his post as executive officer. I in turn asked to be shifted to a rifle platoon in order that Jack might stay with the company and keep the weapons platoon.

My assignment was to the second platoon, and I could hardly have drawn a better command. Tech Sergeant David Barber had been leading the platoon, with Staff Sergeant William F. Hobbs as second in command. They were both competent men who knew their jobs.

The platoon was on the hill the day I joined. The CP was well located, a big four-man hole among an outcropping of large rocks, almost precisely in the middle of the platoon area. Spread in an arc about 150 yards beyond the CP were the scattered outposts. Company E's mortars plus a section of heavy machine guns from my old platoon of Company H were attached.

We were connected with six of the outposts by telephone, while the men in the others had visual contact with those equipped with telephone. Each hole accommodated three men. Every night just at dusk I made the rounds of the outposts, whereupon the men settled down for the night with the knowledge that anything else that moved in the darkness was enemy. Back at the platoon command post, we maintained an all-night vigil by the phone—Barber, Hobbs, me, and Corporal Theodore Haerich, our platoon medic.

Haerich was an excellent soldier, even though, as a medic, he was not in the strictest sense a combat man. Born in Germany, Haerich had left in 1937. He was very religious and always started his letters home with a quotation from the Bible. He was probably one of the bravest man any of us ever met. Any number of times he rescued wounded men under fire, though fully aware that shells and bullets had little or no respect for the Red Cross armband he wore. Also, by using his native tongue to advantage, he had taken numbers of prisoners. He was, in effect, a one-man propaganda bureau, talking and cajoling to convince the Germans he was one of them and that all was much better on our side of the line.

The four of us in the command post hole held many a speculative conversation through the long autumn nights.

"You think you'll ever go back to wrestling?" Sergeant Barber asked one night.

"I'll be satisfied just to go back," I said. "Then again, if I do make it back, I'd like to wrestle again. You don't do a job for ten years and then kick it aside overnight without some regret."

"What the hell would you do if you lost a leg over here, Lieutenant?" Hobbs chipped in. "You wouldn't be much at wrestling then."

"Well," I answered, "at least they'd never get a double toe hold on me."

It was gallows humor, no doubt, but many a man engaged in it, and somehow it helped.

We worked out a system in the hole so that each man had a two-hour watch on the telephone. Each half hour he contacted every outpost to make sure all were still with us. The telephones were sound-powered, without bells, so that to attract the attention of the party at the other end we depressed the sending switch and whistled. At night we had only to breathe heavily into the mouthpiece and to the tense men at the other end of the wire it sounded as if we had set off a siren. We might not be manning the most active sector on the western front, but this did not mean that tension did not grip us, particularly at night.

One night during my turn at the phone I began to make the half-hourly check of outposts. Whistling softly into the phone, I sounded off in a quiet whisper:

"Number One."

Number One whispered back promptly in a similar hushed but reassuring tone:

"Number One Okay."

So it went with Number Two, Number Three, and Number Four,

until at last I came to Number Five. My call to Number Five drew only silence. I tried several times, becoming increasingly concerned, then went on to Number Six and came back again to Five. With growing anxiety, I tried again and again to raise the man at Number Five phone.

"Number Five! Number Five! Outpost Number Five!"

I blew again into the mouthpiece, as loudly as I dared. Still no response. I raised my voice ever so little and whispered again.

"Number *Five!*"

A hoarse whisper came at last from the other end.

"All right, all right, Jeezus Cuhrist, ya don't have to shout!"

Then still in a low, almost inaudible whisper, the voice continued. "It may be all right for you guys to shout—you're way back there!"

I sat stunned for a moment. Way back there! We were way back there!

It was funny at the time, but actually it was an accurate indication of the state of everybody's nerves in those tense days. We were scarcely 150 yards from Outpost Number Five, and if an attack had begun, we might have been even more involved in it than the man in Number Five; but in his mind we were behind him, so we were "way back there." Somebody was almost always a little farther back for the GI to complain about. I suppose the troops at corps headquarters 50 miles behind the line looked on those at army headquarters another 25 miles or so behind as "rear echelon."


While we were on the hill, we received a new item of equipment, a sleeping bag. It was a kind of shroud, a wool inter lining in a water-repellent poplin cover, full length to include the head with just enough opening for the face to protrude. Both the wool lining and the poplin outer sheet had long zipper fastenings.

The first night we had the sleeping bags, I looked forward to a warm night's rest. Confidently, I removed my shoes, a luxury we seldom permitted ourselves this far forward. Outside the air was cold, but inside I felt delightfully snug. Pulling the zippers (located inside the bags) with a delicious sense of warmth, I settled back on the ground to revel in this marvelous acquisition the supply people had so cleverly dreamed up for us at the front.

Panic suddenly seized me. What if the Jerries should come? How the hell would I get out? The sleeping bag became a strait jacket. Looking at the entrance to the hole, I could have sworn I saw a big

German standing there, grinning malevolently at my efforts to free myself. Grabbing almost frantically at the zippers, I fought to get out. At last I was free. I sat bolt upright.

I refused to get out of the bag; it was too warm and comfortable for that. But I knew I had to do something to lick my overworked imagination, or I soon would have to part with the new-found warmth.

First I tried bringing my carbine inside the bag with me, but this was of little help. Next I tried placing it close alongside me, outside the bag, but this too gave me little peace of mind. I tried several more positions, all to no avail, until finally I hit upon the solution of hanging my carbine from the log roof of the hole, its muzzle pointed toward the entrance. If the Germans came, I might reach up, even without freeing myself entirely, and press the trigger. Somehow this helped, whether because I really believed I might fight off the enemy in this manner or simply because I had worn myself out in the process, I do not know. In any event, I pulled the zippers closed and drifted off to sleep, both zippers gripped tightly in my hands.

It was about this time too that we began to experience a cigarette shortage. This was all the more ironic since we had been so free with cigarettes ever since our arrival in France. On the train trip from Brest the men had traded with cigarettes as if the supply were inexhaustible. We had always had enough, issued without charge, just like rations. This sudden drying up of supplies caught just about everybody without reserve stocks, so that I, a non-smoker, discovered I was one of the more popular members of the company. All I had to do was open a K-ration and any number of nicotine addicts were clambering around me in quest of the four little cigarettes the K-ration package contained.

The reason for the shortage of tobacco soon became apparent. Stories in *Stars & Stripes* revealed that a railway company of the Transportation Corps, whose job it was to operate the freight trains which brought supplies forward, had been involved in a scandalous black market operation that was netting the men involved millions of francs. The details of the court martial, which told how the men would run carloads of cigarettes, chocolate, or gasoline onto a siding and then sell the entire car, contents and all, to the black market, made our blood boil and our tempers run hot.

"They ought to hang the bastards," was the usual comment.

"Yeah," another man would add, "and I'd like to be pulling the rope when they do it."

I never saw such genuine anger vented—even against our enemy—as I saw turned against this small band of selfish men who stole the comforts, even necessities, from their comrades who were doing the fighting. To an infantryman, the business of not letting your comrades down is sacred and vital; sometimes it is all that keeps a man going when things are rough. Few of us could understand how other Americans could treat us in such a shabby manner.

We watched the trial with keen personal interest, frequently suggesting to each other the type and length of punishment these culprits should receive. Some of our suggestions, I fear, would have set justice back to the Inquisition, and might even have suggested to those ancient purveyors of torture a new wrinkle or so. But we were never to receive the satisfaction of pulling the rope ourselves or even of hearing that somebody else pulled the rope.

For when the court martial passed sentence, our Supreme Commander, General Eisenhower, gave the morale of all of us at the front a kick in the teeth. He offered to erase the sentence if the thieves would volunteer to be trained as infantry and go into the line to fight alongside the men they had betrayed.

We scarcely could believe what we read!

"Since when is fighting for your country a punishment?" Sergeant Hobbs demanded in a real fury. "I've been in the infantry four long hard years, not to escape jail either."

"Who the hell wants to join the infantry," another man asked, "when they make it the dumping ground for all the dirty bastards in the world? Eisenhower should have kept his damned nose out of this and let those guys rot in jail where they belong."

I could not help but agree. These men were solid American citizens, intent on doing their assigned part in a terrible war, and in the process they had come to respect the branch of service which they learned through hard experience does the bloody job of meeting the enemy face to face. In one ill-advised move, General Eisenhower had done more to damage the morale of every rifleman in Europe than the Jerries with all their high-priced propaganda could have accomplished in a lifetime.

"Just let me find one of those sonsabitches in my squad," one of my squad leaders remarked, shifting a chew of tobacco violently from one cheek to the other. "He'll wake up KIA with a bullet in the back."

To compensate in small measure for the lack of cigarettes, we received an occasional ration of what was classified as "PX supplies." These rations came forward at irregular intervals. Actually, the news of their coming arrived first. We were never told what we would get, just how much our allotted share would cost. Whereupon we did a little quick arithmetic and collected prorata amounts from each squad. Once we had sent the money back to headquarters, we started anticipating what we might be buying. Unfortunately, most of our guesses were wishfully far from the mark.

When the shipment finally reached the platoon, we had all the squad leaders present so they could see we divided the items equally. I usually took what was left. Generally we got candy bars, sometimes cans of fruit juice (perhaps one can to a squad of 12 men), a few cigars, an occasional plug of chewing tobacco, a few packs of cigarettes, sometimes ink and writing paper. Once the items were divided among 35 or 40 men, no individual got very much, but we were grateful even for little things.

What irritated us about the whole process was that we knew when the PX shipment first started out it had contained many choice items like fountain pens, cigarette lighters, lighter fluid, watches, combs, razors, things that the men genuinely needed. But as each succeeding echelon got its hands on the shipment, it dwindled in size and selection. One day we found we had paid for a hundred bars of toilet soap, yet we had nowhere to take a bath. We heard of one man as far down the ladder as a rifle squad who actually got a watch once, but the story had it that he was in another regiment, and nobody ever actually verified it.

The newspaper, *Stars & Stripes* ran into the same diminishing process. It left the presses in great numbers, and in rear echelon units close to the point of origin almost every man had his individual copy. But by the time the paper travelled forward, we in the rifle platoons were lucky to get one copy per squad. Even then the paper was a day or so late, but we thumbed the precious print until it wore thin from fond handling.

While in Luxembourg, the officers and some of the senior sergeants received a liquor ration—for a fee, of course. It was another blind purchase. We were told to send back a certain sum for liquor, and we dutifully complied. When the bottles reached us, we divided them in whatever size, amount, and variety the supply allowed. Since I didn't drink, I could have sold my ration at an astronomical profit, but there was much more satisfaction in dividing it free among the men of the platoon. With so many men and so little liquor, no danger existed that anybody would get too much.

Once, when an epidemic of chest colds was plaguing the platoon and the loud coughing at night had become a real danger, I decided to use my liquor ration for medicinal purposes. Tired, muddy, bearded men arrived at the command post, half a squad at a time, for their one hot meal of the day. Their faces lit up when they spied Corporal Haerich standing near the food with a bottle of cough medicine in one hand, a bottle of Vat 69 in the other. A man had his choice of treatment—Vat 69 or cough medicine. We had plenty of cough medicine left.

The nervous strain of being on line continued to be alleviated every six days by a few days in reserve, either in Bettendorf or another village, Gilsdorf. The men looked forward to the break, to hot baths, a few glasses of watered beer.

Chow time during these breaks was always the signal for a horde of visitors, most of them kids. Though we detected no real lack of food among the civilians in Luxembourg, the fare must have been dreadfully monotonous. When we had anything left over, we usually passed it along to the civilians, who appeared exceedingly grateful.

We usually let the kids have the variety of things that came with the 10-in-1 rations, the candy bars, hard water soap, other little items. We put them in a big after-dinner "grab bag." One night after the kids had emptied the bag, we had a visit at our CP from a perturbed village priest.

"Please," the priest said apologetically, "would you please to take away from the children the balloons? Yes? Please?"

"Balloons?" said Sergeant Foy. "We ain't had no balloons."

He thought for a moment.

"Holy mackerel!" he shouted.

In a flash we all knew what had happened. Somebody by mistake had put a box of rubber prophylactics in the after-dinner grab bag, and the kids had understandingly mistaken them for balloons. When the elders saw the kids playing with them, they had blushed to their finger tips and detailed the village priest to set the matter right.

While in reserve on one occasion, Jack and I shared a room, along with Lieutenant Theodore Evergreen, of Pasadena, California. Ted was assigned to Company E but was on duty with battalion as a liaison officer to regimental headquarters. As a liaison officer he had his own jeep and thus had been able to assemble and carry along with him a variety of souvenirs, including a captured Jerry radio. The radio made a most welcome addition to our room. Sweet music coming over the Armed Forces Radio Network brought a flood of poignant memories and produced a wave of homesickness that all but overwhelmed us. I heard the song I had learned to love at Brest, "Good Night, Wherever You Are," and had a chance to hear one that Eleonore had written about, "I Walk Alone." We sprawled on our bedrolls on the floor and wrote long, and probably sad, letters home.

One day Captain McKenna returned from a visit to battalion headquarters and brought with him an enticing proposal.

"Boesch," he said in his pleasant manner, "we can send one officer to Paris along with the enlisted men of the regiment to take care of the convoy. You want to go?"

I thought for a moment. It was a wonderful opportunity, one that might not occur again.

"Captain," I suggested, "Lieutenant Bochner has been in combat as long as I have. I think he'd enjoy the chance. Does it matter to you which one goes?"

"Well, not exactly, except that Bochner is really an F Company officer. But if you want to turn your chance over to him, it's up to you."

I went to Jack with the proposition. As much as I wanted to see Paris, I knew Jack would enjoy it more. He liked an occasional drink, he spoke French fluently, and he had not travelled as extensively as I. His eyes lit up when I made the suggestion.

The next morning we searched the possessions of every man in the company in order to come up with a clean uniform for Jack's trip. When he left he was dressed in a composite, but sartorially correct uniform.

While Jack was away, Ted Evergreen had to make a trip to the city of Luxembourg, about 25 miles away, on regimental business and asked if I'd like to go along. I was delighted with the opportunity and subsequently found the old city a fascinating place.

As we drove down the narrow streets I marvelled at the old-world architecture, but even more entrancing was the sight of normal things like trolley cars, moving picture theaters, crowds of civilians, and stores with their wares displayed in the windows.

As we rode down one street, I saw a bakery with a window full of pastries that looked more than simply appetizing. I prevailed on Ted to stop while I went inside to make a few purchases. The pies and cakes turned out to be not quite so tasty as they looked, for they were made of substitute materials for the most part, but back at the platoon this would hardly be noticed.

Shortly after my visit to Luxembourg we moved out of reserve and back on the hill where I was destined for one of my more narrow escapes of the war.

It was an unwritten rule that any time you installed a new booby-trap, mine, or other lethal device, you passed along this information to those who followed you in the position. But the troops we followed apparently ignored the rule, for after they left we discovered any number of devices they had installed with never a word of warning to us.

One day as I was returning from an early morning patrol, I decided to use a path I had not taken before. As we approached our position, I called ahead to the man on guard to ask if the trail had been checked for explosives.

"Sure has, Lootenant," he called back confidently. "Come on in."

I walked ahead, well in advance of my patrol. I suddenly felt my foot catch against something, then heard a loud POP! I recognized the sound immediately as that of the safety lever disengaging from a hand grenade. Almost without thinking I realized I had exactly four seconds to put some distance between me and the grenade. I ran, counting instinctively. Taking three giant steps, I hit the ground heavily. Just as I fell, the grenade exploded. The air around me filled with dirt, metal fragments, smoke, and pieces of brush.

I lay for a moment where I had fallen, tightly clutching my helmet and trying to regain my breath. Rising rather gingerly to my feet, I felt around my body for the wounds I was sure I had, but to my amazement, I was unharmed. I shook pieces of branches from my uniform and tiny, hot pieces of the grenade that had hit the trees and then fallen down on me, but I didn't have a scratch.

When Jack returned from Paris, he brought things he had bought for the two of us to send home as Christmas gifts. I need not have made my elaborate plans with my sister Margie after all.

But Jack's return also brought some unpleasant developments. He was to return to duty with Company F. Several new officers arrived in Easy Company to bring us up to strength, Lieutenant Martin Weinberger, of Bayonne, N.J., and Lieutenant James J. Gillespie, of Philadelphia.

Battalion also made a surprise change, removing Lieutenant Zienke as executive officer and replacing him with First Lieutenant Nikolai Von Keller, a Russian-born American from New York City. Von Keller was a big, affable Russian, a particular favorite of Colonel Casey's. Since he was the oldest lieutenant in the battalion, Colonel Casey had decided, probably correctly, that he deserved an executive officer post.

Von Keller had a thick accent and a good sense of humor.

"I just got so the guards in Fox Company will not shoot me," he said in his garbled way, "and now maybe I will be shot in Easy Company. They think always I am a German. Always I am saying the password upside down and backwards and too late."

Lieutenant Zienke came to the second platoon, since it had been his before he was wounded. I moved to the weapons platoon to take Jack's place.

The days passed slowly, and the nights changed from chilly to genuinely cold. One night a blanket of snow descended on the hills. The Luxembourg natives assured us it was the earliest snowfall in many years and made dire predictions for a fierce, long winter ahead. It was far from reassuring.

During that first snow-capped morning, I had a telephone call from battalion. The man at the phone whispered to me as if the Lord himself was on the line.

"It's Colonel Casey," he breathed.

I picked up the phone with some trepidation, wondering just what I had done to warrant a chewing out from the battalion commander himself.

"Boesch," the Colonel said, short, to the point. "I've got space open for an officer to go to Paris. Do you want to go or don't you? I'm asking you to go, not just any officer from E Company, and I don't want it passed on to somebody else. Is it yes or no?"

"It's yes," I blurted out, "that is—yes, sir!"

He hung up, and I turned around with a wide grin on my face.

"That was short and sweet, lieutenant," said Sergeant Abbot "You look as pleased as a man who just got told he was going to Paris."

"That's just what I was told, Sergeant," I replied. "Just what I was told. And I said yes!"

# 16

The trip to Paris got off to a start that was something less than auspicious. Hardly had our convoy assembled with men and officers from all three regiments of the division when a heavy snow began to fall. Sharing a cab of one of the trucks with the driver and Captain Samuel Rabinowitz, of the Bronx, a battalion surgeon, I was comfortable enough, but the men in the rear, though bundled in sleeping bags, were miserably cold. They nevertheless kept up a constant joking chatter, with the thought of seeing Paris obviously providing some measure of warmth. The same prospects must have inspired our drivers too, for they successfully defeated every effort of the treacherous snow to hold us in Luxembourg and brought us out of the mountains onto a broad, flat stretch of road which eventually led to Rheims, France.

We stopped for the night in Rheims. After storing the trucks in an army motor pool and seeing that the men were billeted in a barracks provided for the purpose, I set out with four other officers to find a hotel. Besides Dr. Rabinowitz and myself, there were three lieutenants, one from each regiment of the division.

The lieutenant from the 28th Infantry, insisting that he spoke French fluently, appointed himself our interpreter. Since none of the rest of us claimed any linguistic ability, we accepted the offer without protest and made our way to a small hotel which someone at the motor pool had recommended. As we entered, the proprietress was cleaning the stairs. She came toward us with a rapid flow of French accompanied by easily understandable gestures which made it obvious we were most welcome. We thumbed her toward our interpreter.

"Ah, oui," she said, obviously pleased, "parlez vous français?"

The lieutenant stared at her quizzically. She repeated the words slowly. At last he shook his head and turned to us with wrinkled brow.

"What the hell did she say?" he asked.

Our faith in our interpreter somewhat shattered, we made our own arrangements for rooms by means of a kind of universal sign language.

After washing up, we set out to find a place to eat and, for my companions, a place to drink. The lady at the hotel recommended a nearby bistro, but we obviously did not understand her instructions too well, for we soon had to stop to ask a passing Frenchman new directions. Our self-appointed interpreter took over. In slow, carefully chosen, labored phrases, he posed a lengthy question. Several times he had to stop and start over again, but through it all the Frenchman listened patiently. At last, making sure our interpreter had finished, the Frenchman pointed a thumb over his right shoulder and smiled broadly.

"One block down," he said easily, "and two to the left."

At this point, our interpreter had had it.


Arriving at the motor pool at the appointed hour the next morning, we found all the men present. No one was taking any chance on being left in Rheims when Paris was the next stop.

It was November 11th, Armistice Day, a fact which soon became apparent. We were travelling historic ground which had been fought over at great length in the previous war. Chemin des Dames, Soissons, Villers-Cotterets, names which we had known only from history books now became vivid and real. All along the road groups of people with flowers in their hands thronged toward the big military cemeteries where the dead of the 1914-18 war were buried. Some of the cemeteries were close enough to the road for us to see that ceremonies were underway at each of them. Everywhere flew the tri-color of France.

It was just before noon when we hit the outskirts of Paris. In each of us, excitement was mounting. In the rear of the trucks the men now showed no ill effects from the exposure. In fact, they hung over the sides whooping and whistling with delight at everything they saw. The French good-naturedly returned the greetings and waved a vigorous welcome.

Arriving at the Place de l'Opera, our convoy turned down a side street to the Red Cross headquarters in the American Express building. Here everything had been arranged in advance so that red tape was cut to a minimum. In a few minutes the men emerged, meal and hotel tickets in hand, eager looks on their faces.

"Well," I told them, "Paris is yours. For two days anyway. I'm not going to tell you anything except to be careful and remember one thing—you're due here at 11 a.m. Monday. It's now Saturday afternoon, you have a full 48 hours. Have fun, stay out of trouble and out of jail and don't do anything I'm going to do. So long!"

With a whoop they set out for their hotel to clean up and escape for two days.

Checking in with the Red Cross, we received our tickets and left for another hotel. As we were cleaning up, trying to make ourselves presentable for the street instead of the foxhole, I detected that most of my companions looked on a visit to Paris in large measure as a tour of the bars. Deciding quickly that I would do better if I set out by myself, I left the others the first time they turned into a bistro. I walked the streets alone, looking at people, at store windows, at buildings. People were everywhere. At last it came back to me that this was Armistice Day. This explained the jammed sidewalks, the impromptu parades forming in every street, the singing of the Marseillaise at every turn. Along the Champs Elysees the masses of people made it almost impossible to walk. It had been so long since I had seen colorful crowds in civilian clothes that I found myself caught up with tremendous, intoxicating excitement.

At the Arc de Triomphe interminable lines of sober citizens stood for hours to pass by the Tomb of the Unknown Soldier and the eternal flame that burns there to pay their humble respects. Under the Arc and over the tomb flew the flag of France that was said to be the largest flag in the world. Somehow the French had managed to hide it through the German occupation, and now it flew majestically in inspiring splendor.

I stood near the Arc de Triomphe for a long time, deeply impressed by the reverent solemnity of the people. It was only with effort that I pulled myself away to walk along the banks of the Seine toward the Eiffel Tower, reaching high and lace-like into the sky. It did not take long for me to come to understand something of the magic spell which this city casts over all men who approach it with open heart.

When we assembled at the hotel for our evening meal, I discovered that I was the only one of our five who had any idea of what

Paris, other than the bistros, looked like. During dinner— which we were obliged to eat in the U.S. Army-operated hotel because of the food rationing program among civilians—we planned our attack on Paris by night. Before leaving the front, we had been urged by others who had made the trip before us to be sure to visit Le Lido, a swank night spot on the Champs Elysees, but when we inquired about reservations, we learned that a French army unit had taken over the place for the night. In the end we had to settle for the Paradise Club in Montmartre.

At the Paradise Club we were ushered to a good table right down front. The floor show began almost immediately, and before we realized what had happened, a bevy of girls, naked from slightly below the waist up, were shaking their bare bellies in front of our widened eyes. Our table was so close, they were so naked, and the ballroom was so cold that we could count the goose bumps that formed on the exposed parts of their anatomy. So little distance lay between us and the show that I felt like part of it.

Ambitious ladies of the evening later came by our table to ply their trade, but our group stuck together. The others stuck to their drinking and I stuck to my sightseeing, though at this point it was reduced primarily to analyzing one naked navel after another. But it was fun to relax and watch the uninhibited GI's whoop and holler as they let loose with steam that had accumulated over weeks on end in the front lines. Almost all the men in the place were combat soldiers on short passes, making the most of their brief freedom, and it apparently made little difference to them that the entertainment was of obviously poor quality. I drank water—though I bought champagne—and over my glass watched the men as they made Paris a poor substitute for the place they really wanted—home.

Most American soldiers arrived in France stuffed with highly colored tales their fathers had told them of French women during the earlier war, so that they expected loose morals to be the rule. Since most of the men rarely had time to meet any girls except those in honky tonks, they obviously met the kind they had been led to anticipate, but instead of realizing that the same situation would have applied at home, they condemned all French women as loose. Yet even in the Paradise Club there was virtue if one chose to notice it. When one gaily-painted broad enticed her GI friend onto the dance floor, the rest of the girls in the place hissed her off the floor.

"Zey have no respect," the other girls explained, "for Eleven Novembaire."

"Just goes to show you," philosophized Dr. Rabinowitz, "there's honor even among whores."

In a moment the doctor was busy defending his own honor. A girl approached him with a more than pointed suggestion, but he brushed her off.

"You are not sympathetic to me?" she asked coquettishly.

"Very sympathetic," Doc laughed, "but please peddle your wares someplace else, won't you?"

We left the Paradise Club late and walked darkened but well-peopled streets back to our hotel. Though a few of the boys needed help occasionally, Doc and I managed to herd them all to bed in the end and finally turned in ourselves.

Having made plans for a sightseeing tour of the city the next morning, Dr. Rabinowitz and I were both on time with clear heads while our comrades of lustier tastes still slept soundly. The sight-seeing bus was full of GI's as it pulled away from the Red Cross center. A garrulous but entertaining guide tolled off the history of each spot as we rode by: the Eiffel Tower, the Hotel des Invalides with Napoleon's Tomb, Arc de Triomphe, Place de la Concorde, Place Vendome, Notre Dame Cathedral, Church of the Madelaine, the Louvre, all the famous buildings and squares we had seen and read about so many times in pictures and stories that we felt we knew them even without the explanation.

In the afternoon I traded a couple of packages of cigarettes—which I had brought along as barter material—as rent for a "beeceekil" and went on my own tour. All through a pleasant, sunny afternoon I pedalled along both banks of the Seine, along the Grands Boulevards, and through winding back streets. Lingering for a long time in the Cathedral of Notre Dame, I reverently said a prayer for Eleonore. I rode under the Eiffel Tower and though I wanted to go to the peak, no one was being allowed on it because of a rumor that the Germans had weakened it. Though pedalling the old bicycle mixed hard labor with my pleasure, I enjoyed every minute.

I might have continued my sightseeing until dark had I not felt compelled to go shopping. Before leaving the company, I had been besieged by requests to bring back perfume or something to be sent home to wives, sweethearts, and mothers, and I was determined to follow through. Though it was Sunday, a number of shops were open, all jammed with GI's buying everything in sight with little regard for price. Those who had preceded us already had created enough of a dent in the supply to give inflation a real start.

Blessed with neither any real knowledge of perfumes nor a selective sense of smell, I picked out brands whose bottles seemed sturdy enough to stand a rough trip home, pretty enough to be treasured as gifts, and labelled brazenly enough to fairly scream "Paris!" It gave me great satisfaction to fill my shopping list, despite the problems involved, for it meant making a lot of other men happy by sharing—in a small way, admittedly—my good fortune in getting the trip.

That night I again joined forces with the other four officers to see Paris after sundown, but this time we succeeded in making reservations at Le Lido. In distinct contrast to the Paradise, the Lido was an elegant place. The music was soft and pleasant. The drinks were correspondingly more expensive, of course, but we considered the surroundings worth the extra francs. The floor show began at 8:30 and continued well into the morning with breaks for customer dancing. Since Armistice Day was over, dancing again was in order. Gone were the painted ladies of the evening who had flaunted their price at the Paradise, though word had it that a lonesome soldier could do well enough out at the bar.

We stayed at our table.

Nakedness again was a major part of the floor show, perhaps even more than at the Paradise, but it was molded into the show with a smoothness and beauty that made it enjoyable rather than embarrassing. So genuinely lovely were the girls in the show that I found myself joining the others in whoops of appreciation. When we finally left the Lido well after midnight, we were convinced we had seen a real sample of first-class French night life and knew what people were talking about when they spoke of the gaiety of Paris.

Gaiety was considerably less in evidence the next morning when we assembled with the men in front of the Red Cross club. In addition to the normal weariness brought on by the high pace of the past 48 hours, we could not avoid the awful realization that the holiday was over and that we were headed back to the nerve-wracking outposts in Luxembourg. There were the usual jokes about how various men had achieved their idea of fun, the inevitable tale of the man who had paid far too much for his pleasure, and the equally inevitable account of the naive GI who had been "rolled" of every franc he possessed within an hour of the time he had left us. But all the men were there, and that's what mattered. Nor were there any drunks or even any black eyes. We piled in our trucks, alert for any incident that might legitimately delay our departure. But none came.

As we rode down the broad boulevards, bordered by big, winter-bare trees, I could hear some of the conversation from the back of the truck.

"Just imagine those poor guys," one man said with a gesture toward an MP we passed. "They got to stay in this town day in and day out with all this champagne and all these sexy women. They may never be privileged to see a dirty, stinking, German from a muddy, stupid foxhole."

"Say la guerre, pal," consoled one of his buddies. "Say la bloody goddamn guerre."

Arriving back at the Company E CP, I could do nothing before I was plied with innumerable questions about the trip. With the experience of a born liar, I began to enthrall my questioners with bawdy tales of Paris and its dens of sin. They would have been disappointed had I let on that I hadn't gotten drunk, hadn't cavorted with the babes, and generally hadn't made a damned fool of myself. So I didn't let them know. Besides, who would have believed me?

The First Sergeant, Sergeant Foy, had handed me an accumulation of letters which had arrived during my absence and I was getting ready to depart for my platoon when a messenger arrived with the day's official distribution of paper work from battalion headquarters. Sergeant Foy fingered through it idly, then stopped suddenly and chuckled with pleasure.

"Well, looka here!" he exclaimed. "The Lieutenant has gone and won himself the Silver Star!"

He turned toward me and shoved out his hand. "Congratulations, Lieutenant Boesch," Foy said. "They sure picked the right man to hang this medal on."

My surprise was tempered somewhat by appreciation of Sergeant Foy's obviously sincere congratulations. This kind of remark coming from him was almost as welcome to me as the Silver Star award itself.

"Pardon me, boys," I said at last, "those Paris lies will have to wait. This is something to write home about."

My heart was full as I sat down to write the longest letter I ever managed to compose in a long correspondence career. Through page after page I took Eleonore on the trip to Paris with me. Together we saw all the sights I had seen, strolled hand in hand along the Seine, rode the bicycle through the snake-like streets of Montmartre. Then I brought her back to Luxembourg, right into the command post where I tossed at her the pleasant bombshell of the Silver Star. As I wrote I imagined the excitement the letter would create and, I hoped, the pride.

"This," I thought as I finally eased my cramped fingers and put the envelope in the mail, "will really be a piece of news."

I was, as it turned out, wrong. Though I did not learn of it until much later, division headquarters had a policy of writing a letter home each time a man was awarded a decoration. This official notification reached Eleonore ahead of mine. It was nice of them to do this, but I still think it would have been better had they not spoiled my surprise. I worked too long and hard with the letter for that.

The next day the company held a simple ceremony in the yard of the old chateau where the regimental commander, Colonel Jeter, presented my award to me and other decorations to nine others of the company. As I watched Colonel Jeter walk along the line of men, I felt privileged to be in this exceptional company. When he stood in front of me, my chest swelled so with pride that I thought it might burst.

Inevitably my thoughts flashed back to the last night I had spent in New York with Eleonore before embarking for Europe. As the Colonel carefully inserted the pin of my medal in my field jacket, I thought of Eleonore's warm arms about my neck and her face upturned in the half light of early morning.

"Remember, darling," she had whispered, "no medals. Just do your job and come home to me."

For a split moment I wondered what Eleonore would think of my disobedience, though in my heart I knew she would be every bit as proud as I was.

The voice of the Colonel snapped me from my reverie.

"Well, Boesch," he said, "it looks like you won another bout."

"Yes, sir," I responded, "but I had an excellent manager for this one."

With a twinkle in his eye that told me he was susceptible to knob polish, the Colonel passed on to the next man in line.

Hardly had I returned to my platoon and recovered from the excitement of the award ceremony when word spread that men wearing the bright red shoulder patch of the 28th Infantry Division had been seen in our division sector. Rumor soon had it that we were to change positions with the 28th, to move from our hilltop defenses in Luxembourg to a place inside Germany called the Huertgen Forest.

Huertgen Forest—where had I heard that name? Somehow it

sounded menacing, foreboding, almost evil.

I shrugged.

Imagination, Boesch, imagination.

## 17

As one eventually comes to know in the army, all really persistent rumors have at least some basis in fact. Word soon arrived officially that the 28th Division was to relieve us and we were to go north into the Huertgen Forest.

Captain McKenna promptly called the officers together.

"There're a lot of rumors going around about this place called 'Huertgen Forest," he said. "Most of them aren't true. The area we go to is just a little more active than this one, but I doubt if we'll be called on to attack. I want you to tell your men that, and I want you to do everything you can to keep them from speculating about what we're getting into. If you don't, they'll be so keyed up when we get there nobody'll be worth anything."

It was sensible advice, but it was hard to adhere to, and particularly hard to convince the men that what we said was true. That night, for example, when an officer from the 28th Division's 109th Infantry arrived at our company to serve as quartering officer, he was dirty, bearded, utterly fatigued—a man who obviously had arrived from no part of the front "just a little more active than this one." His eyes were red-rimmed, his movements nervous, almost jerky. Looking around at our clean-shaven faces and our relatively comfortable positions, he obviously took us for a greenhorn outfit. While putting him straight on that score, we fed him well, and I relinquished my bedroll to permit him a decent night's rest.

Before the officer turned in, we asked him what it was like, frankly, this Huertgen Forest.

"It's hell," he said flatly. "Pure, unadulterated hell. That's the only word for it. It's hell." A kind of wild light seemed to come to his eyes.

"You haven't heard anything about it because they're afraid to talk about it. That's it, they're afraid to talk about it. The Germans tore up our division. Tore it up. They kicked the crap out of a lot of other good outfits too. I've been with this division since we landed in France, and I never saw anything like it. It's artillery, tanks, mines. Everywhere mines. Godalmighty, the mines. And Jerries. Everywhere stubborn, stubborn Jerries."

When he finished, we sat quietly for a while, partly because we wanted to give him a chance to get to sleep but mainly because his words produced sombre thoughts. As the candle burned low, I wrote a long letter home.

The next morning we sent a quartering party forward, my mortar section leader, Sergeant Andy Senuta, of Cleveland, Ohio, doing the job for Easy Company. Then we concentrated on getting our equipment ready as we were to leave the area that same afternoon. We took special pains to see that everybody had items of warm clothing—long underwear, overcoats, and perhaps most important of all, overshoes. It was not until we were almost ready to pull out that every man was outfitted, every man except one officer with big feet who could not find a pair of overshoes to fit him. The officer's name was Boesch.

During the early part of the afternoon, Captain McKenna called me aside.

"Boesch," he said, "battalion tells me the chaplain may not make it to us before we push off. I want you to hold a church service for the men."

I gulped, but one look at the Captain's face convinced me he was serious. Nevertheless, I had definite doubts that I could provide the words of comfort needed at a time like this; I needed someone to give me words of comfort myself. I was still leafing through the Bible and a GI church book, totally unprepared, when word arrived that the chaplain would be there in ten minutes.

Never have I received a more timely reprieve.

The appointed time for moving out was fast approaching when I made a last-minute check on my weapons platoon. The men were putting the guns together after a final cleaning. When

I reached the barn where they were quartered, I found a bustle of activity. Everybody was on hands and knees searching through the hay.

"What in the world is the matter?" I asked.

"That stupid sonofabitch over there," said Sergeant Abbott, "let the barrel plunger spring shoot the barrel plunger out into the hay and we can't find it."

Finding a needle in a haystack would have been nothing compared to finding the little two-inch machine gun part in the load of hay the men had been using for bedding. Yet we had to find it, for without it the machine gun was worthless, and now that we were to be on the move we would stand no chance of getting a replacement part.

"Wait a minute," I shouted, convinced we had to use some kind of system or we had not a prayer. "Get some helmets over here and fill them with hay and bum the hay till we find it, even if you have to burn every last straw in the loft."

As smoke began to curl up from the helmets, I sent a messenger to tell Captain McKenna we would be there shortly. One helmet-full after another we burned, then carefully fingered the ashes. Smoke began to fill the barn and we began to cough and choke, but still no barrel plunger. Eventually, Captain McKenna sent a message that the company was waiting on us.

I was about to give the word to admit defeat when I heard a jubilant shout and a fat-faced private rushed toward me in triumph.

He held a smoky barrel plunger in his outstretched hand.


The men of the 28th Division had begun to arrive when with the weapons platoon I joined the rest of the company outside. Each of the newcomers was a replica of the tired, bearded officer who had arrived the night before. Lest our men be unduly impressed by the sight, I tried to remind them that they too had looked like this many times in Normandy and Brittany and that the Jerries the 28th had been fighting were no different than the Jerries we had met before and licked. Yet somehow I knew in my

own mind that these men of the 28th Division were different. There was something about the way they carried themselves, dispirited, heavy, the way some of them flinched at the slightest untoward noise. Nobody could deny that these men had been through something terrible, something close to hell itself.

Relinquishing our warm houses and barns to these men, we moved into a nearby field to pitch our tents for the night. Captain McKenna went to Battalion to get the movement order. We were to load on trucks at daylight the next morning.

Orders many times appear to be issued only so they can be countermanded. This was the case that night. About midnight I gradually became conscious that somebody was nudging me, urging me to get up.

"Hey, Lootenant," the man said, "we're pulling out right away. Hey, Lootenant, get outa the sack."

Even as I sought to shake off the stupefying effects of my short nap, I gathered my section leaders to alert them for the move. By one o'clock we were sitting in the backs of the trucks, a biting wind whipping cold rain around us. For what seemed an interminably long time we sat there. We had almost decided the orders had been changed again when the drivers began to warm up their motors.

It was pitch dark, the road deserted. Gone were the well-wishers and signs of welcome which had greeted us when we first arrived in Luxembourg. Now the towns seemed dead in the darkness and the noise of the heavy trucks rumbling over rough, cobblestone streets was mournful, depressing.

Through a long and sleepless night we tossed and shivered in the rear of the slowly-moving six-by-six truck. The weather could hardly have been worse. A biting wind raced mockingly through torn seams and patches in the tarpaulin which stretched above us. The rain pelted down, finding the same openings. As we moved farther north, the rain changed to snow. Hour after endless hour we huddled close, hoping only that the coming of day would bring some relief from the cold, but the dawn arrived reluctantly behind great gray clouds and did little to improve our lot.

But at least we could see where we were going—that is, more correctly, where we had been.

"Join the army and see the world through the rear end of a six-by-six," quipped someone in disgust.

One man stood watch through a hole in the front of the truck to tell us when something of interest was coming up, then we all would strain to see it out the back of the truck as we passed.

One man, though, would have no part of it.

"What the hell is there to look at and what the hell good is it going to do you to see it?" he asked. "Does a guy that's headed for the electric chair walk down the aisle making complimentary remarks about the paint job on the walls?"

It was a defeatist philosophy we had no choice but to try to ignore. Doggedly we continued to watch for things of interest. At least it made the time pass more quickly. That was important, for packed as we were in the truck we soon became uncomfortably stiff. The cramped condition when added to the cold made every minute seem incredibly longer than sixty seconds. Yet for all our misery we saw men behind us who would have traded places with us any time. They had drawn trucks with no tarpaulins on top.

Slowly, inexorably, the hours passed and so did the miles. Finally we crossed the border into Germany. Though no immediate change in the scenery was evident, we seemed to sense a kind of tension in the air. As we passed through a wide gap blasted in the dragon's teeth of the Siegfried Line, I had the same feeling of gratitude to the men who had pierced this line as I had experienced when I first climbed the high bluff overlooking Omaha Beach in Normandy. What was there in the vast, unpredictable lottery of assignment in the army which had accorded these tasks to someone other than me?

At the town of Roetgen, we followed orders we had received before starting and donned our field packs. Roetgen, we had been told, was near where we were going. At any time now we had to be prepared to get out of the trucks with little or no warning.

Beyond Roetgen our progress slowed considerably as we deserted the main highways for back roads and trails. Incessant rain had made quagmires of the roads. In some places engineers, hard at work trying to drain off the water and keep the roads serviceable, had to stand aside to let us past.

At one of these bottlenecks, a group of engineers was laboring with pick and shovel trying to get enough gravel into a hole in the road to allow us to get through. A young lieutenant carried on a fierce tirade of bitching about the work, the weather, the war, everything in general. When he tired of ranting at his own men, he turned toward us with his indignant monologue.

I interrupted him.

"Hey, buddy," I said, "would you like to change places with us? We'd be glad to get out and fix your road for you."

He looked hard at us, huddled together for warmth like so many cattle. For the first time he seemed really to see us.

"What are you," he asked hesitantly, "infantry?"

"You're damned right we're infantry," shouted one of my men before I could reply.

"No thanks," the lieutenant mumbled. "No thanks."

With this he turned slowly and went about his business, this time in silence.

Minutes later we became aware we were approaching a vast forest of evergreens stretching away to the east as far as we could see. Daylight already was fading fast, even in the open, but as we entered the woods, night rushed at us with gloomy and alarming suddenness. On either side of the narrow road big evergreens with thick, dripping branches almost engulfed us. It was cold, eerie, uninviting. For the first time the truck we had cursed all night and day seemed warm and friendly. We were loathe to leap from it into this forbidding unknown.

Though we had been expecting the order to detruck for miles, it caught us by surprise when it came. I had to force myself to get down from the truck, and the shock of 220 pounds landing on legs that had been cramped for interminably long hours was sharp and painful.

Some units, we noted, were already bivouacked under the trees — men who looked depressingly wet and cold as they sought to force the inhospitable forest to provide them some measure of protection from the elements. We set out past these men in a long, ragged file, stiff-legged at first but gradually walking with more ease as exercise restored our circulation. Finally we turned off the road into the thick of the woods where we found my mortar section leader, Sergeant Senuta, who had preceded us with the quartering party.

Andy waited until I had dropped my musette bag to the ground before he tried to tell me what was in store for us.

"We jump off, lieutenant," he said, hushing his voice so the others would not hear, "at nine in the morning."

Nine in the morning! The news hit me with a revolting shock. I personally had suspected, despite Captain McKenna's repeated insistence otherwise, that we were not moving into the Huertgen Forest to sit on our rears in defensive positions. But to learn that we must attack so quickly after arrival from a long, arduous journey was something totally unexpected. I could hardly believe it. Surely somebody was mistaken.

"Well," I said, deciding to borrow a leaf from Captain McKenna's book, "don't spread the word until I can get some facts and let everybody have it straight."

While awaiting further information, I tried to speed the issuing of rations in order that the men might have a chance to heat their food before it got too dark for any kind of fires, but company headquarters informed me a hot meal was on the way.

"That's well enough," I told Lieutenant Von Keller, the executive officer, "but who the hell wants to stumble around in the dark to eat hot food when he could be heating up a K-ration right now?"

"Orders, friend Boesch, orders," said the big Russian in his thick accent. "You know what's best, I know what's best, the men know what's best. But the General says we got to get fed hot food, and we get fed hot food, whether we like it or not. You know that."

Utter darkness soon enveloped us. It was a clinging, impenetrable darkness. Lights of any kind were forbidden so each of us stayed right on top of his pack lest we lose our equipment. When word at last came that chow was ready, we groped into some kind of formation that resembled many things more than it did a chow line, but by holding to each other's belts and following the voices that called us, we eventually arrived at the spot where Easy Company's cooks were dishing out the meal.

In war and in peace I have eaten many a meal in many parts of the world and under many conditions, but this one remains unique. Until you have stood in a long line of muddy, tired, disgruntled men, holding onto the belt of the man in front of you and feeling the tug of another man at your own belt; until you have stood before a cook you cannot see and who cannot see you, who cannot see even the pot from which he is serving nor the messkit he is supposed to fill; until then, you cannot know the full foul sensation of this meal.

None of us had any idea what we were being served, and by the time we had groped our way to some spot where we could squat on the ground, the food was cold and soggy from rain. In seeking some place to settle, each of us stumbled over other men who had gone ahead of us. In the end we had to give up and take the food in our filthy hands and cram it in chunks into our mouths. Few of us would argue with the theory that before an attack a man should have a hot meal, but neither would we endorse a hot meal under any circumstances, least of all these under which we found ourselves. A crust of bread and a little water would have been preferable to that uncertain, unpalatable repast in the darkness of the Huertgen Forest.

While we were attempting to eat, Captain McKenna was at battalion headquarters for a briefing on the job ahead. Returning just about the time I stumbled back from chow, he called a meeting of company officers. Somehow I found my way to his side.

"I think some of you already know," he said, soberly, "that we attack at nine in the morning. We relieve elements of the 12th Infantry of the 4th Division tonight, then jump off from there."

Then it was true what Sergeant Senuta had said. I still found it hard to believe. I was so stunned that I involuntarily interrupted.

"You mean we occupy their positions on a black night like this and jump off first thing in the morning with never a chance to see where we're going?"

"That's right, Boesch. And I know what you're thinking. I voiced the same objections and raised the same questions at battalion. I have no doubt Colonel Casey did the same at regiment. But we were supposed to arrive here early today. The fact that somebody goofed some place and we got here late hasn't changed the original plan."

As he went on with his instructions, I could not even make out the outline of his helmet. Lifting my hand in front of my face, I literally could not see it, and only when my cold fingers touched my dripping nose could I be positive my hand was there. Yet we were going to move forward through the woods in this blackness, right in the face of the Germans, and then try to drive the Germans back with no more preparation than a loathsome all-night march after a miserable night and day on the road from Luxembourg. I thought of the things the army had gone to great pains to teach us—that relief of a unit at night in close contact with the enemy is tricky and hazardous under any circumstances and must be prefaced by detailed and careful daylight reconnaissance, with guides and markers posted so the relieving column would not get lost, blunder into the enemy, degenerate into noise, confusion, even panic. If the enemy hears you, he may counterattack, hitting when you are thoroughly disorganized and incapable of fighting back.

But after my abortive objection, none of us said a word. This was the way things were, this is the way they would be. It was as inevitable as the night that enveloped us, clung to us.

We were, it turned out, to move immediately, for we still had six or seven miles to walk before we reached the positions held by the 12th Infantry. As soon as I could find my way back to my platoon, I issued instructions quickly, then set out to find the jeeps which had brought our mortars, machine guns, and ammunition from Luxembourg. To my astonishment, I found the vehicles readily, but satisfaction left me when I discovered both jeeps were mired deep in clinging mud. No matter how hard we tried, we couldn't budge them. Knee deep in gurgling slime, we pushed, pulled, and puffed, but to no avail.

Reluctantly, I sent for my platoon and gave the unwelcome order that we would have to carry the heavy weapons and equipment by hand. It would make the long trek through the wet and the dark even more arduous, but machine guns and mortars were vital and my platoon would be of no use in the attack without them. We had no choice but to write off the jeeps as a luxury we could no longer afford.

With considerable effort, we hoisted the weapons and ammunition to our shoulders. Holding fast to the man ahead, we slowly, painfully made our way to where the rest of the company had assembled on the road.

Down the narrow trail of a road between towering trees on either side we moved. The night seemed to get even blacker if that was possible, and the rain came in great wind-driven sheets, drenching every thread of our clothes.

It was not easy to hold onto the belt of the man in front while slipping and slithering forward under the weight of a machine gun tripod or a mortar tube. I constantly patrolled the wavering line of men to patch up the inevitable breaks. Whenever I found a gap, I would rush to the rear until I came upon the man heading the broken segment, then urge him on to greater efforts so that we might catch up with the man he had lost.

The only light to pierce the blackness came from artillery pieces located in clearings in the forest. The big guns belched their shells with thunderous, unannounced, ear-splitting roars that reverberated against wooded hills and echoed and reechoed until it seemed we were caught in the middle of some giant cauldron with hundreds of Satanic monsters banging sledgehammers against the sides with fiendish glee. For an instant as each gun fired, the sky would light up with a blinding flash. After the sudden, brilliant burst of light, it was hard to adjust your vision again to the darkness. Circles and stars danced before your eyes, and you had to struggle to keep from losing your balance. Far off on the horizon answering reports from the enemy's big guns appeared like quick little flickers of heat lightning.

We had no breaks or rests as we marched, just the maddening accordion action of the long, single-file column. At times we would come to an abrupt, complete stop, whereupon you sought to take advantage of it to adjust your burdens, only to have the man ahead of you invariably take off with never a word of warning. In turn you generally reacted by bounding forward at a run, leaving the man behind you to do the same. Up and down the line the exasperating process was repeated over and over, yet there seemed no solution.

The road was full of holes, and the holes were full of water and rocks, and it was almost impossible to keep your feet at times as you stumbled on the rocks or stepped with no warning into a deep hole. Men slipped and fell. As they fought to regain their footing, they knocked into others. One minute we were standing and marching, the next we were sprawled on the muddy road cursing in language that elegantly fitted the situation, some of it invented on the spur of the sodden moment.

For hours we fought for breath and struggled to maintain the exhausting pace. The knowledge that at the end of the march we faced the ticklish problem of relief in the face of the enemy, then attack, dragged at our feet at first; but as time passed we welcomed even this prospect as a way to end this nightmare walk-a-thon.

Suddenly the line halted. Though we braced ourselves for the usual accordion motion, the men ahead did not move. One man turned his head toward us.

"This is as far as we go tonight," he said. "Pull off the road and get some sleep. Pass the word along."

I turned and repeated the message, then worked my way forward to check that it was authentic. Lieutenant Weinberger confirmed it.

"Captain McKenna said we still have to jump off at nine in the morning," he said, "but they've decided it's impossible to make the relief tonight. We've got to fall back in on the road just as soon as it's light enough to see anything."

Thanking him, I returned to my platoon.

"Okay," I said with little conviction, "just get far enough off the road so you'll be dry and not get run over. As soon as it's light, we move out again. Try to get some sleep, you'll need it."

Sleep? The rain pelted down with a fury. Several inches of sloppy mud covered the ground. The perspiration we had worked up on the march quickly dried and made us colder than ever.

I elected to bunk with my section leaders, Sergeant Abbott and Sergeant Senuta, so they would be at hand when the order came to get moving. We made no effort to establish any kind of defense, no guards, no password. I simply made sure the squad leaders knew where their own men were, then spread my raincoat on the ground. Abbott and Senuta lay down with me on my raincoat and we pulled theirs over us.

It was a thoroughly miserable night. Puddles of rain quickly formed in the folds and dents of the raincoats, so that any move brought water pouring into our faces and down our necks. Though we tried pulling the raincoats over our heads, this merely exposed more of our legs and feet. The coldness of the ground soon added to the other chill so that our teeth began to chatter, and I could feel my companions press close against me in futile expectation that my big frame might exude some measure of warmth.

It was a forlorn and frozen hope.

# 18

We lay there courting sleep until the first faint light of day showed above the trees and the word to assemble passed like a dirty thing among us. Down in the woods where we lay, the dark was still almost as impenetrable as ever, but we stirred our rusty joints, picked up our meager belongings, and headed in the direction our instincts told us was the road we had left the night before.

As we moved to assemble, we became aware of the presence of a big tank only some ten feet from where we had spent the night. We had not seen it before. It might have been one of ours, maybe a dead one, or perhaps it was German. We would never know, though we figured if it was German it would have fired at us.

Counting noses as we hit the road, I found that my platoon was ready to obey when the signal came to move forward. Though the darkness would not be fully dissipated for an hour, the marching was considerably easier, for even a little light eliminated the awful problem of keeping physical contact and we could make out most of the obstacles in the road and avoid them.

The trail led down between a pair of giant concrete pillboxes which had been blasted into big heaps of jagged rubble. The incredible thickness of the concrete awed us as we passed. Battalion had taken over one of the blasted structures as a headquarters and aid station, and additional ammunition for our mortars and machine guns was waiting for us just outside. I picked up a carton of mortar shells, slung it over my shoulder, and then hoisted two boxes of machine gun belts with my free hand. Despite this added load, it was easier now to keep pace with the column, for a gray, cheerless light had begun to filter through the trees to dispel a measure of the gloom in the morbid woods.

As visibility increased, we looked about with sobering revelation. The fighting here, on both sides of the road, obviously had been bitter, fierce, and destructive. Once magnificent trees now were twisted and broken; indeed, it was hard to find a single tree which had not been damaged in one way or another. Mutilated limbs torn from the trees spread a rough, grotesque carpet on the floor of the forest. The country was hilly, almost like a rollercoaster, with steep rises projecting in some places close from the edge of the road.

Everywhere we saw discarded equipment—gas masks, ammunition belts, helmet liners, helmets, rifles. Here and there were articles of clothing with great rents and clotted scarlet stains. One man kicked a bloody shoe from his path, and to our revulsion we could see a foot still in it.

Soon the signs of battle turned into sounds—mean, nasty, personal sounds. The noise of Jerry artillery crashing along the narrow valley through which we marched reverberated incessantly against the wooded hills, making it impossible to detect where the shells landed. Nor could we see where the shells hit because of the rises in the ground and the thick matting of the branches of the evergreens. One of the protections an infantryman needs and soon acquires is an ability to distinguish the various sounds of battle and recognize those that mean danger to him, but in the Huertgen Forest we began to realize that the forest usurped this sixth sense. We would grow slow and uncertain in our reactions. Uncertainty means delay, and sometimes the difference of a split second is all that separates life from death.

Despite the emotional conflicts that raged inside us, we continued forward like the soldiers we were, a long, worried column moving to an inevitable rendezvous with destiny. And death.

When we reached a place where the road crossed a timber bridge over a small, muddy stream, Captain McKenna was waiting to give me further instructions.

"Boesch," he said, "I'm taking the company up that hill ahead to relieve a company of the 12th Infantry. We still jump off at nine o'clock like our orders said. I don't think your 60's will do a damned bit of good in an attack in these woods. I want you to stay here and cover this valley. It's our responsibility, and I figure you can do more good here than you could up on the hill. You'll have to use your ammunition bearers as riflemen to protect your position—do the best you can."

As the rifle platoons and my machine gun section moved ahead, I went about the business of getting ready for Jerry should he choose to advance along the line of the stream. There were no positions really suitable for mortars, but eventually I settled for a location near a fork in the road where the road split to follow both banks of the stream. Here we placed the mortars in battery.

The ground around the bridge was a sea of mud at least a foot and a half deep and of a consistency slightly thicker than plain water. Engineers working to make the road passable for vehicles, particularly for tanks, were bringing up truckloads of gravel to fill in around the bridge. Nearby a tank destroyer watched over the proceedings, affording some measure of reassurance against the concern that the enemy might advance down the valley.

After marking out the places for the men to dig in the mortars, I set about the job of picking possible target areas. Hardly had I begun when Lieutenant Zienke stumbled down the hill, his face ghostly white and contorted with pain. With his right hand he held a bloody left arm. He had been on the hill less than 15 minutes when a German bullet caught him in the left forearm.

"Is it bad?" I asked solicitously.

"Not too bad," Zienke replied with a grin, but every movement made him wince and it was obvious he was slipping into a state of shock. "It didn't touch the bone."

"Hey, looka guys," one of my men shouted to the rest of his squad, "the lieutenant's went and got hisself a million dollar wound!"

Crowding around to have a look, the men made no effort to conceal the envy in their glances or their remarks. A million dollar wound was one that did no permanent damage to bone or structure yet still was serious enough to put a man in the hospital for a while. Hospital was a magic word which meant rest, attention, beds, hot food, and—what was most important— nobody shooting at you.

(Zienke's wound did, in fact, prove to be of the million dollar variety, but a few months later, after he had returned to duty, he took a Jerry bullet in the throat and died within a few minutes).

Hardly had Zienke departed toward the aid station when Captain McKenna came staggering down the road, his messenger helping him to walk. He had suddenly been taken violently ill and was doubled up with stomach cramps. Our amateur diagnosis pronounced it appendicitis, but whatever it was, it was obvious that the Captain needed medical attention immediately. We commandeered an engineer jeep to rush him back to the aid station. It was the last time I was to see Captain McKenna. After several weeks in the hospital, he returned to duty but was killed on Christmas Day.

Nick Von Keller took over the company, and I moved up again to the post of executive officer, though I still maintained control of the mortar section. The changes occurred so rapidly that men of the 12th Infantry whom we were relieving still had not cleared the area.

We dug in our mortars and kept constant watch up the wooded valley for any signs of enemy infiltration. Up on the hill Easy Company joined Fox Company and jumped off in the scheduled attack. They took two pillboxes; that was all. It quickly became apparent that this hastily-mounted attack was stopped cold and would make no further progress through the day. Artillery fire plastered the two companies unmercifully, and a whole rifle platoon of Company F, along with a part of the weapons platoon became lost from the main body and presumably was captured. I was selfishly thankful that Jack was not with them; he had been ordered to stay behind in Luxembourg to orient the men of the 28th who took over our positions.

Throughout the day Jerry's big guns sought the bridge over the stream, and even though they failed to find it, their errors in aim were small enough so that the area around my mortars was deluged with huge shells. Meanwhile, the big trucks carrying gravel and stone came and went, dumping their loads into a seemingly bottomless morass around the bridge. An almost constant rain added to their problems, and the task began to appear hopeless. In addition, continuous turn in of the trucks in one spot was compounding the problem. Eventually the engineers decided that the trucks should cross the bridge and turn around on the other side of the stream in order to spare the road the grinding effect of the trucks* backing, twisting, and turning.

The first truck negotiated the bridge with little real difficulty, found relatively solid ground on which to turn, and started back. Easing off the bridge into the slimy mud, the driver prepared to dump his load.

*Karooom!*

The violent explosion rent the air! Steel fragments flew. Pieces of truck flew. Someone screamed in agony.

We were only about twenty yards away. Diving into our half-finished holes, we waited until the rain of metal ended, then jumped from the holes to help the engineers.

The twisted bulk of the truck had been blown about 15 feet from the spot where the explosion occurred. The front end was demolished. The driver was still behind the wheel, alive but unconscious. We lowered him to the road, onto a stretcher. Six other men who had been close to the truck suffered visibly from concussion.

By the time the last of the engineers had been cared for, darkness was descending, and we slunk back to our holes for the night. It was already too dark to heat our K-rations, and in the freezing, pelting rain we had little desire to eat the food cold. So thoroughly soaked were our overcoats that they were useless for keeping us warm, so we spread them across the top of our holes to help fend off the unfriendly elements. Hardly anyone ever wore an overcoat in the Huertgen Forest. Those that tried had to walk stooped at the waist as if they carried the burden of the world on their backs, so heavy were the coats after soaking up rain and mud.

Everything was cold, wet, clammy. Mud clung tormentingly to our clothes, and even when the rain stopped for a while, which was rare, the soggy mud made sure we stayed cold and uncomfortable. At first I did not have even the protection of overshoes, but within a few days I was to find a pair that fitted me on a man in a ditch who was beyond caring whether his feet were wet or not. As I removed the overshoes from the dead man I felt no emotion other than selfish satisfaction that at last my feet would be protected.

Through the night we shivered while taking turns at standing guard. Our artillery shells came overhead and crashed on Jerry-land to our front; Jerry's shells came and crashed around us with a diabolical roar that made us huddle closer to the muddy bottoms of our holes. We were caught in the middle of what seemed a perpetual two-way stream of messages that spelled violent death.

With the first sight of light in the sky, we crawled from the wet holes, stretched our cramped muscles, and looked at the world through bloodshot eyes. It wasn't much of a world to look at. The rain continued to fall with an irritating monotony, and as a murky light increased, we could see the torn and twisted body of the truck, mute testimony to the violence of the evening before. It was hard to imagine any explosive powerful enough to do so much damage to the truck. We finally decided it could not have been just one mine but several stacked together.

As we discussed the tragedy, a truckload of engineers arrived to tow away the battered vehicle. One of the officers who had been with the engineers the night before recognized me and spoke.

"You haven't seen one of our men around here, have you? We're missing one man ever since the explosion last night. I thought he might have stayed with you fellows."

"Haven't seen a stranger around at all," I said.

The wrecker moved in and towed the big wounded vehicle out of the slimy road. When it moved away, I helped the engineer lieutenant search through the muck for equipment. We had found several shovels when my foot hit something soft and yielding. It was the missing man. He either had been crushed to death by the truck or drowned in the oozing mud. We helped carry him up to higher ground and laid him where the trucks could not disturb his peace.

Now that daylight had come again, more trucks began to line up with loads of gravel, and a new squad of engineers arrived to take over the task of filling the hole. The tank destroyer moved ahead of our mortar positions and took up a post where it could sweep the intersection and cover both roads. A new day had started in the Huertgen Forest with a bustle of work, but it looked very much like the same dismal day before.

After checking the mortars thoroughly and conferring with Sergeant Senuta on targets, I moved ahead to the rear command post of the company. In a situation of such close contact with the enemy, it was important for the company to have two CP's in order to coordinate communications and movement of supplies. Only about 200 yards separated the spot chosen for the rear CP from the front lines, but those 200 yards afforded a slight measure of protection which enabled the men to go about various supply tasks out of sight of the enemy.

The 200 yards from the rear CP to the front led up the side of a steep hill, made almost impassable by fallen trees and brush and the slippery, ubiquitous mud. With some of the men from my mortar section, I formed a carrying party to move rations, water, and ammunition up the hill. Huffing, puffing, bitching bitterly, we followed the telephone lines to guide us. Shells fell frequently not far away, but so thick was the forest that we never actually saw a burst. The noise of the explosions bounced against the sides of the hills and echoed up and down the valley with a fury that left us concerned and perplexed, never quite knowing when to drop to our bellies for protection. So steep was the hill in some spots that we would progress for five feet, then slip back six. We had to crawl under some broken trees and over others, passing our burdens to willing but weary hands on the other side. By the time we reached the top we all were sweating profusely despite the chill in the air and the steady rain.

In the face of the unpleasant situation, Nick Von Keller still greeted me with apparent warmth when we reached the pillbox he was using as a command post. If he was worried over the way things were going, he was far too clever to convey his feelings to his men. I admired him for it. Briefing me on what had been happening on the hill, he told of the noisy night they had spent under the German shelling. I wanted to stay on the hill with him and leave the rear under the guidance of Sergeant Foy, but Nick would not hear of it.

"I will feel better if you are there to come up and take over if I am hit, old man," he said. "Keep the supplies coming and be sure to stay in touch with the situation. That will be just what I need."

A little reluctantly I turned and found my way back down the hill. On the way I resolved to make the path easier for the men to climb. As soon as I got to the rear CP, I telephoned battalion to send the Ammunition and Pioneer Platoon to hack out a clear path. Within an hour the men were at work.

The real terror of the Huertgen Forest lay partly in the number of casualties we absorbed but also partly in the type of injuries. The Germans had sown the forest lavishly with mines. Mainly they were *Schuh* and box mines, scattered in no apparent pattern. The mines contained about a half pound of TNT, just enough to blow off a man's leg or foot. It was impossible to probe for them with bayonets or knives, for the area was too large, and it was equally impossible to use mine detectors to find them. Since these mines were encased in plastic or wood, mine detectors, which are designed to pick up the presence of metal in the ground, would not react to them. Besides, so many shell fragments littered the floor of the forest that mine detectors were constantly buzzing even though no mine was present.

Men became afraid to walk except on well-beaten paths, and even these sometimes disclosed mines that had failed to explode even though hundreds of feet had passed over them. The parade of men wounded by mines was so constant and depressing that the thought of getting a foot or a leg blown off was with us at every turn. This specter haunted us day and night.

Up on the hill Easy Company jumped off in another attack, only to run into a well-defended stretch of concertina barbed wire which the men could not cross. As they stopped at the obstacle, the German machine gunners caught them in a terrible cross-fire while mortars, and artillery rained down on them with deadly accuracy. Soon the wounded were slipping and slithering down the muddy hill in a painful, bloody procession. Lieutenant Gillespie slipped and fell during this attack, taking a bullet in the leg from his own carbine.

We checked them through our command post and added their names to an ever-growing list of casualties which we noted each day on our morning report. At times we laid down our pencils and picked up our carbines to try to even the score against individuals or small groups of Germans who wandered down the valley, sometimes errantly, sometimes on reconnaissance, sometimes with the specific purpose of surrender. It was a feeble, futile effort to balance the casualty lists. To us, we had no way of estimating the damage our artillery and planes were doing to the enemy, it seemed a cruelly one-sided battle.

On the opposite bank of the creek, Company G went into action in an attempt to outflank the opposition which was holding up the other two companies, but the advance platoon soon hit mines and the platoon leader had both legs blown off. Machine guns and mortars then started cutting down the remaining members and it was only with painful difficulty that any of the men made their way back.

As I look back on the action in the forest, a curtain of time tries to minimize the cruel length of the days and nights and run them together in one broad picture. It is difficult to recall the sequence in which events occurred. Each episode appears to claim precedence over the others. But though it is hard to recall exactly when a thing happened, it is impossible to erase the events themselves, for the sheer, stark, exhausting terror burned them inextricably in our memory.

The next day following the thwarted attack of companies F and G, I looked up from something I was doing on the road and saw Jack approaching. For a moment I was crestfallen and may not have greeted him with the enthusiasm the reunion deserved,

for in the back of my mind was the knowledge that now he would be exposed to the same terror and dangers as the rest of us. Shaking off this morbid thought, I pumped his hand vigorously. For a few happy minutes we talked like a couple of voluble Frenchmen, but duty beckoned, and he turned, picked up his equipment, and made his way slowly up the blood-stained hill.

I saw another familiar face on the road that day, a pleasant, clean, smooth-shaven face belonging to brand new Second Lieutenant James H. Kee, of Newberg, Tennessee. Only the day before Kee had been a dirty, bearded, but capable sergeant who had left for the rear to be awarded a well-deserved battlefield commission. At division headquarters General Stroh had presented him with shiny gold bars.

"Hey, look, lieutenant," one of the men said to me. "Kee got a shave and a gold bar. They had to give him a bath so the general could get close enough to pin the bars on him."

I shook Kee's hand with sincere enthusiasm.

"I won't congratulate you," I said. "I'm not sure congratulations are in order. But I do wish you every bit of luck in the world."

Kee smiled, his clean face offering a strange contrast to the rest of us. He obviously understood why I would not congratulate him.

Lieutenants, he knew, too often received the honor of being among the first to be killed. (Kee became proof of that axiom when he was caught by the burst of a mortar shell. He was evacuated with more than 400 wounds. After the war we met in Houston, Texas, and he still had more than 200 pieces of shrapnel in him. In 1959 he died and at the funeral home I said a prayer from each of us in the One-Two-One.)

Company G pulled back from the halted effort to force a way through the woods on the opposite side of the creek and reformed its battered platoons to our rear. The next day one intrepid platoon moved down the road on the left side of the creek in order to avoid mines, then, upon reaching a point believed to be about even with Easy Company's hilltop position, left the dangerous road and turned toward the creek. Fording the stream, the men began to climb the sheer face of the hill. It was a difficult and brilliant maneuver. In some places the incline was so precipitous the men had to pull themselves up by tugging at trees and bushes, but they made it and forced the Jerries to abandon several positions along the road.

The Company G commander, Captain Black, the tall, blond Westerner whom I had come to know in Brittany, then led the rest of his company straight up the road past our little foxhole CP in an effort to reach the platoon and strengthen and exploit the advantage the platoon had gained. But Black and his men had not gone far beyond us up the steeply rising road when machine gun fire cut down the two men who were preceding Black as scouts. Black nevertheless pressed forward, urging his men all the way until at last they came to a roadblock covered by three machine guns. The ground was so steep on either side of the road that the men could not deploy and could find no cover except in a shallow ditch on the right of the road.

The ditch turned out to be false protection, at least for one man, Lieutenant Joe Kowalewski, who had left his job as Battalion S-2 to become Company G's executive officer. As Joe stepped into the ditch, he set off a mine that severed one leg midway between the ankle and the knee. Medics responded quickly to the call to carry the lieutenant back, and Captain Black helped them bundle the big, genial fellow on the stretcher. As they carried Joe past my mortar positions, I tried to think of a joke, some pleasant remark to make. "It's a suicide mission," I started to say, but I could not speak. I had to turn my face away.

Unable to penetrate the roadblock, the remaining members of Company G began to stumble back by our command post. I could see as Captain Black approached that he was under some terrible strain. At the sight of me, a fellow officer whom he knew, he gave way to a volume of pent up emotions.

"Why did it have to happen to them?" he cried. He dropped his head in his hands and began to sob. "Why didn't it happen to me? McCarthy gets both his legs blown off. Men get killed and wounded all around me. Those two sergeants were with me ever since I got here. I made them sergeants. Now they're dead. Joe loses his leg. Why doesn't it happen to me? Why, dammit, why?"

I could appreciate how Black felt. He was a man who took his immense responsibilities seriously, and the ever-lengthening casualty lists inevitably had a strong effect on him. I tried to comfort him, to make him understand that we all felt the same way. But he was inconsolable.

At last I put him in my hole, stretched my blanket over him, and telephoned battalion.

"Colonel, it's me, Boesch," I said, keeping my voice low so Black could not hear me. "I've got Captain Black here in my foxhole. His nerves are shot. He needs a little rest, else we're going to lose a mighty good man."

The Colonel listened, then said to keep Black with me for a few hours to see if he might not snap out of it.

"Okay, sir," I agreed. "His men are stretched out along the road here now. I don't want to parade him past them in this condition anyway. I'll make sure he's okay before I bring him back."

When I hung up, I heard Black sobbing again. I went to him.

"I heard you, Boesch," he cried accusingly, sitting up in the foxhole. "You're ashamed of me. You think I'm yellow. I'm not yellow. I'm not afraid of these sonsabitchin' Germans. I'm not afraid of their goddamned artillery. But why do all these good men get killed while I stay here and see them go? Why wasn't it me instead of them? Why wasn't it me? Answer me that, dammit. Why?"

How could I explain to Black that I often had pondered the same thing, that I had concluded that somewhere in Heaven they used a strange method of selecting who would go and who would stay. Most of the men at the front explained their narrow escapes with the laconic phrase that their "number had not come up," but I wondered how many believed in their own bravado. To many a man in other foxholes I had recited a poem on the subject:

> *It does not matter when I go.*
> *    Nor how nor why.*
> *Each day a million roses blow,*
> *    A million die.*
> *For every bird that lives to sing,*
> *    A song is stilled.*
> *I go ... a brief remembering ...*
> *    My place is filled,*
> *I'll live and love and dine and drink*
> *    The while I may,*
> *And when my number's called,*
> *    I think I'll say "O.K."*

I knew now was not the time nor the place to recite this poem to Black nor to try to explain it to him. Nor was it any use to try to comfort him. I left him in my hole, covered him with everything I could find that might provide some warmth, and hoped that he might sleep.

── **19**

Hardly had Captain Black quieted when I received a phone call from battalion. It was Captain William S. Freeman, of Philadelphia, our S-3 (operations officer).

"Boesch," he said in a voice that was supposed to radiate cheerfulness, "happy Thanksgiving. We've got a hot turkey dinner here for every man in the outfit. I'm sending Easy Company's up now."

"A turkey dinner?" I asked incredulously. "Are you guys nuts? It's almost dark and my carrying parties have already made the trip up the hill with rations and water. I can't send them up there again. Besides, they can't feed a hot meal in the positions they're in now. Good God, they're right on top of the Jerries." "It's the General's orders, Boesch," Freeman answered. "We've got to do it. You want to see the men get a nice hot meal, don't you?"

"Well, Jeezus Christ, that's a fine way of putting it. Of course I want to see them get a hot meal. I want to see them get three hot meals a day and a dry bed every night and a babe to sleep with, but let's save the turkey until they can pull back where they can enjoy it. Who the hell knows it's Thanksgiving except some silly bastard in the rear who gets hot meals anyway and just wants a change of diet?"

Freeman had had enough. He put Colonel Casey on the phone. "Colonel," I argued, "division headquarters hasn't been up on that hill. They have no idea what it means to try to get food to those men, not to mention the trouble of trying to eat it. Why can't we wait until we pull back and the men can enjoy the food?"

"Boesch," said the Colonel, "I used the same arguments at regiment, and I have no doubt Colonel Jeter used them with division, but those are the orders. There will be no change. The meal is here. I'm sending yours right down. You will see that it gets served."

"Yes, sir," I said, defeated.

Resentment seethed inside me. What the hell difference did it make when a man ate his Thanksgiving turkey? One day was like any other to us.

Nevertheless, I sent a messenger to round up the carrying party. When I told the men their assignment, the assortment of bitches that greeted it were in no way softened by the prospect of a turkey dinner when they would get back.

One private, bolder than the rest, looked me square in the eye.

"Lieutenant," he said, "don't you think it'd be smarter to have a meal like this when we come off the line and can enjoy it?" "Today's Thanksgiving, Joe," I said—curtly, I'm afraid. "Division wants us to remember our blessings and be thankful. So we eat turkey and like it."

When the food arrived the men shouldered the marmite cans and started up the hill while I turned my attention to Captain Black's company. Except for a lieutenant with the isolated platoon up on the hill, Company G had no officers left.

The men of Company G had just begun to congregate for their Thanksgiving turkey when on the other side of the creek a noisy distraction broke loose. Just about even with our position on the other bank stood a disabled tank. Though knocked out, it remained on the road. Because patrols passing near had claimed they had been fired on from the tank, the tank destroyer near my mortar position had been given the job of sending the tank up in flames. Unfortunately, the tank destroyer crew chose this particular time to do the job. The sudden bark of a direct fire weapon so close to us and the explosive crash of the shells caught us by surprise and sent us diving for the ground. Jerry heard the racket too and began to smother the valley with artillery fire.

Then all hell broke loose, not only around us but up on the hill where the men of my carrying party probably were just arriving at the company command post. In almost no time the wounded began streaming down the hill. It took little checking to determine that many of the wounded were from my carrying party.

"What happened?" I asked.

"Just when we got there with the goddamned turkey," one man told me, holding a bloody bandage against his arm, "the artillery began to come. A lot of guys were killed and wounded, Lieutenant.

They need some litter bearers up there, need 'em bad."

I quickly called battalion for litter bearers, then tried without success to contact Von Keller at the forward company CP. The telephone line was dead.

It was completely dark by the time the litter bearers reached us, and I was reluctant to start them forward. I knew that if we tried to bring wounded down that steep, slippery slope at night we probably would do more damage than by letting them wait overnight for evacuation. Von Keller, I was certain, would assemble them for the night in the pillbox he was using as a CP.

When Colonel Casey telephoned saying he had heard what happened, I told him my decision to wait until daylight. He agreed with me.

"And Boesch," he added, "I'm sorry. Very sorry."

It proved to be a miserable night. Through the course of it Captain Black sobbed and moaned. His pitiful condition was almost contagious, and I found I had to fight myself to keep from becoming thoroughly maudlin. Across the creek the tank burned with a steady flame while at intervals the ammunition inside exploded. The noise and fire kept Jerry on his toes, prompting him to bombard the valley with even more shelling than usual. Since Black had my blankets, I found it impossible even to try to sleep. Through the night I went up and down the lines of G Company's men, checking to make sure none was hit in the shelling. Between times I slumped in the foxhole with Black and did what I could to comfort him. As dawn approached, the cold rain started again.

As soon as I could see well enough to distinguish one tree from another, I summoned the litter bearers and some wiremen who were to repair the telephone lines and we started up the hill.

As we reached the small clearing where Company E's command post was located, I jolted to a halt. Near the entrance to the pillbox lay two men, side by side with helmets over their faces. Close by stood the unopened marmite cans containing the turkey dinner.

Inside, Nick greeted me.

"My friend Boesch," he said with a grin on his dirty face, "welcome to our CP and we are sure glad to see you."

I could not return Nick's effort at pleasantness, so anxious was I to learn the details of the tragedy the night before. One shell, it developed, had come in just as the carrying party arrived with the dinner. The shell hit a tree, thus heightening the impact of the explosion and sprayed deadly fragments over a wide area. Seven men had been wounded and three killed, an awful price to pay for a Thanksgiving dinner that nobody wanted to eat.

Of the three men killed, one was Hobbs, the staff sergeant in the second platoon with whom I had spent so many nights in the big foxhole back in Luxembourg. Hobbs was one of the finest soldiers I ever met, certainly the most conscientious enlisted man I ever knew. He had received many chances for a battlefield commission, and I had urged him to accept, but he was concerned that it would mean transfer from Company E's second platoon. He had started his army career in that platoon—and that was where he finished it. Sergeant Hobbs' death affected me more than any had before; Hobbs was a real friend, and it is difficult to apply the stoicism with which a soldier accepts the inevitable when it applies to good friends.

Before we left Luxembourg, Sergeant Hobbs had mailed home some perfume which I had purchased for him in Paris. As I stood looking down at his lifeless body, the thought ran through my mind again and again that the people at home would get the notice of his death before they received the perfume.

Lying alongside Hobbs was Staff Sergeant William C. Gant, my machine gun section leader, a particularly capable soldier. Gant had always handled his men well and quietly, and almost to a man they would look on his death as an ill omen for their future. Gant and Hobbs, good friends during their time together in service, lay stretched out side by side where they had fallen, victims of the same shell.

The third man killed was a little old man who never had belonged in the infantry. He was Private Robert Fullerton. This man's age and physical condition had made it impossible for him to pull his own weight in the company, even though he always tried hard. It was a shameful waste of life, it seemed to me, for he never should have been in the infantry. Careful screening would have resulted in his serving in a job within his capabilities.

While I was at the CP, Sergeant Pople approached me with news of another death.

"Well, lieutenant," he said in a tired voice, "they got Melgoza yesterday. I guess we won't be going out on any more patrols with him now."

I put my hand on Pople's shoulder. There was little I could say since I knew he and Melgoza had risked death together many times and Pople felt that now that Melgoza had lost the toss, his own time was much closer. I recalled the daylight patrol to the Our River in Luxembourg when Melgoza had been one of the four of us. Still I could not speak to Pople, for I could think of nothing to say. I patted his shoulder and turned away.

As for the wounded, Nick told me the comforting news that he had gotten every man down the hill the night before except one. He was in Company F's CP in a pillbox about a hundred yards away.

Leading the litter bearers along a forest path, we came to a pillbox similar to that occupied by Company E's command post. Inside we found our casualty. He had been hit in a number of places. A bandage wreathed his head, and his left arm was in a sling. As we lifted him gingerly to a stretcher, he appeared to be a critical case.

With utmost care we started with our burden down the hill toward the road. The going was rough all the way. Several times we slipped on the steep wet slope, but with the greatest possible concern for our miserable, moaning charge, we kept the litter on an even keel. We gently passed the man over some fallen trees and under others, while he groaned in pain. He seemed to be bordering on unconsciousness every step of the way.

We were about half-way down and just about exhausted when Jerry began to throw in huge shells that landed with resounding crashes. With a smoothness that showed long practice, my three litter-bearing mates gently laid down their ends of the stretcher, then dived into the deepest holes they could find. Somewhat taken by surprise at the alacrity of their maneuver, I suddenly found myself alone with the patient. Lying down close to the stretcher, I rolled near him, intent on comforting him during the danger if not actually protecting him from the deadly shell fragments.

But as I hit the dirt, I got quite a shock.

Our patient, who had been as still as death except for a few groans, leaped to his unsteady feet, bandages trailing, and with the unerring instinct of the infantryman, dived into the nearest empty hole.

In spite of continuing shelling, in spite of the horrors of the preceding night, in spite of my own exhaustion and the danger, I could not help laughing. While the enemy barrage poured out a venomous and far from humorous message, I roared with laughter.

When the shelling stopped, the medics reassembled, our patient hobbled back, climbed again on the stretcher, and placidly resumed his recumbent role. We picked him up without comment and carried him the rest of the way, but on several occasions when we came to especially difficult obstacles, the corporal in charge of the medics would tap our patient gently on the shoulder, point to the tree barring the way, and say with a grandiloquent gesture of politeness:

"Would you mind?"

Without a murmur, the patient would get off the stretcher, walk around or climb under the tree, and then get back on the stretcher to be carried the rest of the way.

# 20

By the time I got back to the rear command post, events had begun to happen with astounding speed. Company G already had left to go around the opposite side of the creek and repeat the heroic climb which the single platoon had accomplished the day before.

Colonel Casey, it developed, had pulled back this platoon during the night lest it be captured or annihilated, a move not fully appreciated at higher headquarters. As it was explained to us at company level, withdrawing this platoon was what cost both Colonel Casey and Colonel Jeter their commands. The 121st Infantry was the poorer for this decision, for both were excellent officers. General Stroh, who stood by Casey and Jeter, received the fate reserved for those of the rank of General and went home on sick leave, but he never returned to the division that loved him so well.

The news took time to filter down to us, and I first learned of it in an embarrassing manner. I had reason to call battalion. When a strange voice answered, I asked who it was.

"This is Kunzig," the voice said.

"Who the hell is Kunzig?" I shot back bluntly.

"This is Lieutenant Colonel Kunzig, your new battalion commander."

It was several days before I actually got to see Lieutenant Colonel Henry B. Kunzig, and during that time he remained but a voice on the telephone.

The new regimental commander for the 121st Infantry turned out to be Colonel Thomas J. Cross, who had been chief of staff of the division. Colonel Cross was a considerate, thoughtful man who had the best interests of his men and his outfit at heart. He was soon to gain the respect of the regiment despite the fact that he faced a handicap in following in Colonel Jeter's steady footsteps.

Command of the 8th Division passed to Brigadier General William G. Weaver, known as "Wild Bill" because of earlier exploits with the 90th Division. Like Colonel Cross, General Weaver was one who looked after those under his command. He was to do an excellent job and to be promoted to Major General before having to relinquish the command some months later because of a heart attack.

When Company G finally got to the top of the steep slope without any real trouble, the lone officer with the company, Lieutenant Rollie Moore, sent a messenger to my CP with the news so that I in turn could notify battalion. Having delivered the news, the messenger headed back. I saw him walk across the road and start to descend to the creek through a stretch of battered trees along a route which no one, to my knowledge, had used before.

I called out to him.

"Hey, soldier, where the hell are you going?"

"Back to G Company," the man answered.

"Hadn't you better stick to the road and take the same path your company used?" I asked. "You never know what you'll find down in those woods."

"That way's too damned long, lieutenant," the man replied. "I'm pooped. Don't worry about me. I know what I'm doing."

Before I could say anything else he disappeared beyond the road and over a deep drop. Something inside me said to call the man back and order him to take the regular route, but for some inexplicable reason the words stuck in my throat and I said nothing.

It was only a matter of minutes before a loud explosion rent the woods. Then a terrifying scream. Then two more explosions. More screams.

I knew instinctively what had happened. The man had set off one mine and then others as, in agony, he thrashed about.

Several of us ran to the spot where I had seen the messenger disappear into the woods. Though the screams continued, we could see no sign of the soldier through the gloomy forest. Hastily, I looked about for a patch of fairly clear ground that might lead me in the direction of the cries. As I started to descend the slope, an engineer lieutenant joined me. Together we started down the side of the hill, trench knives drawn, probing the ground in front of us. It was an almost impossible task. Leaves and fallen branches and bits of trees had laid a heavy carpet which completely hid any mines.

"Look, lieutenant," the engineer officer said to me finally, "we'll never get there this way. It'll take hours. Look, I'll take some litter bearers down to the bridge and we'll follow the stream. They wouldn't have mined the stream."

It seemed the only chance to reach the man. I stayed where I was in order that the engineer officer might know when he reached a point in the stream opposite where the man had disappeared.

The screams already were growing fainter as the lieutenant and four litter bearers slipped over the side of the bridge into the icy water. Slowly and carefully, testing occasionally for mines, each man followed closely behind the other as they made their way down the creek. All went well until one of the medics grew careless and stepped out of the narrow stream of water. A mine erupted with a roar. With a vicious thoroughness, it snapped off the man's leg.

Sorrowfully, the lieutenant and the other three men put the medic on the stretcher and retraced their steps. By the time the wounded man had been removed to the aid station and another recruited to take his place, it was getting dark and the cries of the wounded messenger had ceased. Without his cries to guide on, it would be impossible to find him, and any number of other men might lose limbs in the process. We had no choice but to leave the man to die a lonely, forsaken, painful death.

It did not pay to get off the beaten paths in the Huertgen Forest. Up on the hill Company F's supply sergeant was delivering rations when he strayed from the usual path, stepped on a mine, and died instantly. As Easy Company renewed the attack and again ran into the murderous fire at the concertina wire obstacle, one of the men in Lieutenant Weinberger's platoon spotted a mine and yelled to the lieutenant to watch out for it. Weinberger took a step backward and with that one step set off still another mine. The explosion severed his leg just above the ankle. They carried him down the hill on a stretcher with the bloody stump protruding from under the blanket— solemn, grim evidence of the dangers which lurked in the forest.

Reports like these came in constantly from every part of the front.

With Company E's second failure to break through the concertina wire and with Company G's success in its flanking maneuver, the attack plan was changed. Company E came down the hill with orders to force a way straight up the road past the roadblock which earlier had halted Captain Black and the main body of Company G. The two companies then were to join forces for a new attack.

It was late afternoon when Easy Company came down from the hill and the next morning before the company was ready to attack. Once begun, the advance was deliberate. The roadblock was destroyed and several light tanks moved forward to reinforce the riflemen. I prepared to go forward too to help Nick now that he and Kee were the only officers left, but just as I started up the road, one of the men called me back to the telephone. It was Colonel Kunzig.

"Boesch," Kunzig said, "can you take over G Company? They just evacuated Captain Black. He won't be back for some time and they don't have an officer left."

Colonel Kunzig seemed to be asking me whether I could do the job rather than ordering me to do it. The thought flashed through my mind that he knew nothing first-hand about me, so he really was questioning my confidence in my own ability.

I replied quickly and with conviction.

"Immediately, if you want it, sir."

Picking up my raincoat and musette bag, I started up the road. On the way I passed along the line of men of Company E stretched on the sides of the road. They were in good spirits and ribbed me about my unkempt appearance. Since laughs were few and far between those days, I encouraged this kind of joking. My own favorite, though admittedly feeble, attempt at humor generally consisted in going up to some stoop-shouldered, shuffling GI and asking him sternly, "Soldier, did you shave this morning?" Invariably the man would stare at me as if he thought I was crazy until eventually he would realize that my beard was twice as long and twice as black as his. Then he would manage a wry smile.

Continuing past the men of Company E, I reached the light tanks when a barrage of mortar shells began to fall. I dived under the nearest tank, grateful for the tons of steel over me. It was an accurate concentration, zeroed with what seemed incredible accuracy on the twisting forest road. Several men of E Company were hit in the shelling; one man not ten feet from the tank where I hid was killed.

Without further incident, I reached my destination, but the sight that awaited me there was not one to inspire satisfaction or confidence. George Company's casualties had been extremely high and the company's last officer—Rollie Moore, whom I had known well back at Camp Van Dorn—had been killed that morning. Rollie's body lay in a ditch beside the road. As I looked down, paying him a silent tribute, one of his men spoke.

"He wouldn't have been killed," the man said, "if he had stayed in his hole, but he was always worrying about the rest of us and going around in the open to check on how we were."

No officer, it seemed to me, ever received a more effective tribute to his ability and devotion.

Gathering my squad leaders around me, I took a physical count of the men we had on hand for duty—less than 30. Instead of about 190 men in the company with the usual 160 of them available for fighting, I had less than enough to make up a full platoon. It was not an encouraging prospect for the difficult jobs ahead.

One of the platoon sergeants was not so pessimistic.

"Lieutenant," he said, "I think some of them sonsobitches are still in the rear. They can't all be dead. When Captain Black went back it knocked hell outa this company, and a lot of yellow belly bastards took advantage of it."

I resolved to look into his charges at the first opportunity, but for now there was no time—we had a job to do. I checked to see what weapons were in operating order and appointed several men as temporary non-commissioned officers. Next I directed that all the weapons from casualties be piled together for collecting and servicing by the supply sergeant. I checked every man for ammunition and made sure he was ready to fight. Although Easy Company now had passed through us to take the lead in the new attack, we might be called upon at any time.

Looking around at the position Company G held, I could see at a glance how impossible was the route up the steep slope which the company had followed to get there. The men obviously could not have made it except that Jerry himself had considered the route impassable and therefore had neglected to defend it adequately. I admired these men—and Rollie Moore— tremendously for having accomplished it.

As the tanks passed through to join Company E, I hurried my reorganization. Though Company E was to lead the new attack, Nick Von Keller and his men were only a hundred yards beyond us, and I was to follow them closely. Thus, time for preparations was short.

When Lieutenant Bob Murphy of Company H joined me by the roadside, we examined his map carefully to see what fires his 81mm mortars could provide. Together we went forward to meet Nick and make final plans for the attack. We found the big Russian in a quandary. He had orders to move out immediately, but he wanted to wait until mortar fire could be brought to bear on the woods directly ahead. Murphy said it would take almost an hour before the mortars could get into position to fire.

To me it seemed ridiculous to wait, thus giving the Germans that much more time to get ready. As evidenced by the condition of the forest all around us, this part of the woods had already been hit by everything from hand grenades to 500-pound bombs.

"If all that shelling hasn't driven them out," I argued, "a few more mortar shells aren't going to do it."

Nick was unmoved. Only a few minutes before, he had experienced real and terrible verification that the Germans still were around when one of his best non-coms, Tech Sergeant Eugene L. Craig, Jr., had moved around the next bend in the road only to be cut down by machine gun fire.

I still could not agree with Nick.

"Look, Nick," I said. "Let's use the tanks as a base of fire. Let them fire their cannons and machine guns for all they're worth, and we'll move right along with them. The edge of the woods isn't so far away. Maybe with a little noise and surprise we can burst right through."

When I left Nick to make his decision he was rubbing a stubbled chin in a dirty hand, thinking over the advice I had given.

Back at my CP—which was just a couple of green boughs slanted against the side of the hill in lean-to fashion—Murphy and I had resumed our close examination of the map when mortar shells again began to bounce with unerring accuracy on the road. Bob and I scrambled into the water-filled ditch until the bombardment was over. As we began to pick ourselves up, I noticed that the water in the ditch was red with blood. I thought at first the blood must have come from someone wounded or killed by the shelling, but as I looked farther up the ditch I realized with horror that the blood came from my old friend, Rollie Moore. What a horrible thing, this war. Here I was virtually bathing in the blood of an old friend. The goose flesh stood up in great patches down the middle of my back.

We had one man wounded in the shelling, and I made immediate arrangements to have him taken to the aid station. Like most tragedies though, this particular shelling had its lighter moments. When I had first arrived at Company G's position one of my first tasks was to clear the road of debris so the tanks could get through without difficulty. I was, somehow, proud of my nice clean road. Now when the shelling stopped, I raised my head to find that my road was blocked by a medium-size tree.

"Now where in the hell did that tree come from?" I demanded.

Bob Murphy thought it was the funniest remark of the war. Almost every time he saw me after that, he chirped in comic mimicry:

"Now where in the hell did that tree come from?"

Soon after the shelling, I looked up to see Jack approaching down the road. With him was Captain John R. Cliett, of Bainbridge, Ga., one of the original officers with the One-Two-One who had returned from the hospital while we were in Luxembourg to take command of Company F. Leaping from my foxhole, I greeted Jack enthusiastically in the middle of the road. The men around us must have thought we were crazy, carrying on that way in this God-forsaken spot.

Jack and I never had held morbid conversations about what each was to do should the other be killed. On the other hand, we knew instinctively that we could trust each other, should such a tragic occasion arise, to care for Norma or for Eleonore, whichever it might be. It was something we did not have to talk about.

The fact is, I never had the feeling that I would not come home from Europe. For me, my journey was a round-trip affair. A man did not dare let his thoughts wander too far from the gloomy present into the even more dismal realm of what might happen. Somewhere there had to be a ray of hope to enable you to carry on from one bloody, muddy, miserable day to the next. Most of those who cracked under the strain were those whose imaginations grew too fertile when the shells began falling and the bullets cracked closer and closer. All of us held the fervent hope that ours, if and when it came, would be the million dollar wound. Some of us had to be wrong, of course, but who would concede that it might be you?

I always thought that the purely apocryphal tale we heard during our training days at Camp Van Dorn perfectly illustrated the attitude of the average soldier toward death. The story had to do with a battalion commander who stood in front of his men before an attack and painted a picture of impending doom.

"By tomorrow morning," the commander presumably had remarked, "every man here, except one, will be dead."

The remark bit deeply into every man present, and each glanced at his comrades with undisguised compassion.

"Gee," each man thought to himself, "those poor fellows."

When Jack and I had exchanged a few remarks, we began to talk with Captain Cliett about resuming the attack. Jack and Cliett both agreed with Murphy and me that the best thing to do was to move ahead with the tanks immediately.

Realizing that the consensus was against him, Nick decided to move. As the tanks opened up with their machine guns and cannon, the stalled column shook off its inertia. The incessant chattering of the machine guns spitting their messages of death coupled with the staccato bark of the cannon gave the men confidence and support. They surged steadily ahead. So many bullets filled the air that ricochets became a menace.

But if we were alarmed, then Jerry was thoroughly upset. The sudden thrust obviously took him by surprise. We flushed Germans out of foxholes which under normal circumstances might have served them well for days or even weeks. The big tank guns got in their work with deadly aim. As the road straightened out in the direction of the edge of the woods overlooking the village of Huertgen, pillboxes on either side fell rapidly.

We might yet get out of this forest in hell.

## 21

Because darkness was approaching as we neared the edge of the woods, battalion called a halt to our advance. A quick reorganization for defense of the ground we had won gave Easy Company the left side of the road, while Fox Company pulled ahead of us to defend the right side. Company G was to fall back and watch the rear against any Germans that might have been by-passed or who might approach around the flanks of the other companies.

Since I had less than a platoon, putting my men in defensive positions was no major task. Scattering them to cover as wide a sector as possible, I led a small group farther to the rear to form a roadblock. By this time, rain was pelting down again and an impenetrable darkness settled quickly in the forest. Fearful of getting off the road into the woods lest I set off a mine, I remembered a battered shelter I had noticed earlier by the side of the road. I checked into it and found it would serve as a home for the night. Shelter was hardly the word for it, but the fact that a few boards were still standing gave my messenger and me the vague impression that we had some protection from the driving rain.

I had just crawled into the shelter when a voice called my name from the darkness.

"Lieutenant Boesch."

There was a trace of a sob as the man spoke.

"Here," I answered.

Following my voice, the man came close enough to grab me tightly by the arm. It was Sergeant Lawrence, the platoon sergeant of the Company H machine gun platoon I had commanded back in Brittany.

"Lieutenant Boesch," he said in a voice that was hard to control.

"Osterberg just got killed."

It was depressing news. Bob Osterberg was the "kid" of the machine gun platoon, one of the two men whose narrow escape inside the sentry box near Brest had amused the entire platoon. Like the others, I had come to love Bob Osterberg. From Chicago, he was only 19 years old but already had part of his college education behind him. He was a sincere and religious youth who earned the respect of all his buddies by sticking close to self-imposed high standards. Bob's death was, somewhat miraculously, the first to hit the machine gun platoon since I first had taken command of it back in July. Having established this enviable record, Sergeant Lawrence would have been deeply affected by the death of any man in the platoon, but the fact that the dead man was Bob Osterberg made it all the worse.

I encouraged Lawrence to talk in the hope that this might ease some of the tension within him. He told me the platoon had moved off the road to set up its machine guns when Bob stepped on a mine. The explosion blew off a leg. Though the rest of the men tried to get to him, he refused to let them come near lest they too step on mines. Instead, Bob tried to work his way to them. Despite his wound, he managed to pull himself upright and start toward the other men, but he lost his balance and fell. This time he landed directly on a mine that blew him apart.

It was hard to think of anything to say that might soften the blow for Sergeant Lawrence.

"Bob was only one man, Lawrence," I said finally. "And he's dead now. You've got 35 others back there depending on you, even more now than before. You and I have tough jobs. We've got to forget the dead and lead the living, no matter how much we hate the thought."

Whether because of my words or simply because he had poured out the story to someone else, Lawrence appeared to get better control of himself. He turned and shook my hand. Without another word he disappeared in the direction of his platoon, into the oppressive night.

As Lawrence departed, I went back to the impossible job of trying to get comfortable. In the crude shelter my messenger and I found a few small pieces of board and put them on the mud as a bed. I tried to place my massive frame on a board that was only about six inches wide. What is more, I might have made it had I not had to share it with another man.

My companion, it turned out, was a philosopher.

"Maybe we can't sleep," he said, "but we can't toss and turn all night either."

After a few minutes of silence, disturbed only by the distant thunder of artillery and the swirl of the wind and the rain, he spoke again.

"Gee, just imagine, lieutenant, somewhere in this world guys are laying in soft beds with soft-breasted girls, listening to soft music."

Again he was meditatively silent. Then he erupted with an eloquent snort.

"I hope the dirty bastards choke!"

As we lay there shivering, one of the men at the roadblock called me. Several officers from the tank destroyer unit we had left back at the bridge had arrived and had no idea where to position their vehicles. Having seen the ground briefly by daylight, I could remember several likely positions and set out to help.

It was eerie, moving along the road with its borders of pine-concealed death. At any moment we expected the big tank destroyers to set off a mine, for engineers had not yet been able to sweep the road. Our artillery shells passed overhead in regular procession to hit the town of Huertgen, and flames from burning buildings lent a flickering glow to the sky. At long last I finished the job and made my way back to the six-inch board and asked my bedmate to move over.

As soon as it began to get light the next morning, battalion called to give me a new mission. Company G, with a pair of tanks for support, was to proceed down a firebreak off our right flank to establish contact with men of the 1st Battalion. From a map it appeared to be easy enough, for, as Captain Freeman pointed out over the phone, the firebreak "looked nice and wide." It was an entirely different proposition on the ground. The firebreak was criss-crossed by a maze of fallen trees. The tanks obviously could not get through.

My report on the condition of the firebreak came as a revelation to the battalion staff. Contrary to the practice when Colonel Casey was around, none of the staff had been anywhere near the actual front positions. Since the tanks could not go with us, I insisted that it was ridiculous to use all of Company G on the assignment as we might run into considerable opposition and get the entire company inextricably involved. Battalion at last bought my idea that a patrol could do the job. I breathed a deep sigh of relief when finally the patrol returned, having accomplished its mission without losses.

Meanwhile, word arrived from battalion that we were to dig in where we were, and to "make the holes good and substantial with overhead cover—we'll be here a while." When I passed the word along, the men relished the possibility, as was quickly demonstrated by the resounding clank of shovels and picks that soon echoed through the trees. For my command post I found an excellent dugout already prepared, just 20 yards from the miserable shelter in which I had spent the previous night. In the dripping darkness of that night, however, it might as well have been 20 miles away.

As we learned from reports which gradually filtered down to us, Combat Command R of the 5th Armored Division was to take over the attack now that we had reached the edge of the woods. The armor was to sweep down another road on our battalion's right and capture the key town of Huertgen.

Faced with the prospect of at least a short stay in one place, I decided it would be a good time to try to tie up all the loose ends of the company I had inherited. I selected one man, whose name I recall only as Dave, to go with me. Together we set out on a roundup of the rear areas to try to find other men of Company G who might have taken advantage of the confused situation to stay behind. Because Dave knew every man in the company, he would be able to help considerably.

Back past the spot where I had taken over the company, down the road through what once had been the deadly roadblock, past my old foxhole CP, and across the bridge over the creek we made our way toward battalion headquarters. It was a thoroughly depressing trip. At one place on the road, the tank destroyers on their way forward in the darkness had run over the body of a man killed the day before, adding mutilation to the already grim tragedy of death. Corpses that once had been fearful, hopeful, fighting GI's now littered the Huertgen Forest at every turn. I had never seen so many dead men. The sight of death and the foul stench which accompanies it, even in cold weather, had, I thought, ceased to disturb me. But the presence of so many dead men wearing the shoulder patches of the 28th, 4th, and now the 8th Division, proved deeply disturbing.

In the area around battalion headquarters we started our roundup. As Dave pointed out the men he knew belonged in Company G, I would pounce on them with uncompromising suddenness. I demanded from every man an immediate explanation. Almost invariably they insisted they had been "trying to find the company." Most of them had, in fact, reported their presence to battalion and thus were covered legally, but I cursed battalion soundly for failing to assemble the stragglers and send them back to duty.

To my surprise I also came upon the moustached second lieutenant whom I had come to loathe when he had been so reluctant to lead his men during the fighting on the Crozon Peninsula. He was, I knew, a G Company officer. He had been left behind in Luxembourg and had returned in the same vehicle which had brought Jack back to duty many days before. When I asked him why he had not come back to the company, he said he had been detailed "to protect battalion headquarters."

"From what?" I shouted.

The next surprise came when I discovered George Company also had a rear CP complete with first sergeant and executive officer! The revelation astounded me, for I had been sent to command Company G because, after Captain Black's evacuation, the company presumably had no other officers.

I asked the executive officer for an explanation.

"Well," he replied lamely, "Captain Black told me to stay right here, and battalion never asked me to take over the company when Black left. So I stayed right here."

The first sergeant, who was filling in for a hospitalized regular topkick, impressed me as being a capable man. I could not understand his failure to be more aggressive in getting the men up front where they belonged.

"Get all these men together, Sergeant," I ordered. "G Company moves out from now on in one body."

As the men began to assemble, a second lieutenant sought me out. He had just returned about an hour earlier from the hospital. I was sure I had known him some place before, but every question drew a negative response until he told me he had been wounded with Company G back at Dinard. It suddenly came to me.

"You're the lucky bastard," I said.

"What's that?" the officer asked, puzzled.

"You're the guy I called a lucky bastard because you got shot in the leg when we were going into the attack back in August." I was right. The officer was Lieutenant Bill Carroll, who now made the fourth officer for a company which only a short while before had ostensibly had none. Now there was the executive officer, the craven lieutenant with the moustache, Carroll and a big guy with wrestler's ears who was trying to do the best he could as the company commander.

As we were about to leave, I decided to have the battalion surgeon,

Captain Arnold S. Moe, of Bellville, Ill., take a look at my left ear. For several days, since a shell had landed fairly close with terrific concussion, the ear had been bothering me. After looking it over Dr. Moe pronounced that it would be okay within a few days even without the normal treatment with pills. However, my companion, Dave, proved to have more serious trouble.

As long as we were at the aid station, he had the medics take a look at his feet, which, as he put it, had been "bothering the hell out of me recently."

He came back somewhat shamefaced.

"I guess you'll have to go back without me, lieutenant," he said. "They're sending me out. Trench foot."

Trench foot was a disease—or perhaps more correctly an affliction—which had been taking a heavy toll of our troops and removing a lot of veterans whom enemy bullets had failed to stop. It could be attributed to the fact that the men had to stay in tight, wet shoes for long periods in cold weather without moving around. The feet would swell, thereby interfering with circulation and bruising the blood vessels.

Recommended treatment and prevention was to remove the shoes daily, massage the feet well, and change to dry socks. Though the idea was excellent, most of us found it impractical and at times impossible to comply with. In my own case, I made every effort to conform, yet I still almost came down with the affliction. It could be serious business, for it was painful, the swollen feet turned a distasteful purple, and amputation sometimes was the only recourse.

Returning to the battalion command post, I joined the men I had rounded up and started again for the front. I was returning with as many men as were presently manning the company positions.

As we passed the foxhole near the bridge in which I had spent several days, men from Graves Registration were hard at work bringing a body down the hill. They obviously had no concern with harming the remains, for they were dragging him to their trailer on his back with stout ropes tied to his wrists and ankles. The sight shocked me at first, but when I remembered what a tough haul it was up and down the hill, I could scarcely blame them. I was nevertheless glad that the body they dragged in front of me was not someone I had known. Almost hypnotized, I watched as they crammed the dirty, bloody remains of what had once been a fine young man into a clean white mattress cover they had brought along as a shroud. Once they had tied the strings, they lifted the sack and tossed it in the trailer to lie with the others.

I stared at the bodies, stacked there like so many bags of potatoes. As rugged and tough as was the infantry, I decided I would not trade jobs with the men in Graves Registration.

Returning to the positions high on the hill near the edge of the woods, I set about trying to turn Company G again into a fighting outfit. We now numbered more than 60 men and four officers. Although this still was only about one-third strength, we had to be ready momentarily for some other combat assignment. I put Carroll and Lieutenant Moustache in charge of rifle platoons, and despite my disappointment with the executive officer I kept him in that post in the event something should happen to me. I took special precautions to see that he knew everything that went on in order that he might take over on short notice.

When I found a few minutes to spare, I checked every man in the company to make sure I knew them by sight if not by name. Looking into the foxholes at the men, I tried to get the feel that Company G was really mine so that I might mold it back into the combat company it had been under Captain Black's leadership.

It would not, I knew, be long before my efforts would be put to the test.

# 22

Word reached us in mid-afternoon that the attack of Combat Command R on Huertgen had failed. The tanks had crashed out of the woods only to come upon antitank mines as they headed across open ground toward Huertgen. A mine knocked a tread off one of the tanks, blocking the narrow exit of the road from the forest. German antitank guns in Huertgen then made quick work of the leading tanks, and no others could get past the disabled tank on the road. The attack ground to an abject halt.

Along with this discouraging news came a fresh rumor that the One-Two-One was to take Huertgen, whereupon the armor would again take up the fight on open ground beyond the town. The rumor became fact late in the afternoon when a party of jeeps stopped on the road near my CP and the assistant division commander, General Canham, came in to use my telephone.

I asked the General about Huertgen.

"We're getting ready to move in right now," he said. "The fact is, F Company has already pushed off. I'm sure the town is empty. Air saw a long column marching away from it."

The word became official a short time after the General left. I received a call from battalion directing me to move into Huertgen as soon as Fox Company made it.

But Fox Company did not make it. The General's feeling that the enemy had abandoned Huertgen was sprinkled liberally with wishful thinking. A pilot may well have seen a column moving away from the town, but what he failed to note was that many more Germans apparently had stayed behind. On the theory that Huertgen was ours for the asking, Company F had gone about the job under strong pressure from higher headquarters without time to make any concrete preparations. Somehow the staffs in the deeper dugouts felt that all Captain Cliett had to do was form his depleted company into a column of twos and march down the main street. The chatter of machine guns and the pounding of artillery which reached our ears soon made it abundantly clear that somebody was wrong.

As night came, plans underwent hasty change. Fox Company was to send out night patrols to get information for a concerted attack by the entire battalion at seven o'clock the next morning. I headed for Nick's CP where Colonel Kunzig had arrived to formulate the attack plans.

I found that on paper the plan for the next morning's attack was simple and sensible. Companies F and G were to attack side by side with a road which F Company already had reached as a clearly defined line of departure. We were to cross the road at seven o'clock, advance on the town, and take it. It was that simple—on paper.

Cliett and I discussed our plans carefully. Huertgen was an elongated, omnifarious collection of drab gray houses grouped primarily along one main street, which was in effect a winding road stretching more than half a mile before emerging again in open fields. My company, we decided, would clear the left side of the street, Company F the right side. Where the street made sharp bends, we designated points of contact beyond which one company was not to advance without coordinating with the other, lest we end up shooting each* other. Then with blissful optimism we traced the attack to a successful conclusion.

What disturbed us most was the necessity to cross a thousand yards of flat, open field, virtually devoid of any cover or concealment, before we could gain the first buildings in the town. We obviously would be ripe for annihilation once we left the concealment of the forest unless we could devise some means of keeping Jerry occupied while we crossed the open ground. At our insistence, Colonel Kunzig promised ample support from mortars and artillery before we started and for several minutes thereafter while we moved across the fields. This was vitally important.

As Cliett and I mulled over our plans, two men from Company F arrived with two prisoners they had taken while on patrol. Corporal Haerich, Easy Company's German-speaking medic, came in to question the prisoners in the hope of gleaning some information which might be of use in the attack.

After beginning the interrogation, it soon became apparent that for every question we received two completely disparate answers, so that in the end we were left more confused than if we had asked nothing. One of the prisoners insisted, for example, that about a hundred Germans were in Huertgen but that all were ready to capitulate.

"Only because their Nazi officers have threatened to shoot them do they stay and fight," he concluded.

His bedraggled companion did not agree.

"There are more than four hundred men in Huertgen," he averred. "They will fight to the last as they have been ordered by Hitler."

The only point the pair could agree on was that everybody in the town was hungry, but even on this subject their opinions showed some divergence. One insisted this would lessen the Germans' will to fight, the other said it would sharpen it.

"You pay your money and take your choice," grunted Cliett, "and we won't know which of the bastards to shoot until it's too late to do us any good."

Colonel Kunzig, for his part, believed the man who thought the Germans were ready to surrender.

"What he says goes right along with the report from General Canham," he insisted. "Those one hundred are just a rear guard."

"Pretty big rear guard, wouldn't you say, Colonel?" Cliett asked dryly.

"Which man do you believe, Haerich?" I asked. It seemed to me that Haerich with his knowledge of the Germans must have formed a personal opinion which would be based on something more than ours.

Haerich was quiet for a moment, looking from one to the other of the prisoners in the flickering candlelight in the musty dugout. At last he cleared his throat and spoke.

"Well, Lieutenant Boesch," he said, "I think this man sounds more honest than the other."

He pointed a gloved hand toward the man who promised a small force with only token resistance.

"I hope to God you're right, Haerich," I said.

With that, the meeting broke up.

It was well after midnight by the time I got back to my own CP to be greeted by my officers and sergeants, whom I had previously instructed to assemble there. In the CP dugout we all gathered around a map. Lighting an extra candle, we talked long and searchingly about every phase of the attack. I gave them every scrap of information I had obtained, and several offered suggestions which we incorporated into the original plan. At long last I was satisfied that everyone knew his job and I had done all I could to insure success of the attack. The others scattered to take advantage of the few hours remaining to let their men know what we were to do.

When they left, I sat quietly for a while, then stretched out on a small strip of bunk which the others in the headquarters group had politely reserved for me. Around me I could hear the rhythmic breathing of those who were lucky enough not to bear responsibilities that kept them awake. Now and then a troubled snort broke the cadence.

Relaxing with a deep sigh, I went over in my mind the various details of the attack, searching for flaws, but I could detect no error in the preparations as we had made them. Our chief difficulty lay in the fact that our rifle squads were drastically depleted. I bore a personal difficulty in knowing too few of my men, so that I would have trouble calling and directing them by name. Yet for all this, I had no real fear for the job ahead. Combat was not new. This was a particularly hard task, but we had faced other hard ones and won.

Though it seemed days since I last had closed my eyes, sleep would not come. Finally I got up and telephoned Captain Cliett's CP. The Captain could not sleep either. Bit by bit we went over the plans again, but the only improvement we could hit upon was to draw the artillery fire closer during the time we were crossing the field.

"If the artillery doesn't hit those first houses," I said, "we're going to catch hell, John. Why don't you call battalion and check it with them?"

Cliett did call battalion, but Colonel Kunzig would not agree. In order to pull the artillery fire closer, Cliett's men would have to draw back from the road they had reached the preceding afternoon, and Kunzig was unwilling to take responsibility for approving a withdrawal, no matter how strategically important and no matter how short or how temporary the withdrawal.

Because my CP was in a central location, all the telephone lines in the battalion ran through it. Thus, I was able, if I wanted, to listen in on almost any conversation. Unable to sleep and distressed by Kunzig's refusal, I lay on my bunk the rest of the night with the phone at my ear. What I heard gave me an insight into how the big wheels turned. It left me wondering how they managed to turn at all.

At one point Kunzig called the regimental commander, Colonel Cross, to discuss our suggestion that F Company pull back to the edge of the woods to insure that the artillery could hit the first houses. Cross was adamant in his refusal.

"Not one inch!" he said in a tone which convinced me he said it with his jaw thrust forward. "We will not move that company nor any other company back one single inch. Kunzig, I'll hit them with every weapon we've got that'll fire. We'll keep it up all night and then give them a concentrated dose in the morning, just before the attack. But that company stays put!"

From where I lay I could see by the flickering light of the candle that the artillery fireline as we had drawn it on the map was much too far beyond the first houses. I could see it plainly; Colonel Kunzig could see it; Colonel Cross must have been able to see it. It took no genius to recognize that the solution Cliett and I offered was logical and sound. But in order to keep a map in some higher headquarters from registering the fact that men had taken a backward step, even though by going backward five hundred yards they might subsequently be able to advance a thousand, the men would have to stay where they were and let the edge of the objective be a privileged sanctuary for the enemy.

I fretted and fumed at the telephone. At one point I was tempted to open my switch and tell everybody what was on my mind. It was only with difficulty that I forced myself to remain silent.

When the conversation was over, I telephoned Cliett and told him. He was as disappointed and frustrated as I.

Still unable to sleep, I continued my vigil at the telephone.

When Kunzig had talked to Cross, the regimental commander had directed extreme thoroughness in preparations for the attack, particularly in communications. Colonel Cross demanded specifically that double telephone lines be installed to insure against a break in contact between regiment and battalion. Kunzig had promised this would be done and subsequently telephoned his own headquarters to speak to his executive officer.

"Major," he ordered, "I want to keep in constant touch with regiment by phone tomorrow during the attack. I want you to be sure to have double phone lines in operation by daylight."

"Oh, yes, sir," the major spoke up quickly. "I'm 'way ahead of you, sir. I have the men out right now putting them in."

"Damned fine work," applauded the Colonel, "that's the sort of cooperation I like from my staff."

The major swelled up on the phone until I could almost hear his buttons pop.

The telephone line was silent for a while. Then the next voice I heard was that of the Major.

"Hello, operator? Give me the communications officer."

After a pause the communications officer came on the line.

"Look," the Major said, "the Colonel'll be up at Easy Company's CP tomorrow. I want you to get busy right away. Root out the men and start putting in double telephone wires from regiment up to Easy Company. We've got to have them in by six o'clock.That doesn't give you much time, you better shake a leg."

Slowly the luminous hands crept past the dancing numerals on my watch, and still my weary body refused to accept sleep. Three-thirty. Four o'clock. Four-thirty. Five. At last it was time to move. Awakening my headquarters group, I headed through the woods to the spot where I had arranged to meet the rest of the company. It was as black as ever even though dawn could not be long off.

At the road I found to my disgust that my company was not there. Despite the explicit and detailed instructions I had given the platoon leaders only a few hours before, they were all still in their holes. For the next half hour I was a one-man team booting men out of holes and onto the road. The squad leaders, I discovered, had failed to give their men any instructions for the attack. My temper boiled.

As quickly as possible I saw that the non-coms got on with the job of telling the men details of the attack plans. While they were doing it I made a firm resolve to check thoroughly on squad and platoon leaders at the first possible opportunity. Having had the company less than two full days, I had had no chance to impose my own will on them. That obviously needed to be done.

"Something is wrong, radically wrong," I thought bitterly, "when men with stripes and bars fail to get their men ready for an attack."

Speed was vital. Everything depended on getting to the line of departure on time, and we still had a long way to go. Though a hurried check revealed that some men still were missing, I decided to go without them rather than try to find them in isolated foxholes in the blackness of the forest. We set out down the road. Taking the lead, I set a rapid pace.

We had not gone far before we ran into men of the 1st Battalion of the 13th Infantry. They were bunched along the road in a scattered, noisy column which eventually was to move to the edge of the woods, turn north, and then assist our attack by enveloping Huertgen from the northwest. The narrow woods road was clogged with troops. Men coagulated together, talking and milling about noisily like nervous cattle.

Chills ran up and down my back. The spot where the battalion of the 13th and my own men became intermingled was the very place where I had undergone a terrific pounding from Jerry artillery the morning before. If Jerry had hit the spot once, he obviously had a concentration right at hand to hit it again. Had he chosen that particular moment to blast the road, it would have been wholesale slaughter. The prospect prompted me to redouble my efforts to get past. How fortunate it was that Jerry did not suspect how we violated every basic principle of safety as if he were impotent to make us regret it.

This encounter consumed more of the precious time we needed to reach the line of departure on schedule and before daylight revealed our movement to the enemy. Though I managed to keep my men together through the bottleneck, I realized as we passed that if we were to move cross-country through the woods as scheduled, we would never get to the line of departure on time. I decided to gamble. Instead of turning through the woods, I elected to stay on the road. This was a longer way around and no one yet had used it—so that running into mines and perhaps a roadblock and a few Jerries was a real possibility —but if all went well, we obviously could make better time on the road.

Again I lead the column as rapidly as I dared. Fallen trees and branches frequently blocked the way. With an imagination made fertile by the impending attack, I conjured fantastic ideas of guiding my company into a mine-laden trap; of steering them head-on into a strong Jerry position. But the delays we had encountered had left no real choice.

Instead of mines and live Germans, we came upon a ghastly column of dead Jerries which apparently had been caught by one of our artillery barrages. Dead men lay sprawled over the road in various frantic postures of violent death. The stench was overwhelming. Bloated men and bloated horses, one of which had burst, lay all across our path, and we had to step high to shake the entrails from our boots.

It was a terrible thing to lead men through such a depressing setting while en route to an attack. Several vomited at the sight, and some needed stiff prodding to force them through. None of us could help but be affected by the experience, even though the dead were enemy dead. Only the fact that we were nearing the edge of the forest and thus deriving some benefit from the approaching dawn made it possible for us to find a path through the vegetable and animal debris.

As we reached the area assigned to us with ten minutes to spare, I gratefully threw off some of my concern. Already big shells were bursting in Huertgen, some of them white phosphorous shells exploding in weirdly beautiful patterns. I spread out my small platoons, had a last word with Carroll and Lieutenant Moustache, pointing out landmarks in the town for them to guide on, and then left to coordinate with the left flank platoon of Company F.

A tall, red-haired lieutenant from Newton, N.J., Edward Korn, commanded the Company F platoon. Together, as the artillery continued to pound our objective ahead, we quickly checked the more important points of the attack.

As we talked, I noted with satisfaction a marked increase in the tempo of the artillery preparation, but I also noted that the buildings closest to us definitely were unaffected by the pounding. Then the pattern of bursts moved even farther from us.

I felt frustrated, almost condemned. Without artillery fire on those first houses, our only chance of getting across the open before the Jerries awoke to our presence lay in beating the dawn. This was a pitifully slim chance, for already the first vestiges of daylight were beginning to reflect on our helmets and barrels of our weapons. I wanted to swear out loud, to damn all who had stood in the way of our getting the support we deserved.

But it was too late, even for swearing. The hands on my watch said seven o'clock. Signalling my messenger and radio operator to follow, I turned back toward my own company.

A thin olive drab line of burdened men rose from the ground and moved forward. I fell in behind the platoon led by the lieutenant with the moustache. Then out across a treeless, coverless field we marched.

This was the way to Huertgen, elusive objective, key to the Huertgen Forest.

# 23

We only went a few yards across the open field toward Huertgen when the artillery fire suddenly ceased. A few vagrant shells still fell on the far end of the town, but the noise of these explosions seemed merely to heighten the silence around us. It was almost as if the silence itself had exploded. We felt frightened, naked, alone.

Jerry obviously would not ignore the quiet. Coming on the heels of the bombardment, it could mean only one thing to him, that infantry was moving in for an assault. We were 25 yards out of the woods now, 50 yards, 100 yards. Here and there, from a half-dozen different houses along the fringe of the town, German gunners fired bursts from automatic weapons. Two hundred yards we advanced, 300 yards—tracer bullets beat the ground around us, forcing every man into the mud as if the hand of Satan himself had reached up and dragged everybody down at once. One moment I was part of a rapidly moving line of men against an objective that reputedly was deserted; then, in a flash, I was flat on the ground, part of an attack that had bogged down.

Though daylight was fast approaching, night still draped a measure of protective concealment about us. I knew that now the artillery had deserted us, our only hope of getting to the first houses was to continue to move, no matter how much fire we drew. Up and down the line I ran, shouting like a man possessed, urging the men to get up, to keep moving. The men must have realized as I did that it was now or never, for they responded, and once again we were plowing across muddy ground toward the objective. Four hundred yards, 500 yards, just about half way now. The tempo of the German fire increased in intensity the closer we got, but still we moved—

slowly. Six hundred yards, 700 yards. Now the cries of the wounded were all around us as the machine guns and burp guns fired with amazing accuracy in that dim light. Again the thin line wavered, slowed, and dropped to the ground.

Again I moved from man to man, calling now for fire and movement. By this method, one group of men would fire, seeking to silence the enemy gunners, while another group rushed forward 15 or 20 yards. Then those rushing would drop to the ground to cover the advance of the first group.

But it was difficult to transmit any real enthusiasm to the others when I, to them, was almost a stranger. I did not know the names of all of the squad leaders, so that I could not call on them individually to help overcome the inertia. It was maddening. At last I decided to put action to my own suggestion and jumped into the lead, rushing forward, dodging, firing my carbine as fast as I could. But Jerry's return fire sought me out and kept the men burrowed in the mud.

After a time I came upon the platoon leader with the moustache. He was lying face down in a shell crater, his helmet clutched close on his head with both hands.

"Come on, boy," I cajoled, "let's get the hell into that town before we get chewed to pieces."

A trembling voice answered.

"Just a minute, just a minute."

Still the lieutenant did not move. Looking down at him, I longed to run the muzzle of my carbine squarely into his exposed bottom. I might have done it had not my urging at last begun to have some effect with the other men. One by one they began to fire and move again toward the houses.

One automatic rifleman was doing a particularly valiant job. Running toward him, I hoped to help him direct his fire so that we might build his fast-firing weapon into a base of fire to enable all the others to continue forward. I pointed out a number of likely targets to him, but as he crouched against the stock of his weapon and began to shoot, a bullet hit him square in the middle of the forehead. He toppled over without a sound. Dead.

For a moment I stared at the man, half-dazed, hardly able to comprehend what had happened. Another burst of German fire snapped me back to reality. I picked up the automatic rifle, intent either on firing it myself or passing it along to someone else, but the second burst had damaged the gun itself. It would not fire.

As I rose to continue forward, German fire cut loose from at least a dozen new positions. Bullets ripped the ground with unmitigated fury. I tried hard to keep from facing the truth, but we obviously could not continue to advance in the face of this fire. We were, in the language of the infantryman, "pinned down"— a scant 100 yards from Huertgen.

I still was loathe to admit total defeat. Even though this platoon could not move, there was still the possibility that perhaps Lieutenant Carroll's platoon on the other end of the line was not so hard hit. I started in that direction.

Deciding to move and getting there were two different things, however. Not only did Jerry continue to pick us off with small arms fire, but now he added the deadly burst of mortars. Every short bound I took seemed to draw a fusillade of machine gun fire, and as I paused to hug the ground to escape this fire, mortar shells began to come in with deep, crunching explosions. Yet somehow they missed and at last I came up behind Carroll's men, only to discover they were in the same dismal predicament as the others.

Carroll's men nevertheless had some advantage, for they had come upon a narrow communications trench about a hundred yards in front of the first group of houses. The trench was not only narrow but shallow, only some two and a half feet deep. At one end was a small, low, covered dugout. With some difficulty we dragged four wounded men from the trench into the dugout.

Carroll himself was farther forward. I decided to continue until I found him in the hope that together we might work something out. Though the communications trench ran in the direction I wanted to go, it was so packed with men seeking cover from the fire that it would be difficult to pass along it. I tried getting out of the trench and rushing forward by bounds, but Jerry forced me back. With agonizing detail, I had to plan my way past each man in the narrow ditch. Some moved to one side, others doubled up, some flattened themselves on their faces to let me crawl over.

As I came to a bend in the trench, a particularly husky soldier blocked my path.

"Flatten yourself against the trench," I called out, "to the right."

Nodding that he understood, the soldier drew in his breath, hoping to leave room for me to pass. I moved quickly, but for some inexplicable reason, the man shifted away from the side of the trench just as I reached him. We collided. My chest was jammed tight against his back when suddenly we both were hurled backward with stunning violence. A Jerry bullet had caught the GI in the shoulder and thrown us both to the ground. The fact that a bone stopped the round was all that had saved me, for otherwise the bullet would have passed through his body into mine.

Pulling the man behind the bend in the trench where others might administer to his wound, I continued to work forward. As I rounded the bend, the Jerry fired again, but this time the shot was high and struck the earth at the top of the trench, doing no more harm than to send down a shower of mud.

When at last I found Carroll, I realized quickly that my trip had been futile. He and the men close around him were just as immobilized as the rest of us. Reluctantly, I turned to make my way again down the trench and seek some other method for reviving the attack. En route I helped the soldier who had been hit in the shoulder to make his way to the little dugout. He became the sixth patient. I knew of at least four men who had been killed, and obviously there had been others.

I hoped to contact Fox Company, but there was a gap between the last of my men and the first of Captain Cliett's, and I could see none of Company F. A lone house which stood to our right rear may have held some of Lieutenant Korn's men, but it was impossible at the time to check.

Finally I slumped down in the trench, exhausted and thoroughly bewildered as to what I might do to alter our position. It was painfully evident that the attack had bogged down completely and equally evident that there was nothing we could do about it.

After alerting everybody to be prepared for a possible German counterattack, I made the wounded my first job. We had no medics, for they were among those I had been unable to find when we pulled out of the woods before daylight. After checking each man for bleeding and shock, I collected every piece of uniform that could be spared in an effort to keep them warm. Through that long day I made the rounds of the casualties often. We had nothing to make their lot easier, no morphine, no drugs of any kind except the sulfa powder in their first aid packets. There was no way we could move them to rear, for to expose ourselves at all was to invite death. Half a mile of open field stretched back to the woods, and Jerry shells landed in the field all day.

One man, hit in the thigh, had to lie outside the dugout in the trench because there wasn't room inside for him to stretch out.

"How're you coming, fellow?" I asked, crouching near him.

"Oh, boy!" he sighed in a low, satisfied voice, his eyes staring above him at the sky. "White sheets for Christmas!"

"What did you say?" I asked in disbelief.

"White sheets for Christmas," he repeated, not monotonously, but exultantly, "white sheets for Christmas!"

I marvelled at the man's philosophy. For him the war was over. He had done his job well, and now he had received his million dollar wound. Christmas, he believed, would find him far from the mud and the cold and the dying. The thought of not making it from that dismal trench to the hospital apparently never entered his head. Yet he was far from safety. As I looked beyond him, back at the field that led to the woods and the battalion aid station, I wondered just what he would get for Christmas—white sheets, or a white muslin mattress cover.

After weeks of rain, this day turned out fine and bright. An unshaded sun shone in unaccustomed brilliance over the desolate landscape. After being in the woods for so long, we felt positively naked out in the open.

Our planes flew overhead constantly, pausing now and then to zoom down on Huertgen and drop their bombs or to strafe beyond the town. For once I envied the fly-boys of the Air Corps. I could not stand because my protection was little more than two feet deep. I could not sit because when I did mud oozed all over my bottom and made me wet and cold. Though I tried sitting on my pistol belt and canteen, they disappeared quickly into the greedy mud. I spread my raincoat over the slime, but it too sank out of sight. I hardly dared sit on my helmet lest my head protrude unprotected over the rim of the trench. At times my feet became so imbedded in the clinging mud that I had to reach down and pull them clear to keep the mud from passing over the tops of my boots. Though the day was clear, it was bitterly cold.

I would have loved being in the Air Corps.


As time wore on, I tried to make some estimate of the situation which would ease the frustration. But it is more than difficult to make decisions that affect other men's lives when you can't even raise your head high enough to see what is firing at you. Jerry added to our problems by searching for us with mortar and artillery fire. At times, as heavy explosions cracked almost on top of us, I could not see how we could possibly escape further casualties, but each time we burrowed deep in the mud and came through without loss. Our own shells also passed overhead from time to time. The morning waned, and still we were pinned down. We could not move, and Jerry did not venture from his houses to meet us at close range.

Sometime in the early afternoon, the sharp report of a direct fire weapon sounded behind us, followed quickly by the splintering crash of a projectile into one of the houses ahead. It was a solution to our problem. If tank destroyers would spew direct fire from the woods line against the houses, we could easily follow their barrage with a concerted rush.

Crawling hastily through the mud, I reached my radio and contacted battalion, explaining my plan to Captain Freeman.

"The gun that fired is directly behind us," I said. "We're on a line between them and the houses we want hit. I can correct their fire from here."

"Okay, Boesch," Freeman replied. "I'll have them put another round where they put the last one, then you can move it either way you want."

I waited impatiently while he relayed my message. In the interim I alerted the men around me that we would be up and moving shortly.

When Freeman came back on the radio, what he said almost made me bounce straight into the air.

"Boesch," he said, "they can't remember where they fired that last round. Can you give them a landmark?"

"Do you mean," I said slowly and deliberately, "that those stupid bastards have been firing into their own troops without knowing where they were shooting? Let them come up here and I'll go back and fire a few rounds at random over their heads and see how they like it!"

I just couldn't imagine such carelessness. The house they had hit was perilously close to us, very difficult to distinguish from the other battered buildings in the edge of Huertgen.

"Tell them to put another round where they think they fired that one," I said at last, then told every man to hug the bottom of the trench.

But the round never came close to the previous target nor to us. "Look, Freeman," I said, "tell those fellows to be sure not to hit the first house. I think some of F Company's men are in there. But tell them to fire another round for registration and I'll see if I can pick it up. Remember, don't hit the first house."

Before the tank destroyers had a chance to fire again, artillery began to rip into the first house. But it was not our artillery. It was

Jerry's!

It seemed obvious to me that Jerry had picked up our radio conversation. Before the roar of his artillery died down, he began dropping mortar shells around our communications trench with disturbing accuracy. The shells literally rained down.

On the other end of the radio Freeman exclaimed somewhat stupidly, "My God, is that falling on you?"

I gritted my teeth, then answered with savage sarcasm.

"What the hell do you want me to do now?" I asked. "Direct their goddamned mortar fire for them?"

When the mortar shells finally let up, I was amazed that we had only one casualty to add to our dugout hospital. As soon as the noise abated, I again contacted Freeman on the radio and got the tank destroyers back to work. The crewmen responded with reluctance; they felt they were exposing their vehicles too flagrantly by continuing to fire from the same spot, but when I pointed out that we were slightly exposed also, they went to work. After an agonizing guessing game that saw the tank destroyers bouncing shots all over town, I finally managed to zero them in on the group of houses we wanted hit. But even when they hit the houses, they were reluctant to bring the rounds low enough to do any good for fear they might hit our positions. Most of the shells struck the upper stories of the houses. I was convinced that Jerry was firing at us either from the first floors or from the cellars.

"Bring them lower!" I roared in desperation.

The scant inches with which they complied meant little. Though I appreciated their concern for hitting us, our position was fast becoming alarming, and we had to take chances. Cautiously raising my head I tried to assess the effect of the fire, but Jerry drove me back with a burst of machine gun bullets that missed by only inches.

Despite this reminder that we still were off our targets, I decided that we had to make another attempt to rush the houses. I alerted Carroll's platoon. Following several rounds which scattered brick and concrete in impressive fashion we leaped to our feet, but had gone only a step or two beyond the trench when the same machine guns opened fire again and forced us back to cover. We pulled two more men back to the dugout for bandaging.

I called back for more fire immediately. This time we got half a dozen fast rounds, but another attempt at rushing forward met the same accurate machine gun fire. There were so many places the fire could be coming from, so many houses that overlooked us, that it was almost impossible to pin down the source. I determined nevertheless to give it one more try and called back for six more rounds.

This last request brought Colonel Kunzig to the radio.

"Boesch," he said, in the telephone voice that had become so familiar, "don't knock those houses apart too badly or we won't have any place to put the CP."

Choking back a reply designed to tell him where he could shove his CP, I reminded him that unless we took the town there wouldn't be any CP.

I got my six rounds, but they failed to do the job. For a moment I was stumped, then decided on a new approach. Crawling close to Bill Carroll, I told him I was going to call for a dozen fast rounds.

"Count them off, Bill," I said, "and the second that last one hits don't waste any time jumping forward."

Bill grunted in assent and made such preparations as he could while lying flat on his face in a pond of water and mud. I contacted battalion again and told them what I wanted. To my utter consternation Freeman told me the tank destroyers had pulled back to the rear—and safety—for the night! Even as Freeman explained that he had thought we would not want them any more, I slumped wearily down in the mud and cursed out loud.

Goddamnit! Goddamnit! Goddamnit!

I wanted to cry.


It was late afternoon, and I looked forward to the coming of night so we could evacuate our casualties. Though most of the wounded were bearing up well, it was obvious that the long hours of pain and anxiety were beginning to have an effect. My optimistic patient had scarcely stirred from his position in the trench, and whenever I was in earshot he muttered his hopeful refrain about "white sheets for Christmas." But some of the others were not so nonchalant.

"Lieutenant," they would say, "when are you going to get us out of here?"

I took careful note of the way they worded the question. It was not, "When are we going to get out of here?" What they said was, "When are you going to get us out of here?"

I wondered.

Just as dusk was beginning to settle, Colonel Kunzig called on the radio. In an ill-disguised effort to camouflage his meaning in case the Germans were listening, he said he was sending "some of our thick-skinned friends out to help."

"Do you understand?" he asked.

"I do," I said rather curtly, still conscious that Jerry might be listening.

Again I alerted the men to get ready to move, and in a moment I saw them stirring to make weapons and equipment ready. Though I had no success in contacting Lieutenant Moustache to make sure he joined us, I did get word to some of his men and could see them adjusting their equipment.

Looking over my shoulder, I made out four light tanks pulling from the woods behind us. We followed them anxiously every inch of the way as they came racing across the field. Grasping my carbine, I crouched low in the trench, ready to take the lead as soon as the tanks came abreast of our positions. A mixture of emotions churned within me. As much as I dreaded the danger ahead, I felt a certain amount of relief in being able to do something active for a change instead of sitting there like a duck in a Coney Island shooting gallery.

Closer, closer came the tanks, the roar of their motors serving as an urgent signal for us to be ready. Though they were only light tanks, the sight of them racing well dispersed across the field imparted to us a feeling of strength. Eagerly we watched, anxious to join them and break forever this dreadful impasse.

The lead tank was only about 200 yards from us when an explosion rocked it back on its haunches. Part of the left tread flew high in the air. Men spilled from the hatch like upset ants. The tank had struck a mine.

The other tanks paused only long enough to pick up their buddies. Then, without a moment's hesitation, they turned and streaked back toward the woods. We watched with emotions tinged both with disappointment and concern as Jerry chased them back to the woods line with artillery fire.

Then we took off our packs and slumped silently back down in the damnable mud.

## 24

With the coming of darkness I quickly set out on an inspection of my men. Uppermost in my mind was the concern that as soon as it grew fully dark, the Germans would sally forth from the town in a determined effort to eliminate our little band. I vowed to organize a solid defensive position.

One of my first moves was to see what had happened to Lieutenant Moustache. After a prolonged search, I found him deep in his foxhole. He had increased the depth of a shell-hole to at least six feet and was still burrowing when I arrived. It was only with difficulty that I persuaded him to emerge from his hole so I could outline what I wanted him to do.

Hardly had I finished speaking when he began to shake like a leaf in a gusty wind.

"I'm going back!" he cried. "I can't take it any more!"

Shocked, I drew him aside where the men could not hear and tried to reason with him, but it soon became obvious that reasoning was not the way. I grew progressively tougher. In the end, when it became painfully apparent that he intended to disregard my orders completely, I threatened court martial.

He turned on me like a madman.

"I don't care what you do!" he screamed. "I can't take it any more, I tell you. I can't take it any more. I'm going back! I'm going back!"

Then he was gone, racing like some wild thing into the darkness back toward the woods line.

I watched him go with mixed emotions. In one way, it was better he left—the platoon would be better off under a capable sergeant than under a lieutenant who was an out and out coward. On the other hand, I resented his actions bitterly. If the rest of us could stay and take it, so could he. The fact that he was an officer made me all the more furious.

I swore that if I got out of this predicament alive, I would court martial the lieutenant, moustache and all.

Choking back a desire to rush after the lieutenant and beat his head into the ground, I turned to the men he had left behind. I laid out the area for defense and made certain each man knew what was expected of him should the Germans attack.

When I got back to the communications trench where I had spent the day, a call awaited me on the radio. It was Captain Freeman at battalion.

"Hey, Boesch!" Freeman said, "send a patrol back to the spot where you jumped off from to pick up rations, water, and the ammunition you wanted. Send a guide back to Easy Company's CP to meet the litter bearers. And say, send two men back to go to Paris."

I couldn't believe I had heard right.

"What did you say?" I asked incredulously.

"General's orders, Boesch. Two men from every company get to go to Paris."

I stared at the mouthpiece of the radio. There I was with a company less than one-fourth normal strength, in the middle of an attack, cut off from the rest of the battalion all day, and now they wanted me to send two men back to go to Paris. From somewhere the thought came to me that I would be usurping God's powers if I should tap two men on the shoulder and say "You go to Paris. You live while these others stay here and die."

I knew I couldn't do it.

"You can count Company G out," I said slowly. "None of us is going any place except to Huertgen—or maybe to hell. But wherever we go, we go together, and you can tell whoever thought up such an asinine order exactly what I said. If they don't like it, tell 'em to come out here and get me."

When I hung up, I noticed two of my platoon sergeants had been listening.

"It's my turn to go to Paris, Lieutenant," one of them said.

"Mine too," said the other.

They began to chuckle.

"You got to admit, lieutenant," said one, smiling, "it sure would be nice."

Rations and water came eventually—the ammunition was a little slower. The litter bearers failed to show, so I had to send a patrol to try to find them. The patrol located them wandering blindly over the field between us and the woods, searching for us in vain. It was ten o'clock before we finally got the wounded ready to leave for the aid station.

I shook hands with each of the wounded. When I came to the man whose thoughts all day long had centered on Yuletide linens, I paused.

"I hope you get your white sheets for Christmas, fellow," I said.

"Don't worry, Lieutenant," he answered in a voice that showed no sign of strain. "I'll get them."

With that, the litter bearers picked up their burdens and headed for the woods and safety. I was immensely relieved. Through my mind ran the question:

"Lieutenant, when are you going to get us out of here?"


Hardly had the wounded departed when I received another call from battalion. It was Colonel Kunzig.

"Boesch," he said, "I want you to take your men and occupy the houses around the church. Pick out a good substantial cellar for the battalion CP. We'll be out to join you tomorrow."

I listened in amazement. Could the man be losing his senses?

"Are you joking, sir?" I asked in disbelief.

"No," he said curtly. "We got word the Germans have evacuated the town. I want you to move right in."

"Evacuated?" I bellowed. "Who told you the Germans have left?"

"What makes you think they're still there?" the Colonel came back.

"Shooting, sir! Shooting! Somebody in the goddamned town is shooting at me and killing my men."

"It's probably a small rear guard they left behind to delay you," the Colonel said with an air of finality. "We have it on good authority the town is empty."

"Who's a better authority than us?" I argued. "We have proof the Jerries are still there every time we stick our heads out of our holes. Can division offer you that kind of proof?"

But no matter how much I argued, Kunzig insisted that we pick our belongings off the ground, sling them across our backs, and march briskly into Huertgen to occupy the houses around the church.

I just couldn't quite get it across to him that we would be marching against deadly fire which had prevented us from moving all day long and much of the night. The realization came to me gradually and maddeningly that Kunzig thought I was lying.

In the end, I gained a concession. He approved my sending a patrol into Huertgen first to check on his information before risking the entire company.

"Okay," he said impatiently, "but hurry. I'm anxious to report to regiment that the town is ours."

Assembling a patrol hastily, I pointed out to the men the route which would take them to the center of the town. I personally briefed them to make sure each man understood that they were not to return until they could say one way or the other—had the Germans left, or were they still there?

I spent an anxious two hours waiting for their return. Just when I began to figure they must have gotten lost, killed or captured, they came back. They had, they reported, heard Jerries in some of the houses. Though they had not actually seen any Germans, nor had they been fired on, they were convinced the Germans still held the town.

Reporting the patrol's findings to Colonel Kunzig, I unwittingly mentioned that from one house the men had heard moans as well as voices.

Kunzig leaped on it.

"That proves it," he said in triumph. "They've pulled out and left their wounded behind. Get into town immediately. Right away. Occupy the houses around the church. Pick out a good cellar for the battalion CP."

He sounded like a phonograph playing a cracked record. CP, CP, that was all he seemed to care about, an elaborate, shell-proof CP.

I pointed out once more that we still thought the town was occupied and felt that the patrol verified our belief. He still would not agree, but again I argued at such length that he finally granted permission for sending another patrol to attempt actually to occupy a house.

This time I sent Lieutenant Carroll with the patrol to make sure the job was done right. Bill was to occupy a house, leave a portion of the patrol to hold it if possible, then report back. If he did succeed in gaining one of the houses, I intended to move forward rapidly with the rest of the company, enter the town, then come in on the rear of the houses which had been holding us up.

In the meantime, we received reinforcements in the form of two squads of engineers armed with flame throwers. I put them in holes and told them to make themselves as comfortable as possible until Lieutenant Carroll's patrol returned. Later, chafing at my own inactivity, I decided to use the engineers right away against an isolated house to our left front.

We moved through the darkness toward the house, guided by the outline of the roof limned against the night sky. We made good progress and might have achieved our goal had not one of the engineers opened up too soon with his flame thrower. The burst of flame drew a quick return fire from machine guns, wounding two men. We had no choice but to withdraw.

Lieutenant Carroll and his patrol still had not returned when, later in the night, the section leader of the flame-thrower squads approached me.

"Lieutenant," he said, "isn't it time for us to go back? My men are getting cold in these holes."

"My men have been cold in the same kind of holes for about two weeks now, sergeant," I explained slowly. "I expect to use you and your men later tonight—you'd better stand by."

He went back to his hole reluctantly, but before daylight he approached me again.

"Lieutenant, I'd like to take my men now and return to the company area." The tone of his voice made it clear he and the men had discussed the subject at some length and he had been elected to come back to me with the verdict.

I answered in no uncertain terms that we were planning on using his weapons as an important part of the attack when we launched it. We could not spare him.

"Well, gee whiz, Lieutenant," the man whined, "they didn't tell me we were going on no suicide mission."

"What the hell do you think about the rest of us?" I demanded. "Don't you think we get a little sick of suicide missions too?"

"But Lieutenant," the man responded, "you all are infantry "

I sighed out loud. My God, we were infantry. That apparently meant we were a race apart. Maybe we weren't supposed to feel, to hurt, to shiver, to be frightened, to react like other human beings. They were engineers, supply clerks, quartermasters, signalmen, ordnance repairmen—they were above this kind of miserable thing. But as for us, we were infantry.

I started to tell the man to get back to his hole, that I wanted to hear no more from him, that he and his men had better be ready when

I gave the word to move forward. Then I changed my mind. These men had tasted too much warm food and slept in too many dry spots to be of any real use to us. To hell with them.

"You're goddamned right we're infantry," I said. "As for you, you take your men and your fancy equipment and get the hell back to the rear where you belong. We want no part of whiners. We'll get along without you. Don't you worry about that."

A reluctant dragon, even though it breathed flame, would be more of a burden than a help.

I was still awaiting Carroll's return when a burst of flame erupted to our right rear around the isolated house which I assumed men of Fox Company had occupied during the day. In a matter of minutes the entire house was in flames, throwing a flickering orange light and a choking smoke across the field.

I could not imagine what had happened. Earlier in the evening I had sent a small patrol to the house in an attempt to contact F Company and had told the men that if they found no friendly troops there, they were to stay and hold the house themselves. What had happened to these men?

I was not to find out until some thirty minutes later when Lieutenant John Terzella, of Rahway, N.J., leading a small patrol from Fox Company, reached our positions. Captain Cliett had sent the patrol forward in an effort to locate Lieutenant Korn's platoon, with whom he had lost contact during the day. Approaching the isolated house, Terzella had heard noises. Certain that he had been fired on from the house that afternoon, he made no effort to investigate but turned a flame thrower against the house. In the confusion, my men got out uninjured, only to be "captured" by Terzella's men.

In the end, nobody was hurt, but the burning house silhouetted us to the enemy the rest of the night. Terzella's arrival also brought the disturbing news that F Company's attack that morning had gotten nowhere, not even as far as my own, so that now our little band was completely alone in the field.

As the night wore on, Bill Carroll at last came back from his patrol. He had drawn fire, he told me, from several buildings, but had managed to by-pass these and finally succeeded in stationing several men in the church itself. To their surprise, near the church they had come upon men of Company C, 13th Infantry. In fact, they had almost engaged in an internecine fire fight, because neither force had any inkling that the other was in the town.

I was amazed and disgusted. Surely somebody should have had the sense to let us know someone had entered our objective from another direction.

Confusion, I breathed to myself, thy name is combat.

In the face of this development, I tried to contact battalion for new instructions, but our radio had gone dead. Morning was not far away, and if I was going to do anything, I had to do it quickly.

I was just about ready to have the whole company trace the route of Carroll's patrol into the town when I looked up to discover Nick Von Keller hovering over me.

"Hello, friend Boesch," said the big Russian in a voice that was much too loud for the situation. "I have been sent out by Colonel Kunzig to become the Mayor of Huertgen."

"You can be Mayor, Nick, and welcome," I said. "All you have to do is get into town and get elected. But that getting in may be the hard part."

"But they told me you were already in the town and I was to pick out a good CP for battalion near the church."

"They probably told you the town was unoccupied too," I said.

"That's right," Nick answered. "Isn't it?"

"You'll find out if you stand in the glare from that fire a little longer," I warned.

Nick, it turned out, was not alone. His entire company was stretched out in the field behind us. Since his communications men also were along and had laid wire as they advanced, he was able to reach battalion by telephone.

"Hello, Colonel," he said. "I'm sitting here in the palatial CP of Lieutenant Boesch . . ."

That was as far as he got. His words made me mad as hell, joking or not. We were in mud and water past our ankles, battalion was convinced we were having a pink tea, and now Nick was adding to the confusion.

"Goddamnit, Nick," I growled, "tell those bastards back there the truth. Tell 'em exactly what the situation is. They think I've been handing them a bunch of crap."

When Nick saw I was genuinely riled, he sobered in a moment. He told battalion the true situation and asked for instructions. Colonel Kunzig told him to pull back with his company to the edge of the woods. It was growing light too fast to take the town before daylight, and he had no desire to risk getting Easy Company caught in the open without protection.

Nervously, I urged the big Russian to get moving fast. I knew from our experience the day before that if the Germans spotted the company in the open, all hell would break loose. Leaving his telephone behind for my use, Nick rose and promised he'd get away quickly.

Just as it got light enough for me to see that Nick and Easy Company were nearing the woods, a voice came over the phone.

"Lieutenant Boesch, Lieutenant Boesch," the voice said urgently, "send a messenger after E Company. Have them come back and dig in on your left."

Noting the rapidly increasing daylight, I could picture the complete confusion which would result should E Company stop, turn around, and attempt to move back across this hostile, fire-swept ground. Obviously nobody had made any real plan for the company. Nick and his men simply would be inviting disaster, and even if they got back to our positions before the Germans discovered them, they would merely be in the same predicament as us.

It was my job to carry out orders, not to dispute the judgment of those above me. But I knew that in the deep dugout which battalion occupied nobody had any real knowledge of whether it was sunrise or sunset or high noon.

The voice on the phone was insistent.

"Lieutenant Boesch," the voice called. "Lieutenant Boesch. Can you hear me, Lieutenant Boesch?"

I listened and I could hear, but I could not bring myself to press the butterfly switch on the telephone which would allow me to answer.

"Lieutenant Boesch," the voice repeated. "Can you hear me, Lieutenant Boesch?"

I sat there, staring into the growing daylight.

The voice finally gave up.

## 25

Morning found us with part of a squad somewhere in Huertgen along with a contingent, size undetermined, of Company C, 13th Infantry, while the rest of us sat munching a cold, totally unsavory breakfast K-ration in the same muddy holes and communications trench where we had taken refuge the day before. Because of the confounded and unfounded belief that the Germans had left the town, nobody had sent anybody to help us. We were certain now, of course, that the house to our right rear contained no enemy, for it had burned to the ground. I also felt I had improved our defensive posture somewhat. But about the only thing which had really changed for us was that we had fewer men than the day before.

If we had entertained any doubts whether Jerry still defended Huertgen, they were dispelled as soon as it grew light enough for him to see. Any time we showed our miserable heads, he greeted us with accurate bursts of fire. His artillery and mortars continued to plaster our positions in a quantity which revealed no worries about ammunition shortages. But we stuck to our holes and the shelling caused us little harm except to fray further already ragged nerves, although it did cut our newly-acquired telephone communications with battalion. Though my radio man, Sergeant Leon D. Larus, of Naylor, Georgia, worked faithfully in an effort to revive our radio, his efforts appeared to be hopeless and we remained out of touch with the rest of the U.S. Army. Jerry alone seemed to know or even care where we were, though we could hardly appreciate the violent way in which he reacted to us.

As mid-morning arrived I noted an unusual amount of activity back at the woods line, but I could not make out what was happening.

In the hope that something to ease our situation might be in the offing, I urged Sergeant Larus to greater efforts with the silent radio. An hour before noon, as we succeeded in getting all the parts back together after cleaning and working with various components, I spotted a covey of medium tanks heading from the woods line straight up the road toward Huertgen. It was an electrifying sight.

"Get set to move!" I yelled. "Pass the word along. Get set to go with the tanks!"

The tanks were almost upon us when we finally established a weak and inconsistent radio contact with battalion. I asked if they wanted us to go with the tanks.

"Yes," came the reply in terse fashion, "join the tanks!"

I explained quickly to Bill Carroll to take half the men beyond the road and attack the houses on the south side of town; I would stay with the others on the north. While he got ready, I raced from hole to hole explaining to the men what we were about to do. Bursts of machine gun and rifle fire followed my movements, but they merely served to add to my speed. I was careful never to move in the same direction twice and never to emerge from a hole from the same side I went in. I would crouch, figure my next move before I made it, and then race like a mad man for the next cover.

In one hole I found a man alone. He was getting his pack and rifle ready, slowly, deliberately. I explained carefully to him, as I had to the others, to advance by bounds, picking out the next hole before he moved. In his case I pointed out a hole only ten feet away. I told him to get to his feet quickly, take two long steps, then dive for the hole. From there he would have a protected approach to the communications trench and could continue forward under cover. The man listened to me with a fixed stare.

"Do you understand?" I asked.

Licking his lips, the man nodded. Slowly, like an automaton, he began to get to his feet. But instead of moving    immediately,   he stood still and gazed around him.

"Move man!" I yelled. "Move fast!"

But he did not move fast. He seemed not even to hear me—he was paralyzed, hypnotized by the fantastic situation in which war had plunged him. Climbing from his hole, he stood fully erect. Ever so slowly, as though pulling his feet out of clinging mud, each movement taking an eternity, he made a step forward.

It was the last step he ever took. A bullet caught him flush in the face. With the same slow motion he had used to get out of the hole, he sank to his knees and slumped forward on a blood-smeared face.

I stared at him unbelievingly, a motionless bundle of muddy olive drab. For what must have been a full minute, I did not move. I could only think over and over and over that I had done it, I had sent this man to his death. Yet gradually a sense of resentment began to surge through me. He need not have died, I argued angrily. He had only to listen to me and understand what it took to stay alive. It wasn't my fault. It could not be my fault. I had tried. I had tried.

The sudden barking of direct fire weapons aroused me. I had to move. Using the same technique I had so carefully but futilely explained to the soldier, I dashed from the hole and back to the dugout at the end of the communications trench.

By this time Carroll had assembled his men, and the tanks were among us.

"Better get going, Bill," I urged. "If we time this right, we'll have a much better chance."

Bill sat on his haunches in the narrow trench. His face was pale, dirty, unshaven; his eyes were set. I knew exactly what was stirring within him and, knowing, could not find the words to give him confidence. He licked his lips nervously. Finally, squaring his shoulders, he rose to his feet and motioned for his men to follow. Running, bobbling, weaving, they rushed across the road.

Watching only briefly as Bill and his men ran, I hurried to the closest of the medium tanks. The machine guns on the big tank were smoking from the heat of firing so long and so often. Just as I approached, the turret gun blasted away with a roar. Jerry artillery began to fall in the field. It was sheer pandemonium.

Beating on the side of the tank with the butt of my carbine, I shouted frantically for the tank commander. At last the lid of the turret raised an inch or so and a man peered out.

"What do you want us to do?" I shouted, hoping to be heard above the din.

"Don't get ahead of us," the commander shouted back, "and, hey, don't get behind us!"

Bending low, I raced back through the mud to the communications trench. The men were ready to go, almost eager, it seemed to me, to get the dirty business over with, win or lose. Somehow I felt G Company was snapping back. We would do a good job in Huertgen.

Before we could leave, one of the sergeants who had gone with Lieutenant Carroll ran up to me. He was Staff Sergeant James C.

Nutting, a tall, lanky boy who had been very ill the entire day and night we had spent outside Huertgen. I had wanted Nutting to go to the rear with the litter bearers, but he had argued that his place was with the men of his platoon. I had relented and let him pass the night in the little dugout, bundled up in my overcoat.

"Lieutenant Boesch," Nutting gasped, out of breath, "there's a colonel in a house on the other side of the road. He wants you there immediately. He said bring your radio."

I looked at Nutting in amazement. A colonel? Up with us? With all this action going on? It was incredible.

"You sure you're feeling all right?" I asked, half serious, half facetious.

"I'm sick as a dog, lieutenant, but honest to God, there's a chicken colonel on the other side of the road. I never saw him before, but he said for you to get over there right away. He ain't kidding, lieutenant."

Turning to follow Nutting, I passed command of the left side of the road to one of the platoon sergeants who had missed out on the trip to Paris.

"Looks like you'll get to town anyway," I said.

"Yeah, but this ain't Paree, lieutenant," he shot back.

For a sick man, Nutting used his long legs well. In a matter of minutes we were inside a battered house where I saw a full colonel wearing the big Indianhead "Blushing Apache" shoulder patch of the 2d Infantry Division. He was a short, powerful looking man who stood with one eye glued to a break in the wall watching the progress of the attack.

He turned.

"You got your radio?" he asked.

Instead of replying directly, I responded in distinctly non-military fashion.

"Who are you?"

The colonel grinned.

"Don't worry," he said. "I'm on your side. I'm P. D. Ginder. I'm in command of the task force that's attacking this town. I'll need your radio and your operator. Tell him to stick with me."

The officer impressed me. Here was a man who knew what he wanted to do and was determined to do it.

"Yes, sir," I said. "Anything else?"

Colonel Ginder looked me full in the eye and answered forcefully.

"Yes," he said. "Get with your men. Keep them moving and don't stop. We're going to take this town."

I gave him a snappy and sincere "Yes, sir!" For the first time, I could genuinely believe that we were going to take Huertgen. I raced from the house, across the road to rejoin my men.

By the time I got back, the platoon sergeant and the other men had overrun the group of houses from which the Germans had terrorized us for a miserable day and night. They took close to 75 prisoners. Even the most pessimistic among us had never suspected that these houses contained more than 20 well-placed Jerries.

This, I thought to myself, should answer for all time whether or not the Germans had evacuated Huertgen.

As we started forward again, a heavy barrage of German artillery began to fall. All of us raced for shelter, and I found myself taking refuge in a house with the prisoners and the men assigned to guard them. Jerry either had written off his own men or figured that we, as the attackers, would be moving in the open while his own troops would be protected by the buildings. The roar of his artillery grew tremendous and awesome.

As the barrage decreased in intensity for a moment, a strange procession approached our house, seeking shelter. It was the medics of Easy Company, carrying what was left of a man on an improvised stretcher fashioned from a piece of board. The man had been badly hit. One arm hung by a thread of flesh that seemed reluctant to let go, one leg was bloody and twisted curiously, and gory gashes poured claret from various holes in his body. Yet somehow the man still lived.

Staring at him, I was seized suddenly with an almost uncontrollable hatred for those who had caused this unbearable misery. Lifting my eyes, I fixed them on three German officers. I wanted to empty my carbine into them. Subconsciously I must have fingered the weapon, for the enemy officers began to fidget nervously as though they had read my thoughts. My physical appearance alone was probably enough to frighten them—uniform hopelessly stained with mud and blood, filthy face covered with a heavy beard, eyes bloodshot. One of the officers took a step backwards, almost involuntarily. His move snapped my trend of thought as suddenly I realized how close I was to murder.

Leaving the guards with the prisoners, I rejoined the attack at the next row of houses. Here, intermixed with men of Easy Company, who, I learned, had come forward with the tanks, we were temporarily stymied until a nearby tank began to blast the lower floors of the next houses. This enabled us to dash forward, plunge through windows or holes punched in the walls by the tank's big gun, and come up with ten prisoners.

It was a wild, terrible, awe-inspiring thing, this sweep through Huertgen. Never in my wildest imagination had I conceived that battle could be so incredibly impressive—awful, horrible, deadly, yet somehow thrilling, exhilarating. Now the fight for Huertgen was at its wildest. We dashed, struggled from one building to another shooting, bayoneting, clubbing. Hand grenades roared, rifles cracked— buildings to the left and right burned with acrid smoke. Dust, smoke and powder filled our lungs making us cough, spit. Automatic weapons chattered hoarsely while the heavier throats of mortars and artillery disgorged deafening explosions. The wounded and the dead—men in the uniforms of both sides—lay in grotesque positions at every turn. From many the blood still flowed.

From house to house we fought, each house a determined strongpoint until the Germans inside at last became convinced they could hold out no longer and still live. First the tanks would spray the houses with machine gun fire, driving the Germans from the openings. Then they would open fire with their big cannons, blasting holes for the infantry. At a signal from us, the tanks would raise their fire to the next houses to prevent other Germans from opening up on us as we rushed forward. Tossing a hand grenade as a deadly calling card, we hurled our bodies through the holes or through windows or splintered doors. Then it became a battle from floor to floor—from room to room. Many times the Germans retreated to the cellars. Another hand grenade tossed down the steps often was sufficient to produce frantic cries of "Kamerad! Nicht scheisen!"

One problem was to keep the men from hunting souvenirs, thereby delaying the attack. These were the first houses we had taken inside Germany, and it was hard to convince them everything was not theirs for the taking. It had belonged to the enemy, thus now it belonged to us.

The mounting toll of prisoners posed a problem too, for each man sent back to guard a batch of PWs meant one man less to carry on the fight. Pausing briefly in one alley I consolidated several groups under Staff Sergeant Paul E. Grosch, a German-speaking soldier, then later Colonel Ginder assigned a staff sergeant from Company E to take all the captives to the rear. Now that the Germans had done their dirty work and then surrendered, they were anxious to get out of Huertgen, for the village was a death trap that recognized neither friend nor foe.

Emerging from one house, I bumped into Captain Cliett, who had been as busy as I since the attack started. We exchanged a few words about the attack, noting particularly what enthusiasm this strange colonel, P. D. Ginder, had generated in all of us.

Cliett, it turned out, had had no more prior warning about the attack than I. He had been hiding in a hole while mortar shells burst about him when he heard a voice suddenly bark at him:

"Captain, why the hell aren't you up there with your men?"

Cliett had looked up in amazement to see a chicken colonel.

"My company's right here, sir," Cliett stammered, "what's left of it."

"Well, damn it, round them up and get into town."

"Isn't it a little too hot out there right now, Colonel?" Cliett asked.

"Well, damn it, Captain," the colonel replied, "if you get wounded, you'll get a nice rest in the hospital. If you get killed, you won't know anything more about it. If neither happens, you have nothing to worry about. Let's get going!"

Cliett had met P. D. Ginder.


Captain Cliett and I were about to part company, each to get on with the task of mopping up the Germans in Huertgen, when without warning, Cliett tossed a bombshell full into my heart.

"Well, Paul," he said, "they got your buddy."

I stopped in my tracks. My knees grew weak. I could feel the blood leave my face.

They got your buddy! They got your buddy! That's what Cliett had said.

He could mean only one thing.

He meant Jack.

## 26

Cliett realized in an instant what a blow he had dealt me.

"He wasn't killed," he hastened to add. "He wasn't killed. Just wounded. He got hit in the side. It wasn't bad. Not bad at all. I swear it, Paul."

I hardly knew whether to believe him or not. Once he had seen the effect his words had on me, his voice had assumed a tone which, to me, was far too reassuring.

"He's okay, Paul," Cliett continued. "I swear it. They've taken him back to the aid station." He told me briefly how Jack had gone out in the open to help a seriously wounded man and had ben hit in the side by a rifle bullet.

My first thought was to abandon everything, to run to the rear and see for myself. What would I say when I wrote home? How and what could I tell Norma? Surely I would have to see him, to verify his condition. In the span of a moment I pondered a million things.

"Oh, dear God," I prayed fervently, "please be with Jack. Don't let them kill him on the way back. Guide him to the aid station. Don't let him be hurt bad. Please, God! Please, God!"

Not far away one of the tanks let go with a blast; the noise snapped me back to reality. What was it I had told Sergeant Lawrence back in the forest? Jack was only one man, one more lieutenant who had gotten in the way of a Jerry bullet. The war would go on without him. The war was still going on, even now, and I was responsible for the men of Company G. We were nearing the church, and I suddenly remembered the men who had come into the town the night before and now were in position somewhere around the church. I had to hurry, to warn the tankers, to warn the men of Companies E and F.

I could not put my concern for Jack out of my mind, but I would have to control it.

I hurried forward.

Contrary to my expectations, we experienced no real problem with the friendly forces around the church. The first men we came upon were from Charley Company of the 13th Infantry. I tried to get them to join us.

"No, sir, lieutenant," a spokesman answered. "Our C.O. told us to stay right in the church, and that's where we got to stay till he orders us out."

I wondered what the hell good they thought they were doing sitting on their butts in the church, but I did not press the issue. Technically, I might have assumed jurisdiction over them, but again I saw no point in augmenting our force with reluctant dragons.

When we at last came upon my own men who had gone forward the night before with Lieutenant Carroll's patrol, the difference in their attitude was quickly apparent. They were enthused and eager to join in the fight. One man in particular, a bazooka man, had knocked out a Jerry machine gun with his rocket launcher and could hardly have been restrained from firing "a few more rounds at the bastards."

The houses in the vicinity of the church were more spread out, some of them well back from the main street, so that assaulting and searching them took more time and slowed our pace. Because the threat of approaching darkness hung over us, this was disturbing, but there was little I could do about it. We were not many. By now I had gathered a group about me which consisted of men from all the rifle companies, E, F, and G, yet the group numbered less than a squad in size. On the other hand, we had developed a practiced system of assault and had grown quickly into a cohesive team. We might yet make it before dark.

We had progressed a few houses beyond the church when we came upon a big chateau-like house, standing relatively isolated. Leading the men in the assault, I rushed through a front door just as two Jerries emerged from the basement and headed out the back. Almost without thinking, I dashed for the back door and into the open. It was a foolish, careless move.

Just as I emerged from the house, one of the Jerries stopped, turned, and raised his machine pistol to fire. Only the fact that the second man still was running and was between me and the weapon delayed his shooting. I instinctively opened fire with my carbine. Almost at the same time I dropped into a low crouch and pulled back to the doorway. The German fired, but his burst of bullets flew past me, knocking pieces of brick from the side of the house into my face. Loud screams told me my own shots had found a mark.

Retreating to the protection of the house, I found my men emerging from the cellar with eight prisoners. When I again looked through the back door, cautiously this time, I saw one German lying on the ground. A few minutes later we captured the other Jerry. Tossing aside his machine pistol, he surrendered meekly.

We permitted our prisoners to go outside and bring in the man I had shot. He was badly wounded. A bullet had entered his chest near the heart and emerged from the back. He obviously had not long to live.

As the Germans applied first aid, the man moaned pitifully. Looking at him and knowing that it was I who had done this thing to him, I realized I should have felt some kind of compassion, yet I had none.

Here, I thought to myself, is the first man I can truly say without doubt that I killed. It is strange how much war a man can see without ever being certain he has accomplished the primary purpose of killing the enemy. I had fired at many Germans, of course, and I had presumed in a number of cases that I had hit them. But never before had I had definite proof. Of this one, there could be no doubt. Yet I could stand there and watch him die and feel absolutely no qualms of any kind.

This seemed particularly strange to me, for I was a man who had never gone hunting simply because I had neither the urge nor the heart to kill an animal. But I could shoot a man and then watch him die without feeling either sorry for him or for the fact that I was the one who had done it. It was as if I were a carpenter and had driven home a nail which secured one beam to another, the job I was assigned to do. As I continued to watch the Germans administer to the man, my only real passion was irritation that he was taking such a stupidly long time to die. We had work to do; we could not sit here waiting for him to take his own time about passing away. At last I told the Germans to wrap him in a blanket and take him with them toward the rear.

He was dead before they got to the main road. They dumped his body beside a house.

It was getting dark fast, so it was with relief that we rapidly neared the last houses. Most of the buildings were empty now. Sticking close to our tanks, we kept moving even though we were dragging from fatigue and the heavy coat of mud on our boots. Despite the nip in the air, I was sweating from exertion, and only the sight of our goal prompted us to keep at the job.

We were down now to five or six men, plus Lieutenant Terzella, Lieutenant Carroll, and me. Where the others were I did not know. I suppose a good company commander would have had the whereabouts of all his men at his fingertips, and I suppose too a really good company commander would have been directing his troops from some strategically sound location in the rear. On the other hand, we had all but taken Huertgen. And if you take your objective you can hardly be criticized for the methods by which you did it.

As we approached the last house, the tankers fired a few more rounds. We dashed forward.

"Go get the bastards," someone yelled, "and let's eat!"

It proved to be no difficult task for a dozen Jerries were waiting for us just inside the door, hands already raised in surrender. I was just about to go down into the cellar to search for stragglers when another German emerged, hands raised but an arrogant look on his face.

"The commander," he said in English, "is in the cellar. He will surrender, but only to an officer."

Terzella and I exchanged glances, pushed the commander's emissary with little ceremony into our group of captives, and headed down the cellar stairs. With our fingers on the triggers of our carbines, we entered a big basement room, damp and dimly lit by a candle. There, sitting at a table, slumped mournfully forward on his elbows, was our man.

The German officer looked up slowly—a small, pale, scrawny man.

"I will surrender only to an officer," he said with haughty independence that was badly misplaced under the circumstances.

Terzella and I exchanged glances again. We were filthy and neither of us had shaved for two weeks. The only man I ever met who could raise a thicker and blacker beard than me was Terzella. Surely we bore no resemblance to what most people think an officer looks like.

I was in no mood at this stage to dally with arrogance. Thinking of General Canham's treatment of the German general back at Brest, I thumped the butt of my carbine down on the table with a tremendous force.

"You will surrender to me," I thundered. Shoving the muzzle of my carbine close to the German's face, I added, "These are my credentials as an officer."

Laughing in appreciation of my performance, Terzella yanked the German to his feet and snatched his pistol. How badly the little Nazi wanted to play soldier to the end, to execute a final Wagnerian surrender. We would have none of it.

"That's a nice looking belt and holster," Terzella said sternly. "Take it off."

Though the German looked at us as if to protest this treatment, what he saw in Terzella's grim face must have changed his mind. Meekly, he complied.

Without further ceremony, we hustled the officer upstairs and out into the street where we herded him along like the defeated Nazi he was.


Heading back toward the church, we passed the tanks which had given us such excellent support. Reaching into a bulging field jacket, I took out several German pistols and tossed them to the men in the hatches of the tanks.

"Gee, thanks," squealed one of the men. The others smiled their appreciation.

"It's okay, boy," I said with sincerity, "you earned it."

I meant it. If they were grateful for the pistols, I was more than grateful for the help they had given us. It was all too easy to remember the open field outside Huertgen before the tankers came on the scene. If it had not been for the men of Company A, 709th Tank Battalion, we might have had no part in the capture of Huertgen or any other place. This was the only way I could express my gratitude, to give to these men the one souvenir which the American soldier cherished above all others.

Now Huertgen was almost deathly still, as though those who had wielded the scythe of death had had such a field day they finally decided to let the lifeless bodies which littered the streets have a few moments of real tranquillity before cutting loose with another deadly swath. Except for exploding ammunition erupting intermittently and the constant warm, almost cheery crackle of burning buildings, Huertgen was silent. An acrid pall of smoke blanketed the town. Whenever the wind blew the smoke aside, I could look up and see a sky sparkling with stars, peaceful, inviting. It made me think of other times, other nights, when stars in such magnificent profusion and brilliance meant things like tenderness and being with the one you loved.

With a few directions from men we met along the street, we at last came to battalion headquarters, located, as I might have suspected, in a substantial cellar near the church. Inside men were milling about, and Colonel Kunzig was making plans for defending the town against counterattack. I personally turned over to him my captive officer.

When the German heard the word "colonel," he snapped to attention and proffered a vigorous Nazi salute, obviously still intent on playing soldier and executing a formal, text book surrender. To my intense satisfaction, Kunzig ignored him except for a casual, disinterested glance. The little German was crestfallen. I could only wonder what the word surrender actually meant to him, for he had nothing to surrender. We had forcibly taken the town and his command away from him. We had forcibly taken him too.

Leaving the headquarters building, I set out to round up what I could of my company, but the blackness of the night made any real search impossible. When we started the attack that morning, I had had about 40 men—now I could locate only eight. These were waiting for me with one of the platoon sergeants, Technical Sergeant Charles Galloway, an Irishman with a big moustache who had done an excellent job. I led the men to a pair of houses which I had selected during the day for their commanding view of the terrain to the east. I put four men in each house, wished them luck, and continued to search for more of the company.

I subsequently came upon Captain Cliett, Lieutenant Jack Christiansen, and Terzella in the cellar of a big house. At their invitation, I decided to stick with them for a few minutes rest. The cumulative effects of exertion, tension, and lack of food had taken an inevitable toll. In addition, my anxiety about Jack was gnawing insistently away at my insides.

I questioned all three of the officers about Jack's condition, and they all tried to convince me that his wound had not been serious. I hardly knew whether or not to believe them. The very persistence with which they sought to allay my fears made me suspicious. I decided to keep right on worrying until I could talk with Doctor Moe, the battalion surgeon, through whose hands Jack probably passed on his way to the rear.

My feet were aching and felt as if they might burst through my shoes. Indulging myself, I removed my muddy overshoes, my tight GI shoes, and two pairs of socks, drenched from perspiration. Easing my weight onto a slab of broken concrete, I began to massage my feet with delicious pleasure. Almost coincidentally, I began to tremble all over.

I couldn't stop shaking. Sweat broke out on my forehead, under my arms, on my legs. I knew the others must have been wondering what had come over me. I made hollow little excuses and apologies, but my trembling voice belied my words. I realized what was the matter. I had been so busy that I could not remember having been frightened a single time during a day which had been replete with hair-raising experiences. Now that the pressure was off and I could stop to think, the memory of all that had happened, the near misses, the shells, the men dying, proved too much.

Only with time and a conscious effort to reassure myself that the day was over, that I had, after all, lived through it, that we had, after all, taken Huertgen, did the trembling and the sweating pass. But even then I could not sleep. The four of us simply lay there and rested, trusting that Jerry would be unable to muster sufficient strength for a counterattack. I had eight men; Cliett could put his hands on two men, three officers, and himself. Company E, which had come into the attack that morning with about 125 men, presumably was better off, though we had no way of knowing for sure. We simply had to trust that Colonel Kunzig had positioned the tanks and the remaining men of Company E that they could beat off the Germans should they come back. We could do little ourselves.

Hardly had we settled down when Jerry artillery began to turn the town into an inferno again, but since we now were the ones in the cellars with a thick cover of bricks and cement over us, we did not mind it in the same way we had minded it when moving through the streets and alleys. It did not take long for us to appreciate how the Germans could have been so tenacious despite all the shells we had thrown at them.

"I'd have been brave too," muttered Jack Christiansen, "if I had been wrapped in a brick kimono."

With the coming of daylight, the incoming shells became even more frequent. The reason soon became apparent when we saw that tanks and other armored vehicles had begun to pass through the town en route to the next objective, the village of Kleinhau. The main street soon became clogged with vehicles. Tanks and trucks pulled off the road into the mud, seeking some protection from the shells against the battered walls of the buildings. Armored infantrymen, hunched in half-tracks that provided some measure of protection with light armor on the sides but none on top, pulled their heads down on their knees and sat there, miserably hoping no shell would fall directly inside their vehicle.

I soon set out again on my search for men of Company G. The first few I found explained they had taken prisoners to the rear and had been caught by the darkness, but they had come back with the first light of day. With these men I began to set up a defense based on the big house where I had killed the Jerry the day before. I chose the house for a CP, and as soon as possible, sent to the rear for my first sergeant and the few men who comprised my CP group. With them came water and rations. We got our first bite of food in more than 24 hours. It was an ever-lovin' K-ration—but good!

I noticed immediately that my executive officer had not come forward.

"Lieutenant," explained the first sergeant, "they evacuated him yesterday with combat fatigue."

"Well, I'm a sonofabitch," I wheezed unbelievingly. "We do the combat and he gets the fatigue."

It was an unkind remark, perhaps it was unjust, but I just couldn't resist.

## 27

When everybody even remotely connected with Company G was assembled, we still had well under 40 men. Yet no matter what our strength, we had to assume a large share of the responsibility for defending Huertgen against counterattack. I personally went with each squad or half squad to see that they occupied the best possible defensive positions.

When the last position had been designated, I turned to various other matters which I considered pressing. One was promotions. I believed firmly that if a man held a job calling for a certain grade, he should be promoted to that grade immediately.

With the aid of my first sergeant, I examined the company roster in considerable detail. I studied each platoon and each squad, seeking to fit names to faces in an effort to recall what I knew of each man's performance in the Huertgen attack. Those whom I credited with having shown ability and a willingness to do the job, I promoted promptly. I also made several changes in the case of men who had fallen down on the job when we needed them critically. It was my first opportunity to tailor the company to my own ideas and my own needs, and I worked to take full advantage of it.

After promotions, I looked into the matter of awards for heroism. I realized that if I did not act promptly, many men would fail to receive the recognition they deserved. In a number of cases, it seemed to me, their performances had been not only exceptional but far above and beyond the call of duty.

Getting a battlefield decoration was generally a matter of being lucky enough to have someone see you do something and then have that someone submit a recommendation for an award.

Recommendations could be submitted by either officer or enlisted man but had to be formally certified. The recommendations then were thoroughly screened by a reviewing board. The higher the award, the more scrutiny the recommendation received. The Congressional Medal of Honor is the highest award, followed in order by the Distinguished Service Cross, the Silver Star, and the Bronze Star.

I felt without doubt that every man who had participated in the attack on Huertgen should have been awarded at least the Bronze Star, but it obviously would have been impossible to obtain approval for a blanket award. I concentrated my efforts on a few men whose actions I personally had seen. I also forwarded several recommendations from Lieutenant Carroll. One of the men I recommended for the Silver Star was Sergeant Nutting whose fine work that day when he should have been in a hospital bed far to the rear had impressed me tremendously. But a board of review far from the scene eventually decided that Nutting's devotion and gallantry deserved no more than the Bronze Star. (Yet the review boards would not take all recognition from us for the work we did at Huertgen. The 121st Infantry later was to receive the highest recognition awarded an entire unit, the Presidential Unit Citation, for this successful attack.)

While I was hard at work on the list of recommendations for awards, the telephone rang. The first sergeant answered.

"Battalion wants you to get busy," he said with a grin as he put the phone down, "and submit a list of men who have earned decorations."

"Situation's normal," I answered. "They're still a step behind."

It was a busy day. As I paused in my work and looked around the command post to see privates and privates first class sleeping, loafing, preparing cups of coffee, I wondered why any man ever would want the responsibility of being an officer. I toiled over the paper work and whenever stragglers returned, I questioned them about where they had been the preceding day and night, then sent them out to the squads where they belonged. I checked the defenses several times. Hardly a moment was free.

Meanwhile, Jerry continued to pound the town with artillery fire, and the big house we were using as a CP seemed to come in for a particularly heavy share. We realized why when we found a Jerry map showing our enemy's prepared artillery concentrations. Our house was in the exact center of one of the plotted concentrations.

I showed the Jerry map later to Lieutenant John Sanky who had come forward as our artillery forward observer. Sanky was using the dangerous upper floor of our CP as an observation post. He in turn showed me a similar map of the area on which our own concentrations had been plotted. The contrast was amazing. Compared to us, Jerry was a mere amateur in the artillery field. Sanky's map showed every conceivable spot covered with small numbered circles, any one of which he might call for in a matter of seconds, whereupon our big guns would put down a quick barrage of deadly fire.

When darkness came again, I looked forward to getting some sleep. I actually could not remember when I had slept last. Certainly I had slept no more than a couple of hours during all the days I had commanded G Company, and the preceding days in the Huertgen Forest had been almost as bad. Since the night before Thanksgiving— more than a week before—I had scarcely closed my eyes.

I had reserved a spot on a filthy Jerry mattress and was eyeing it covetously when word came from battalion that we were to receive replacements. No matter how much I wanted sleep, I could not allow these men to arrive at the company unwelcomed and to be assigned willy-nilly to fill up the gaping holes in the platoons. In the end it was to mean almost a full night's work, but I was determined to interview the new men and place them within the company in keeping with their individual qualifications.

We received 45 replacements, all but a few totally inexperienced in combat. As soon as they had deposited their equipment along the walls of the big cellar, I called them together for a briefing.

It was a strange scene. The only light came from a crude lantern made by sticking a piece of rag in the neck of a bottle of gasoline. It burned with a dull, flickering light and let off a thin, dirty stream of smoke. A few feet away from the lantern, it was so dark that the men's cigarettes glowed like beacons. Most of the new men wore relatively fresh uniforms and were clean shaven, in marked contrast to me and others of the CP group. Outside the sounds of battle continued unabated. Occasionally the cellar seemed to vibrate with the explosion of a nearby shell, and dust fell from cracks in the ceiling.

To welcome the men, I stood on a chair so that all of them might see me. I told them a little of the history of the company and what we had done in this last fight. I wanted to build up at least a little pride of outfit as soon as possible, for this is a vital thing in battle.

"To most of you," I said, "this may seem like you're looking at a Hollywood movie, only this time you yourself are in the picture. But believe me, it's not as bad as people have told you. It couldn't be, or none of us would be here. It's not even as bad as it must seem to you right now. There're still lots of us left here, and some of us have been around a long time. We expect to be around a longer time. It isn't easy. It's tough. But if we can stand up to it, so can you."

I continued in this vein, urging the men to get to know their squad leaders immediately, to learn the name and face of every man in their squad, not to worry if they were afraid but to keep the fear under control, to ask questions of the old men, take their advice, and add to it what they had already learned in training. I ended by apologizing for the fact that the situation prevented us from getting to know each other better before they had to join their squads.

"I know this company is going to be proud of you," I said, "just as you are going to be proud of Company G."

It was the strangest speech I have ever made. Perhaps the situation did not really call for a speech, but Company G was my company and I intended to treat men in it the way I would want my officers to treat me. I would, under similar circumstances, have appreciated the welcome. Even though the bursts of artillery fire that punctuated my address sometimes sent the more wary among the audience plunging to the floor, the men were extremely eager to please. They even laughed at some of my very poor jokes.

Immediately after this formal welcome, I began interviewing them individually. I wanted to put each man in the job where I thought he could do the most good; but even more, I wanted each man to know that someone took a personal interest in him and his future—in whether he lived or died. Since most of the men had been in the army only about four to five months, I felt this was particularly important.

After I finished interviewing the last man, a few short hours of darkness remained. I was so tired I seemed to be in a trance. In slow motion, I went through the movements of taking off my shoes. Someone had long since usurped the Jerry mattress I had coveted earlier—now I merely stretched out on the cement floor. A deep sense of personal pleasure swept over me. What a delicious thing to do, to lie down to go to sleep! Then a wave of homesickness immersed me. I had heard nothing from Eleonore since Luxembourg, and I had not even found time to write to her. I longed to see her and talk with her, even if for just a few precious minutes. I longed to see Jack and talk with him, to find out for myself how seriously he was hurt. I wanted the whole dirty war to be over so badly I almost began to cry.

Then I rolled on my side to try to find in dreams the things that were impossible when awake.

## 28

The next morning I awoke with a start, somehow conscious that the whole house had begun to stir nervously. Reaching instinctively for my carbine, I popped to a sitting position. One of the men who had been on guard upstairs half ran, half stumbled down the steps.

"Lieutenant," he said excitedly, "it looks like a counterattack!"

Barefooted and helmetless I rushed up the stairs two at a time. In the distance I could hear a violent eruption of small arms fire, but it was nowhere near our positions. Breathing somewhat easier, I searched the fields ahead of us through binoculars and carefully studied the woods beyond. Still I could detect no signs that the Germans intended to strike. Grateful that it had been a false alarm, I nevertheless put additional men in good firing positions upstairs and sent non-coms to check on the other positions in the company area.

After returning to the cellar for my shoes and a K-ration breakfast, I again climbed the steps and searched the fields. I was about to leave to check on the other positions when I noticed one of the new men standing alone in a corner.

"How're you doing, soldier?" I asked.

There was no response.

Looking at the man closely I saw that he was literally scared stiff. His eyes were staring straight ahead, seeing nothing.

In an effort to comfort the man, I put a hand on his shoulder. I might have been sticking a pin in a bag of air. With an ear-splitting scream, the man collapsed to the floor. He lay there in a miserable, jelly-like heap, trembling all over.

With the help of some of the other men, we got him downstairs into the basement where we made him as comfortable as possible until one of the medical aid men could give him a sedative. The aid man thought, as I did, that we should send the man to the rear, but Jerry was becoming so persistent with his shelling that this would have been asking for trouble.

We at last turned away in the belief that the sedative had quieted our patient. At that moment, a Jerry shell landed particularly close to the CP. In an instantaneous reaction, the soldier leaped from the floor. Standing erect, his hands thrust down stiffly at his sides, he emitted another blood-curdling scream. It was a horrible, nerve-wracking sound from another world. Then again the man slumped to the floor, trembling violently.

There was nothing we could do. We could not send him to the rear until the shelling slackened, yet to keep him there in the cellar as the shells exploded was enough to drive the rest of us at least partially insane. Every time a shell landed nearby, the man would let go with the same horrendous scream. It took little of this to put our already frayed nerves on edge.

It was in self-defense, not in callous disregard for the condition of a fellow soldier, which at last prompted the GI's in the CP to ease their nerves by laughing and joking every time the man reacted to a shell. After a while they began to turn their quips at the man himself, but he was totally oblivious of anything that went on except the shelling. Perhaps we were callous and heartless, perhaps our reaction was an indication of what war does to the souls of men. On the other hand, I think we did the only thing we could have done under the circumstances. However, it was still an immense relief later in the day when we were able to evacuate our screaming patient. The cellar seemed almost deathly silent after he left.

I swore I would not let the day go by without writing a letter home, yet I found it a difficult letter to write. Though I wanted to be cheerful, I knew I could not disguise the fact that something very serious had kept me from writing for the last two weeks. What to write about Jack also disturbed me. In the end I decided to say nothing about Jack, for if his wound was, in reality, minor, he himself might not be saying anything about it in his own letters home. After all, it was his wound; surely it should be his decision.

Later in the day I made another check of the company's positions. The new men, I found, appeared to be mingling well with the old, and I knew it would be only a matter of days before you could not tell old and new apart.

Back in my basement CP things also were progressing smoothly.

We had collected a number of Jerry weapons to add to our arsenal, and the men worked hard cleaning them. I felt better about G Company than at any time since I had taken command. I began to have the feeling that it really was my own company, not just a unit I was running temporarily for somebody else. I was determined to stay with these men, to try to mold them into a really capable fighting unit. I was sure that, given time, I could do it.

In mid-afternoon word arrived for me to report to battalion. The CP, to my chagrin, had been shifted back to the group of houses which had blocked our path at the beginning of the attack, so that I had to dodge shells and heavy traffic all the way through the town to get there. At one point I took refuge from the shelling in what was left of the church. I could not help but ponder about what God would do in retaliation for the desecration of His holy temple. As I gazed on what had been an altar, I felt moved to take off my helmet—but didn't.

While standing in the church I noticed a jeep stop in the center of the street about 30 yards away. The driver suddenly threw the vehicle into gear and stepped on the gas. The jeep leaped forward. Seconds later a mortar shell fell and exploded exactly where the jeep had stood.

It is hard to understand how or why things like that happen. One thing is certain—the men in the jeep did not hear the mortar shell approaching, for incoming mortar shells are almost silent until they burst. I have no explanation except that it was not time for these two men to die, that some higher power somehow transmitted news of the danger to them. Subconsciously, they had reacted. If you were an infantryman, you had to believe in some kind of power like this, else you simply could not continue to exist.

As I continued toward battalion, I came upon Captain Cliett. Lieutenant Korn and his platoon, Cliett told me, still were unaccounted for. Because I had had a feeling that Korn and his men, who had been close on my right when we first set out for Huertgen, had advanced at least into the first house on the right of the road, I suggested to Cliett that we take a look there.

What we found was a pitiful sight. The house was a shambles from shellfire. Strewn all about, inside and out, were dead men. There must have been at least a dozen dead Americans, perhaps more, and a number of Germans, all intermingled. Some of the dead were partly undressed; others bore wounds which had been bandaged. Pockets of some of the men had been turned inside out, as if somebody had rifled them thoroughly. Something terribly unusual and tragic had taken place in that house, but from the grim evidence left behind we could not reconstruct the story. Yet we were able to determine that this had been Lieutenant Korn's platoon, for Cliett recognized several of the men. The lieutenant was not among them.

Years later I was to learn that Korn and his men had, in reality, reached the house. There they had held against overwhelming odds through most of the day we had been pinned in the communications trench on the other side of the road. When ammunition finally ran out, Korn and the few men who remained surrendered. They spent the rest of the war in a PW camp.

At the battalion CP, I saw Colonel Ginder, clean shaven, fresh, getting set for the next attack. I had a chance to thank him for his timely entrance onto the Huertgen scene.

"I want to thank you too," said the Colonel considerately. "You and your men did a magnificent job in one of the toughest fights I've ever seen. How do you feel?"

"I feel fine, Colonel," I answered with a grin, "except for a big black and blue spot on my rear where your big foot kept booting me through town."

I could detect considerable resentment among some of the battalion staff against Ginder, but I personally believed that Colonel P. D. Ginder more than deserved the Distinguished Service Cross he received for his action that day. Indeed, had I had my way, he would have gotten the Medal of Honor. Before he and the tanks came into view, we were hopelessly bogged down, stopped cold. He and the tanks had infused new life and new spirit into all of us. They literally made possible the capture of Huertgen. It did not matter to me that he came from another division. He was there when we needed him and he did the job. That was what counted.

Colonel Ginder informed Cliett, Von Keller, and me that he had recommended the three of us for the Silver Star for our part in the attack. I felt a glow of pleasure with the news and was glad that I already had submitted recommendations for awards to the men who had made my own recognition possible.

I took this opportunity to confront Colonel Kunzig with a demand for a courts martial for my moustached platoon leader who had deserted us when we were pinned down in the field. In fairness to the other men who had done their jobs, some of them dying in the process, I could not do otherwise.

"Can't do it, Boesch," Kunzig told me.

"Can't do it?" I asked incredulously.

"That's right," Kunzig said. "They evacuated him through medical channels with combat fatigue. Whether he was guilty of desertion or not, you'd never be able to prove it now. He's in the hands of the medics."

The reason for our call to battalion soon became apparent. The armored task force which had passed through us in Huertgen was to attack the nearby village of Brandenberg, but a neck of woods straddling the road to Brandenberg had turned out to be infested with antitank guns and mines. The tanks could not get through. We were to attack when night came in order to clear a line of departure from which we might move at dawn the next morning against the neck of woods. We were, in effect, to fight all night to secure a place from which to fight the next day. A pretty stiff order.

Because details of the attack still had not been worked out, we were to wait at the CP for the final order. Sending my messenger back to the company with a warning for Lieutenant Carroll to start preparations for the move, I went outside with Nick Von Keller for a visit to the latrine. As we returned, I met Lieutenant Roy Greene, the medical administrative officer of the battalion.

I pumped Greene for details of Jack's wound. Though Greene had not personally seen Jack, he understood that he was not seriously hurt. There was no reason not to believe him.

Lieutenant Greene and I started together down the stairs into the basement CP. The stairs were wide enough for the two of us to walk side by side, but we had to be careful because of a slippery coat of soft, slimy mud which the passing of many feet had left on the steps.

We had gone down only a step or two when an artillery shell exploded just in front of the CP. Greene flinched; I ducked. The involuntary movements threw us together. My feet slipped out from under me. I went into the air, headed for nowhere.

The next part of my body to touch the steps was my back. I cracked my sacroiliac against the ragged edge of the stone steps, then slid, bounced, and scraped all the way down to the cellar floor.

I felt a sharp, excruciating pain in my back. My right leg lay numb. I could not move.

The men in the CP rushed to my assistance, but when they tried to help me to my feet, it felt as if a bayonet were protruding from my back. Laying me to one side, they sent a hurry-up call for Doctor Moe, the battalion surgeon.

It took Doc Moe only a few minutes to make up his mind.

I had to be evacuated.

Nothing I could say would change the decision. I begged, I pleaded. In the end, I prevailed upon him to give me a few hours in the hope the pain would desist, but as time passed, my back grew stiffen I obviously could do no good here. I had to go back.

They made preparations to turn my company over to Lieutenant Christiansen, Cliett's executive officer. Christiansen was a good man, and I could not argue with this arrangement, but I did insist that I be allowed to stay around a few hours more in order to orient Christiansen about the company.

When Christiansen arrived, I went over the organization of the company with him carefully. As I spoke, my insides were a melange of emotions. I hated war and combat and all the misery that went with it with all my heart, yet I dreaded the thought of giving up my first company, of leaving behind under such miserable circumstances the men with whom I had come through so much, of deserting the new men who needed help so badly. Though I believed my absence would be only temporary—some strong adhesive tape and a few day's rest should get me back on my feet—I hated leaving at all. What of the attack that night? I had gotten to know some of my men now. Christiansen would find them complete strangers, just as I had found them a few days before.

I procrastinated for several hours, stretching out my discussion with Christiansen much longer than was necessary. For one thing, I took the opportunity to ask Doc Moe about Jack. Though he assured me Jack's wound had not been serious, I still found it difficult to be absolutely convinced. I knew then I probably never would be until I got the word from Jack himself.

Several ambulances came and went without me. Night had fallen when Doc Moe returned to issue a specific order that I was to be on the next one.

Before I left, the surgeon gave me a shot of morphine to help me get up the stairs and to ease the rough ride to the rear. Since it was impossible to carry a stretcher up the steep stairway, particularly one bearing my heavy weight, I gritted my teeth and struggled upward with the help of a man on either side. As I reached the head of the stairs, I looked back to see dirty bearded faces turned up toward me and hands raised in gestures of farewell.

In the ambulance, men with bandages sat on the seats while I and another man, his head wrapped in bloody white gauze, stretched out on litters on the floor. Despite the hurt in my back, I felt like a stupid ass. It made me boiling mad to think that I had gone through so much, including the Huertgen Forest and Huertgen itself, only to be put out of action by the kind of accident which many a housewife incurs while doing her chores at home. Not a shell fragment, not a bullet, not even combat fatigue—just a fall on my big prat.


The ambulance creaked out of the courtyard and onto the crowded road leading back from Huertgen toward the forest. Despite considerate handling by the driver, the wounded burden inside groaned at every hole in the road. Inch by inch the vehicle crept through a stygian night toward the protection of the forest. A few shells fell, not far away. I began to think of the man who wanted white sheets for Christmas. Maybe I would get a real wound after all. I wondered even if we would make it.

We were at last inside the forest and the sounds of battle a little farther away when I became nauseous, probably from a combination of the morphine, the pain in my back, the jostling, and an unaccustomed heat inside the ambulance. The driver stopped, got out, and held a helmet under my chin so I could vomit in it. I remember apologizing to the rest of the men for holding them up. They were kind enough to pass it off lightly.

A few miles to the rear we drew up at a huge tent hospital which was the division clearing station. Willing hands helped me from the ambulance into a smaller tent that served as a receiving office. I still wore my steel helmet. An orderly told me to throw it on a pile that grew alongside the entrance.

I took off the helmet and separated it from the liner. Looking at the liner, I saw my name printed across the front of it in big white letters. I had first worn that liner back in the United States at Camp Van Dorn, a million years ago, at the start of the long, seemingly vagrant road that had led to Huertgen. For a moment I would not let it go. Casting it aside would be like discarding part of me, part of all that had happened to me on that road, part of the men I had known, the men who had meant so much to me.

I stroked the liner once, like it was a live thing. Then I tossed the helmet and the liner on the pile and watched the liner tumble back to the earthen floor. There it rested, upside down, my name up-ended, along with the discarded equipment of a lot of other men.

# Epilogue

Most of the hospitals I passed through now seem woven together into a kind of puzzle whose parts all fit together somehow but cannot be separated. Sometimes men lying on either side of me awaiting emergency operations. Occasionally a man clinging to his Luger pistol, even as they wheeled him to the operating room, lest some medic steal his prize possession. Long rows of men with swollen, discolored feet sticking from beneath the covers, cotton between their toes—trench foot. In one hospital, Nick Von Keller, in terrible pain, almost delirious, wounded the day after I left Huertgen. An appetite for food that returned with a rush, and nurses who slipped you snacks of bread and jam between meals. Combat fatigue cases, men who might rise from their beds at any hour of the day and night, screaming and fighting enemies who weren't there. Prisoners of war serving as orderlies, nervous when these attacks occurred. Men laughing and joking in spite of pain, because at last they were out of it, away from a miserable place called "the front." A constant search for familiar faces, for men with news of the One-Two-One, for men with news of Jack, for Jack himself. Long letters home—two and three a day sometimes—but no letters back, because you moved too often for mail ever to catch up. Doctors who pushed and pulled at you, looked at your X-rays, then shook their heads in clucking disapproval and issued the diagnoses which meant, in effect, you'd never go back to combat.

Days passed. I was in a big converted warehouse in Eupen, Belgium. Then I was on a jostling, lurching hospital train en route to Paris, gritting my teeth to smother outcry against pain, for there were seriously wounded men all around me who must have hurt worse than I did. Then Paris and me peering out the porthole at the rear of the ambulance in search of familiar landmarks.

More days passed. I was on a C-47 hospital plane bound for England. I took daily physio-therapy treatments and followed the progress of the Battle of the Bulge from radio news reports.

Weeks passed. I was discharged from the hospital and sent back to the Continent, where, 50 miles from Paris, at Choisy-au-Bac, I commanded a company converting men from rear echelon units into infantrymen.

I was "limited service." I could not return to a combat assignment.

February was waning when at long last I got a letter from Jack. He and I, it turned out, had spent a day's leave at exactly the same time in Birmingham, England. No doubt we had trod the same streets, but we had missed each other. Now Jack was expecting any day to be discharged from the hospital and sent back to the One-Two-One. He swore he would get by to see me en route.

I packed my musette bag and a few things I genuinely treasured and kept them in a corner of my room, ready at a moment's notice. I had thought it out carefully. Every request, every plea for reclassification so that I might go back to my regiment had failed. I would go anyway when Jack came. Since I would be running toward rather than away from the front, I could not believe the punishment would be severe.

But Jack never came. The train carrying him to Germany, I learned later, never came close to Paris. Jack had no opportunity to visit me without going AWOL himself. I unpacked my musette bag and resigned myself to a rear echelon existence until the war was over. Through it all I trained the men assigned to me with an almost feverish intensity, for they might be going to the One-Two-One.

One spring day we were seated in our mess hall when the church bells for miles around began to toll. A lieutenant with me turned to the French orderly who was serving us.

"Charley," he demanded, "pourquoi Français ring all them goddamn bells?"

Charley threw his hands into the air in exultancy.

"Finis la guerre!" he cried.

Charley was right. It was over.

CPSIA information can be obtained
at www.ICGtesting.com
Printed in the USA
LVHW032014050619
620228LV00020B/352/P

9 781497 434479